Challenge and change in the information society

Challenge and change in the information society

Edited by

Susan Hornby and Zoë Clarke

facet publishing

Published by
Facet Publishing
7 Ridgmount Street
London WC1E 7AE

Facet Publishing (formerly Library Association Publishing) is wholly owned by
CILIP: the Chartered Institute of Library and Information Professionals.

First published 2003

British Library Cataloguing in Publication Data
A catalogue record for this book is available from the British Library.

ISBN 1-85604-453-X

Typeset from editors' disks by Facet Publishing in 10/14pt New Baskerville and
Franklin Gothic Condensed.
Printed and made in Great Britain by MPG Books Ltd, Bodmin, Cornwall.

Contents

Part 3 The information society and policy / 129

Part 4 The information society and the information professional / 167

Contributors

Chris Batt OBE BA FCLIP is Director of the Libraries and Information Society Team at Resource: the Council for Museums, Archives and Libraries. He is responsible for strategic advice on the delivery of services to users of museums, archives and libraries. As part of his remit to advise on the use of ICT he is responsible for the implementation of the Government's People's Network programme.

He also leads the development of strategic planning for public libraries, working closely with the Department of Culture, Media and Sport and other government departments to position public libraries at the heart of national policy. Until August 1999 Chris was Director of Leisure Services for the London Borough of Croydon where he had worked for over 20 years. His responsibilities as Director of Leisure Services included libraries, museums and heritage, the arts, sport and recreation, parks and open spaces, and tourism.

Ian Beeson MA MSc is a member of the Information Systems School and of the Community Information Systems Centre at the University of the West of England, Bristol. He came to computing from an educational background in anthropology and linguistics, when COBOL 'seemed something exotic and romantic'. He followed a career in programming and systems analysis before moving into teaching. His main research interests are focused on sociocultural and philosophical aspects of new information technologies, and particularly on how people and communities can make creative and empowering use of them.

Alistair Black BA MA DipLib PhD MCLIP read history at both undergraduate and postgraduate levels. Having qualified as a librarian he occupied professional posts in both academic and public libraries in the 1980s. In 1990 he became a lecturer in information studies at Leeds Metropolitan University where he is currently Professor of Library and Information History. He is author of *A new history of the English public library: social and intellectual contexts 1850-1914* (Leicester University Press, 1996) and *The public library in Britain 1914-2000* (The British Library, 2000).

Peter Brophy Bsc HonFCLIP FCLIP FRSA is Professor of Information Management and Director of the Centre for Research in Library and Information Management (CERLIM) at Manchester Metropolitan University, and is Chairman of the LIS consultancy, LIMC Ltd. He is a former President of the UK Institute of Information Scientists and Fellow of The Library Association, and is now an Honorary Fellow of CILIP: the Chartered Institute of Library and Information Professionals. Until 1998 he was Head of the converged Library and Learning Resource Services at the University of Central Lancashire. He has published widely in the LIS field.

Zoë Clarke BA MA MCLIP is a Research Associate in the Centre for Research in Library and Information Management (CERLIM), in the Department of Information and Communications at Manchester Metropolitan University. Her current research activity is in the digitization area, where she is co-ordinator of the Cultural Objects in Networked Environments (COINE) project. Her previous research activity was in the area of library performance measurement, where she worked on the EQUINOX, EQLIPSE and CAMILE projects. Previously she worked in academic libraries at Liverpool John Moores University, Humberside University and the University of Central Lancashire.

Graham P. Cornish BA FCLIP studied theology and history at Durham and library and information science in Liverpool before joining the (now) British Library in 1969. Since 1983 he has been responsible for copyright issues within the BL and since 1986 has managed much of the BL involvement in IFLA. He was elected a Fellow of both The Library Association and the Institute of Information Scientists, and is now a Fellow of CILIP: the Chartered Institute of Library and Information Professionals. Graham was President of The Library Association for the Year 2000 and is Chair of the LA Disciplinary Committee. He has been closely involved in several EU projects on electronic copyright management; he now heads the Secretariat for the IFLA Committee on Copyright and Other Legal Matters and is chair of the IFLA Publisher Relations Advisory Committee. He is also a member of the Government's Creative Industries Task Force Intellectual Property Working Group.

J. Eric Davies MA PhD FCLIP FInstAM MCMI FRSA is Director of LISU (Library and Information Statistics Unit), and also a member of Faculty in the Department of Information Science at Loughborough University. His experience of professional practice includes over 25 years in academic library management, as well as work in public libraries and special libraries. His main interests lie in strategic management and performance evaluation of services, the impact of IT and legal issues on information management, and scientific and technical information. He has published widely and delivered numerous conference papers and workshop presentations at home and overseas.

Paul Dunn MBA has a background encompassing over 20 years of IT/IS development, and has spent much of the last decade developing IS strategies and business planning. Formerly Head of IS at Oftel, he moved to the Cabinet Office's Central IT Unit to promote Information Management and research better data use within government. Through his leadership of the Government business register project he has become closely involved with the e-Government agenda and the part it plays improving Government KM.

John P. Feather BLitt MA PhD FCLIP is Professor of Library and Information Studies at Loughborough University where he has served as Head of Department, Dean, and Pro-Vice Chancellor. His books include *The information society*, now in its third edition (Library Association Publishing, 2000) and (with James Dearnley) *The wired world: an introduction to the theory and practice of the information society* (Library Association Publishing, 2001).

Margaret Haines BA MLS was appointed Director of Research and Knowledge Management for the South East Region of the Department of Health in December 2000. She is also the national KM Portfolio Director for R&D across England. Previously she was the Chief Executive of the UK's Library and Information Commission, a position she held from 1996. She was the first NHS Library Adviser for the Department of Health and the National Health Service Executive, a position she took on secondment from her post as Head of Information Resources at the King's Fund. Margaret came to England in 1989 from Canada where she had worked in the health and academic sectors. She has also been an information consultant specializing in information policy, research programme design, and knowledge management.

Susan Hornby MA has worked for the Department of Information and Communications at Manchester Metropolitan University since 1990. Her teaching and research interests are the education of information professionals, aspects of the politics and sociology of information, information in the health services, knowledge management and literature and its readers. Her publications include refereed papers in the areas of the information society, education for the professional information worker, information for health and knowledge management. With Peter Stephen she is co-author of *Simple statistics for library and information professionals* (Library Association Publishing, 2nd edn, 1997). She was a member of the QAA Benchmarking Panel for Librarianship and Information Management.

Dave Muddiman MSc BA DipLib MCLIP is Principal Lecturer in the School of Information Management, Leeds Metropolitan University. In the 1980s Dave worked in public libraries in Nottinghamshire and Sheffield before moving into LIS education and research. In broad terms his research interests concern the social dimensions of the information society; more specifically he has focused on the changing nature of the public library service. With Alistair Black he is author of *Understanding community librarianship: the public library in postmodern Britain* (1997) and he was Project Co-ordinator of the Library and Information Commission funded project Open to All: The Public Library and Social Exclusion (2000). Dave is currently working on a major AHRB project on the history of the information society.

Ian Rowlands BSc MSc PhD is a senior lecturer in the Department of Information Science at City University, London. His main teaching and research interests lie in the areas of information policy, science policy (with an emphasis on biomedicine) and bibliometrics. Before joining City, Ian worked as a consultant to various public and private sector clients, focusing mainly on text retrieval projects.

J. Stephen Town MA DipLib FCLIP is Director of Information Services at the Royal Military College of Science, Defence Academy of the UK, and Deputy University Librarian of Cranfield University. Stephen is active in research and consultancy with more than twenty publications in the fields of library management, performance measurement, benchmarking and information literacy, and clients include the NHS, Oxford University and the Swedish International Development Agency. Stephen teaches the management module of the MSc in Information and Library Management at the University of Bristol, and is a member of SCONUL's Advisory Committee on Performance Improvement and its Information Skills Task Force.

Claire Warwick MA MPhil PhD(Cantab) is a lecturer in electronic communication at the School of Library, Archive and Information Studies at University College London, specializing in Electronic Publishing, Humanities Computing and the Information Society. Claire's research centres on societal and user implications of electronic publishing and information society issues in general. Claire has a degree in Classics and English (1986–90) and a PhD in seventeenth century religious poetry (1990–94), both from Cambridge University. In 1995 she joined the electronic publisher Chadwyck-Healey, and worked on the Patrologia Latina database and Literature Online. In 1996 she moved to Oxford University to work for the Centre for Humanities Computing and the Faculty of English. In 1998 she moved to the Department of Information Studies at the University of Sheffield, before taking up her present post at UCL.

Introduction

The 'information society' is a term often used without adequate definition; politicians, those in the media and (sometimes) academics will use it as a 'buzz word' to describe the impact of information and communication technologies. The information society is much more than that: it can be a set of theoretical perspectives outlining the recent changes in society, it can be used to analyse different scenarios for current and future developments in society, and it can be used by information professionals to understand the impact that these changes are having on their role and the changing needs of their users.

When we were originally approached by the publishers to contribute to the discussion about the information society from both professional and academic perspectives it quickly became apparent that there were many different views and ideas and that it would be impossible for one or two authors to give the coverage that the topics deserved. We feel fortunate that so many people who are eminent in their field were willing to contribute and are confident that we have a text that will engender discussion and further debate. Our idea from the outset was to let the authors have their own voice and to allow debate and discussion within the text and between the authors.

This book is intended for those people in professional practice and in the field of academic study and research who have an interest in the information society and its impact on the profession. We hope that this collection will enable the reader to consider different viewpoints and aspects of the information society.

The book is arranged in four parts: the first, 'The information society: fact or fiction?', covers theoretical perspectives, the second, 'The information society and daily life', considers impacts and scenarios for current and future developments in society, the third, 'The information society and policy', discusses the impact of the information society from a governmental and policy perspective, and the final part, 'The information society and the information professional', examines the practical consequences of the impact that these changes are having on the role of the information professional.

In Part 1 the first chapter, by John Feather, is a scholarly overview of the key theoretical perspectives on the information society. He examines and evaluates the economic model of the information society using the work of Machlup and Porat, and the technological model as a development of Porat's work with perspectives added from Masuda. He further considers the sociological model through the impact of information and communication technologies on how people live and work, examining in particular the work of Castells and Daniel Bell. He also discusses the historical model and the continuing debate about how and why society has changed in the past 20 years.

The two following chapters are continuations of these debates that challenge and develop the ideas outlined by John Feather. Alistair Black's 'secular view' challenges the view of the utopian qualities of information. He questions the novelty of the information society concept and argues that there have been many information societies in the past and that human societies have witnessed many momentous developments in the history of information transfer and retrieval. He challenges the technological determinism of many of the debates, arguing that the information society is not 'a value-free, or purely techno-economic concept' but instead a 'continuation of industrialism, modernism and the Enlightenment project'.

Dave Muddiman is again sceptical about the utopian view of the information society. He analyses and challenges Marxist perspectives, arguing that information societies represent a restructured, rather than transformed social order. He evaluates changes in the workplace, relating his findings to the public library and social exclusion. He argues that there is disjuncture and fragmentation in the information society but that the information society is part of postmodernism.

Part 2 moves on from the theoretical perspectives to the effect of the information society on the individual and communities. Chris Batt's chapter is a vision of the future and a signposted way of getting there. He views the advances in information and communication technologies as a potentially beneficial factor in the way that society can change. He discusses the fluidity of information flows and the popularity of the new technologies, and he analyses the capability of people to support, develop and take advantage of networks and networking. He discusses the potential for technological change and the role of governments and public policy in the information society. He debates the social implications of private practice and public policy, and concludes with an optimistic vision of the potential future.

Stephen Town examines the link between information literacy and the information society. He contends that the former flows from the demands of the latter and thus information literacy is an essential skill in the information society. He evaluates information literacy in various national contexts and contrasts these with strategies in the UK, particularly the SCONUL Information Skills Task Force.

Ian Beeson considers how traditional communities can resist submersion in a global information culture. This does not entail rejection of information technology, but rather using it in an appropriate manner to enable local communities to tell their own stories. Theoretical analysis is followed by a description of the True Stories research project which included a case study of the use of hypermedia technology by a community group in Bristol (UK) to tell the story of their annual carnival.

Part 3 examines information policies from a theoretical and practical standpoint. Ian Rowlands discusses the importance of information policies in the information society. He argues that information policy is an important component in the deliberations of national governments and international public bodies; however, it is not yet clearly defined or understood. Information policy is a complex topic and to increase clarity he offers a model to help us think about the values that underpin information policy.

Margaret Haines and Paul Dunn examine knowledge management in government. Their chapter begins with an outline of the public sector in the UK and the impact that technology has on the management of knowledge. They then continue to consider the present government and the knowledge management environment, examining different aspects of knowledge management and the policies and processes necessary. Using the National Health Service as an example, the authors describe how one governmental department has been encouraged to develop knowledge management. They conclude by describing how knowledge management can aid responsive government.

Part 4 examines the implications of information and communication technologies for the information professional and the individual. Graham

Cornish examines one of the more problematic areas of the information society for information professionals, that of intellectual property. He outlines the rights and privileges concerning copyright and evaluates the impact of information technology. He discusses the neglect and abuse of intellectual property rights and ways of overcoming them (licences, using the technology). He considers the dichotomy of freedom of access and copyright. His chapter should be required reading for all professionals concerned with protection of intellectual property and access to information.

Eric Davies explores the relatively new subject of personal data protection, a topic that has became of increasing concern to many as mass data processing has greatly expanded the potential risks posed by the inappropriate use of personal data held on computers. He defines data protection and refers to national and international activity designed to protect personal privacy. He explains the legal underpinning to data protection in the UK and discusses recent research in the field.

Claire Warwick discusses electronic publishing and its predicted impact, and whether this has been realized. She examines the history of publishing and the place of electronic publishing in this process. She contends that while electronic publishing is appropriate for some types of publication, for others its reliance on computer hardware makes it inappropriate. Lack of accessibility and portability has resulted in less take-up than originally predicted of electronic publications.

In our final chapter Peter Brophy discusses the role of the information professional in the information society. He considers the definition of a profession and to what extent these criteria apply to the information profession. Various aspects of the information profession are examined, such as professional and ethical standards, and the challenges of information technology. He contends that professionalism in many of these areas is as yet ill defined and offers us a challenge in the emerging information society.

We would like to thank all of those who contributed to this text for their time, their patience and their good humour, and we hope that the reader finds this an interesting and thought-provoking collection.

Part 1

The information society: fact or fiction?

1
Theoretical perspectives on the information society

John Feather

Introduction

Academic analysis of the societal function of information has inevitably led to the development of theories which attempt to provide a conceptual framework within which such studies can be pursued. The task has been made more complex by the lack of agreement on what exactly is meant by the phrase *information society*, and indeed how it relates to other descriptors such as *information age*, or *post-industrial society*. To compound even these complications, there are issues around the relationships between the information society and the academic disciplines of *information theory* and *information science*, not to mention various other terms which are sometimes used analogously with the latter, such as *informatics, information studies* and *information management*. These terminological issues might, in themselves, be thought to reflect the pervasiveness and visibility of information in contemporary society, and the extent to which it is considered to be a significant subject for study. For that very reason, however, the subject attracts scholars from many different disciplines, and impinges on practice in a number of professions both old and new. The purpose of this chapter is to try to explicate some of the issues that have been identified, and to describe some of the approaches that have been adopted, in the continuing attempt to provide the theoretical framework that will help us to understand the practical issues.

From the large and growing literature that claims to deal with the information society, a search of seven abstracting services (Computing and Information

Science Abstracts; Conference Proceedings Index; Electronic and Communications Abstracts; LISA; Social Services Abstracts; Sociological Abstracts; Worldwide Political Science Abstracts) using the term information AND society produced over 9000 hits (www.csa1.co.uk, 4 January 2002) – from this we can derive four broad frameworks within which scholars seem to work:

- economic
- technological
- sociological
- historical.

We shall consider each of these in turn, and attempt to assess the extent to which they help to explain the phenomenon which we describe as the information society.

The economic model

The essence of the economic model of the information society is that information is regarded as a commodity. Like other commodities it is an object of trade, and can therefore generate profits for producers, manufacturers and distributors. It will reach the consumer or end-user only after a series of commercial transactions of which the full cost is necessarily borne by the ultimate recipient. In this simple formulation, however, the commodity is not really the information at all, it is the physical manifestation or format in which the information is made available. Information itself is an abstract concept. Payment is made for the book, magazine or newspaper, or for access to a database. It may be a direct payment by the consumer, or made on his or her behalf by an employer or other organization, or the costs may be met by the use of tax revenues to provide services and institutions for society as a whole. In practice this is a mixed economy of public and private provision; but even if it were wholly public or wholly private the monetary exchanges would still take place.

The financial dimension of the provision of information media is, however, only one aspect of an economic approach to information. At a more complex level, information itself, rather than merely the information carrier, is argued to have been commodified. The underlying assumption is that information is a construct, which can be understood as an artefact in whose manufacture value has been added to pre-existing material. Theorists of the economics of information use analogues with other industries. When metal, plastic, fabrics and other materials are made into a car, value is added to the original materials at each stage of the process. Cumulatively, they have a value which none of them could acquire separately. It is the value-added element for which the consumer is willing to pay provided that the product can be sold at a price that is acceptable to both buyer and seller. It is argued that the raw material, the steel, of information is *knowledge*. The classic formulation is that information, is constructed from knowledge by a process of selection and analysis, and is then presented in a useful and usable form. Value is added at each stage of the process, and in this way knowledge is transformed into information, is indeed turned into a marketable commodity to which a meaningful price can be attached. (For a more extended introduction to these ideas, see Hayes, 2003).

Economists began to take an interest in information in the second half of the 20th century. This interest was practical rather than theoretical. Knowledge and information were seen to underpin many important economic and social activities, such as education, research, publishing and broadcasting. These activities could not easily be defined in terms of the division of the economy into the three traditional sectors of agriculture, industry and service provision. To some extent the activities on which the economists were now focusing overlapped with both the industrial and service sectors. Education is a service. Publishing is a manufacturing industry. But how do we classify research? Is broadcasting a service in the same sense as, say, insurance or banking? The first attempt at a comprehensive analysis of these issues was undertaken in the late 1950s and early 1960s, and is associated particularly with the work of Fritz Machlup. His *Production and distribution of knowledge in the United States*, published in 1962, was the first systematic attempt to identify the place of knowledge and information in the economy as whole.

Machlup's method was to examine expenditure on goods and services across the economy as whole, and then to relate this to the activities that he considered to be concerned with what he called 'knowledge'. (Machlup was rather dismissive of the knowledge-information dichotomy. He regarded them as essentially the same.) These activities included those that we have already mentioned, such as education, broadcasting and publishing. But Machlup added an important new element: knowledge creation, or research. In other words, he looked beyond the product to the raw materials. Machlup considered that research and development lay at the core of knowledge-related economic activity. On this basis, he concluded that by the late 1950s, rather more than 30% of the US economy was knowledge related, and that it occupied over 40% of the active workforce. (Machlup, 1962, 382–7). Moreover, by looking at the percentage of 16-year-olds who were continuing in school and then going on to college or university, he concluded that this percentage would continue to grow. Machlup's findings were startling. At the time, the USA saw itself (rightly) as the world's leading manufacturing country, and yet here was evidence that the manufacturing of goods was being overtaken by very different kinds of activities which would need a very different workforce.

Fifteen years later, Marc U. Porat, another economist, re-examined Machlup's conclusions, and conducted substantial research of his own. Porat started from Machlup's conclusion: that the production and distribution of knowledge are essential elements in an advanced economy. The task Porat undertook was not to identify its existence, but to delineate it in detail. It was he who formally proposed that the information sector should be added to the three traditional sectors that economists had used. This proposal was itself radical, but Porat went further. He argued that the economy as a whole had become so dependent on knowledge, that it was now most accurately described as an 'information economy', the phrase that he used in the title of his most important publication on the subject (Porat, 1977).

Porat's research suggested to him that about half of the total workforce of the USA was engaged in the information economy by the mid-1970s. To analyse this phenomenon, he constructed a model in which there are distinctions between 'primary' and 'secondary' sectors, and between five areas of activity: information production, information distribution, information transaction handling, information hardware and software, and supporting facilities. All workers were either put into one or other of these sectors and activities, or were defined by exclusion as 'non-information workers'. Porat's primary sector consists essentially of those activities which generate knowledge and information and convey it to others. Thus research and development, education, publishing, library provision and telecommunications all fall in the primary sector. In the secondary sector he placed a combination of activities which were essentially similar to those in the primary sector but took place within an organization (such as staff training), or which supported activities in the primary sector (such as management services).

Porat's economic model of the information economy is still relevant a quarter of a century after it was developed, despite all the changes that have taken place. Indeed, many of those changes have been not unlike the developments that Machlup and Porat envisaged. The advanced economies have shifted even further from manufacturing to service provision, and have become increasingly dependent on the generation of knowledge and the dissemination of information for their economic well-being. In specific terms, we can see this in the various manifestations of those parts of the economy which fall into Porat's primary information sector, especially perhaps in information distribution and information transaction handling. The massive growth of computing, telecommunications, broadcasting, and publishing can already be seen as a key development of the last 20 years of the last century.

The technological model

The growth of some of the key areas of the information sector of the economy in the 1980s and 1990s is associated with technological innovation and the widespread adoption of new technologies in almost every aspect of Porat's information economy. Whether in production, distribution or transaction handling, new devices and systems for the storage, analysis and communication of information have wrought change in the activities that Machlup and Porat described. The issue is whether this change is a fundamental re-conceptualization of activities and their purpose, or whether it is merely a change, albeit very significant, in techniques and mechanisms. Another way of expressing the problem is to ask whether technological change drives social change, or social change demands new technological solutions to new and newly identified problems.

It is incontestable that there has been revolutionary change in the technology of information. Since the first electronic computers became commercially available in the early 1950s, generations of machines have followed each other with increasing rapidity. The ubiquitous devices and systems of the turn of the 21st century were all less than 20 years old in 2000, and some of them had less than five years of history behind them. The personal computer, the key to all of this, came on to the general market in the mid-1980s. The internet spread outside the academic world and a small number of business and government users around 1990. The world wide web became a public facility in the mid-1990s. Digital technologies moved from the leading edge of science and technology to everyday life in the home and the office in ten years. Development periods were becoming very short, devices became cheaper. A generation of people approaching maturity has never lived in a world without networked computers.

The issue is not whether there has been technological change and innovation: that is undeniable. It is rather whether the change has been led by the needs of users and of society at large, or whether technologies and systems have been developed for which uses have then been found. Is the information society essentially an information *technology* society, or is it something more than that? It is perhaps not surprising to find that some of those who pioneered the development of IT are strong advocates of the view that social and economic change was technology driven. The Japanese writer Yoneji Masuda sees technological development as the essential driver of social change, and identifies the information society with an economy transformed by information technology. (Masuda's most accessible work is *Managing in the information society: releasing synergy Japanese-style.*) Masuda was centrally involved in the development of the Japanese computer industry in the 1970s and 1980s. The essence of his view was that computers changed everything by opening up new ways of working and living.

At first sight, this is a tempting and powerful argument. Other writers have identified a consistent delay between the development of information and communication technologies and their large-scale adoption (Winston, 1998). It is argued that there is a consistent pattern of invention followed by a search for an application. The application often turns out to be quite different from that envisaged by the inventor. The most successful inventions are not necessarily those that seem to have the greatest promise at the time. The history of communication is littered with examples. In the late 19th century, for example, the telephone was seen as a medium for the dissemination of entertainment, particularly music, while sound recording was thought of primarily as an educational tool. A related phenomenon is that new media supplement rather than supplant those that already exist. Handwriting continued after the invention of printing; radio broadcasting has found a distinctive role alongside television; telephone and e-mail live happily together performing slightly different functions. While it may be proverbially true that necessity is the mother of invention, it is also the case that the parent can be the sheer curiosity of the inventor. That can lead to dead ends, but some are more apparent than real. When Ted Nelson conceptualized hypertext, there was no technology that could deliver it; 20 years later, it was the key to developing the content and presentation of the world wide web.

The society of the early 21st century is critically dependent on information and communication technologies for a huge number of activities. Very few of these, however, are genuinely and inherently new. Some have displaced older systems, as paper-based correspondence has been largely, although by no means entirely, replaced by e-mail. Some operate in parallel to existing systems, as online databases sit happily alongside traditional reference books. It is, by and large, users who determine the success or failure of particular systems and devices. Choices may be based on social convenience (the mobile phone), business efficiency (electronic mail), or economic necessity (financial information systems), but they are essentially choices. Technology does not determine what happens; it only determines what *can* happen.

There is, however, a broader context. The ICT developments of the last 50 years did not take place in an intellectual vacuum. To some extent, computers have solved problems which had been identified, described and analysed long before there were machines available to solve them. For most of the 20th century, the phenomenon that we now call 'information overload' was of growing concern to librarians and others engaged in the provision and use of the literature through which information was disseminated. Those who considered these issues, and attempted a systematic description of them, were the pioneers of the discipline that we now call information science. In the 1920s, the English librarian (who preferred to call himself a documentalist), S. C. Bradford made a systematic attempt to describe the structure of scientific literature, already growing at an alarming rate. Later theorists, such as Zipf and Lotke, added their own empirically derived laws about how information is disseminated and retrieved. Information science, the study of the collection, processing, analysis and dissemination of information, was established as an academic discipline by 1960, and came together with other intellectual development to provide a theoretical framework within which ICT was increasingly applied to the delivery of information to users (Meadows, 1987; Dearnley and Feather, 2001, 5–7). While the early information scientists were essentially studying how information users behaved, others were publishing more theoretical studies. The development of a universally applicable model of communication by two American mathematicians, Claude T. Shannon and Warren Weaver, was a critical point in this development. Shannon and Weaver essentially described how data travelled from source to recipient, using whatever means might be available (their focus was on voice telephony), and how it was distorted by 'noise'. Noise could be a purely technical phenomenon, such as a bad electrical connection, or, more profoundly, it could be a distortion of the content of the information, either deliberate or accidental at some point in its transmission. Shannon and Weaver were not the only mathematicians working on communications problems. Others included Alan Turing in England, who before World War 2 conceptualized a logic machine to solve numerical problems; John von Neumann in the USA, who in the 1930s began to develop the formal logic that could be applied in such a machine; and Norbert Wiener, who developed a mathematical description of communications engineering and control systems in the 1950s. Information theory – the theory of how information is accumulated, analysed and transmitted – helped to describe what ICT was doing, and perhaps helped to conceptualize its potential (Vakkari and Cronin, 1992). The contemporaneous development of information technology and information theory offered both physical and intellectual tools which could be used to help in the more effective use of information.

The sociological model

The impact of ICT on the way people live and work is undeniable. The question of whether change followed from the development of technologies, or technologies were developed to meet a desire for change, is important when we seek to understand the causes of what has happened. Regardless of the answer, however, the effects of change are visible all around us. It is those effects which sociologists seek to identify and explain. Both economics and technology are called into play as necessary elements in a broad sociological analysis of the information society, but so are wider social issues and social theories. In its most extreme form, a sociological model of the information society argues that the whole of society is changing fundamentally under the impact of the use of ICT. In particular, this approach is associated with the work of Manuel Castells (Castells, 1996; 1997; 1998).

The essence of Castells's case is that new forms of communication and of information storage and processing will ultimately determine everything that we do. Certain kinds of work will vanish altogether, or be squeezed into the margins of the world economy. Leisure activities will take on new forms, both in public and in private. Political systems will evolve which will be responsive to the demands of a more informed population with easy access to a vast quantity of information, and less susceptible to traditional methods of persuasion. At the same time, a new underclass is being created of those who are excluded from the information revolution. This does not only disempower the less educated and less wealthy in the developed countries. It encompasses whole countries and even entire regions of the world, where the national or regional economies are not strong enough to support the development of the essential infrastructure of the information society. The counterbalance to information wealth is information poverty, and, in general terms, it is the financially deprived who are also deprived of information, whether the deprivation is individual or general.

An analysis along these lines is related to the economic analyses of Machlup and Porat. The shift from an economy based on extraction and manufacture, to one based on service provision and knowledge transfer, leaves massive social dislocation in its wake. For over a hundred years from the middle of the 19th century onwards (and somewhat earlier in some cases) many of the great cities of Europe and the USA were essentially places of mass-manufacturing industry. Large numbers of workers were employed by a small number of firms, based in factories or mines. First housing, then transport systems, and – much later – health, education and welfare provision was built around the existence of this workforce. In the first half of the 20th century, the traditional patterns of industrial work were modified into a different kind of mass production, exemplified in the rapidly developing motor car manufacturing industry, and often called Fordism. The essence of Fordism is that every worker has a specific function, and that goods are produced by the combined efforts of large numbers of workers. Individual initiative is stifled; the production line is the effective master of the system.

Fordism at its worst had deeply unpleasant personal and social consequences, but in terms of efficiency and profitability it could work extremely well. Adapted to different conditions and different products, it enabled the USA to play a key role in winning World War 2 by facilitating the mass production of aeroplanes, ships, tanks and armaments. But it contained the seeds of its own destruction. The rebuilding of the economies of the defeated powers, and particularly Japan, was done by imitating Fordism both in structure and in products, and then successfully competing in world markets. By the 1970s, social prophets like Daniel Bell were foreseeing the end of Fordism in the USA, and the coming of what Bell himself called the 'post-industrial society' (Bell, 1974). It was the beginning of the post-industrial society which Machlup identified and Porat delineated. Knowledge and information would indeed become more important than coal and iron ore. What mattered was the accumulation of intellectual and fiscal capital; the mere production of goods would take place wherever it could be most cost effective. In the developed economies there was therefore a decreasing demand for unskilled and semi-skilled labour, and a growing need for knowledge workers. In turn, this made it necessary to promote the growth of educational provision for people beyond the traditional school-leaving age, and for continued re-training throughout a person's working life. The tyranny of the shop floor has been replaced for many by the more subtle but more insidious tyranny of uncertainty and change, redesignated as flexibility and lifelong learning.

The transformation of work, the central theme of Bell's prophecy and Castells's analysis, has had a worldwide impact. Long before 'globalization' became a fashionable buzz word, the interdependence of national economies was an established fact. Indeed, it goes back to the 19th century and even earlier, when the European colonial empires were, in part, a means of supplying food and raw materials for the people of Europe and their industries. Since the 1960s, the increasingly knowledge-based economies of the West have effectively exported their manufacturing industries to parts of the developing world, not least to their own former colonies. This is particularly apparent in the newly industrialized countries of east and south-east Asia. The 'tiger economies', Korea, Malaysia, Singapore, Thailand and so on, have developed significant large-scale manufacturing capacity built on a combination of Fordism and cheap labour. Of course some of these countries (Singapore being a notable example) also have a commitment to the development of a knowledge economy, but all too often their contribution to the information society is to be the source of cheap computers built by labour as sweated as that used to manufacture footballs and trainers.

The impact of these economic changes on the functioning of society, both locally and globally, lies at the heart of contemporary political debate about the information society. The German sociologist Jurgen Habermas has argued for many years that the mass media of the 20th century, by providing a one-way system of mass communication, have effectively destroyed the public space in which public discourse can take place (Habermas, 1989). One can take this argument further by contending that in the industrialized countries, social intercourse is increasingly mediated through communications systems rather than being directly between people. This is perhaps the point at which the development of ICT has most obviously and most immediately influenced the way of life of significant numbers of people. At the simplest level, the near-universal use of mobile phones and e-mail in the developed countries has wrought great changes in the way in which people interact with each other in both personal and professional relationships. Communication has indeed become almost immeasurably easier than it was even ten years ago, but the nature of the relationship between the communicators has also changed.

Inevitably, analysts who seek to explain these phenomena put different emphases on different aspects of what is happening. Castells sees the development of a global communications network as the driver of economic change. Other observers take different views. The British sociologist Anthony Giddens, who had a significant impact on the development of the ideas of New Labour in the 1990s, sees globalization itself as the central phenomenon which is driving social and economic change, including the adoption of ICT which he regards as instrumental rather than causative (Giddens, 1999). There is an increasingly common view that the internet has been over-hyped as a driver of economic change, and that in the end it is simply another system of communication. Moreover, it is one whose economic consequences are far from being universally beneficent (Cassidy, 2002).

The historical model

The continuing debate about how and why society has changed in the last 20 years is, in itself, a recognition of the profundity of the change. Bell the prophet, Habermas the explicator of causes, and Castells the analyst of consequences all have at least one opinion in common: that there has been change and that it will continue. It is precisely this recognition that has led to another approach to understanding the information society, which takes as its starting point the idea that even revolutionary change has its roots in what has preceded it. It is argued that all organized human societies have always been dependent on information, and have been concerned to record it, store it, retrieve it, disseminate it and control it. Whether symbols are incised into a lump of clay and then baked, or digitally imprinted on to a floppy disk, the principles remain essentially unchanged. What has changed is the ease of access to the media and systems, and the widespread (although far from universal) capacity to use them (Feather, 2000).

The key perception is that information has a history. This needs a little further explanation. Any given piece of information has its own history; it has been derived from knowledge through a process of disaggregation from a larger body of knowledge (a single fact taken from an encyclopedia) or combination (making two or more facts into a single piece of information). But information also has a history in a broader sense; there is a history of how information has been assembled, stored and made available. This is a history of public and private provision of systems of communication, and of institutions through which those systems have been put into the public domain. In part, this is an outgrowth of the traditional (and often deadly dull) sub-discipline of library history. But it is far from being merely a history of one aspect of information service provision (Black, 1998).

A broad historical sweep provides a meaningful context for the understanding of the impact of digital technologies and economic and social changes with which they are associated. It also, however, provides a proper context for understanding and analysing the development of the digital technologies themselves. Networked computing may be argued to be the driver of radical and even revolutionary change, but in itself it is merely the latest of a series of innovations in communications systems and technologies. We can begin the story at many different points: with the clay tablets of ancient Assyria; with the invention of alphabetic writing in the pre-classical Mediterranean; with the Western invention of printing in 15th-century Germany; or with telegraphy, telephony, wireless or for that matter electronic computing. The fact remains that wherever we begin, there is a history; we can only understand where we are by knowing something of how we came to be here. Even the argument that the internet is a uniquely revolutionary tool of communication only makes full sense if it can be argued in comparative terms against the significance of the adoption of other communications systems. The importance of historical perspective is too often lost amidst the fierce political and economic arguments which rage around the concept and impact of the global information society.

Conclusion

The question that is implicit in the first sentence of this chapter has no answer that is 'right' or 'wrong', nor even any single answer. The work that has been so briefly surveyed here is no more than the tip of the iceberg of how academics, economists, politicians, journalists and many others have reacted to the change that all can see and seek to explain. There is no single explanation. Indeed, there is probably not even a consensus on the facts of the case. Has the internet fundamentally changed how we communicate? how we learn? how we work? how we enjoy ourselves? how we find our partners? Or is it simply another system of communication which like the telegraph, the telephone and wireless before it simply drives people further apart while apparently bringing them closer together? Has the development of the knowledge-based economy brought greater personal freedom and greater flexibility in how, when and where we work? And how do we set that against the possibility of working all the time, and the pressure to do so? And against the export of semi-skilled jobs, and the creation of a global underclass of those deprived of information who provide cheap manual labour? These questions are so huge, and of such fundamental importance, that there can be no single or simple answer to them. Perhaps we are too close to the phenomena that we are trying to understand. Even taking an historically informed approach, we are still looking at a society of which we are a part and in which we live and work.

It may be that in due course a generally accepted universal theory of the information society will be developed. The history of the disciplines that would contribute to it – economics, sociology, history, information science – suggests otherwise! Indeed, like all disciplines they flourish on debate and disagreement, and tend to atrophy when there is universal assent. Any satisfactory theoretical approach to understanding and explaining the phenomena that we describe – however unsatisfactorily – as the 'information society' will have to be multi-disciplinary, and have a clear relationship to the observable (and sometimes measurable) developments in wealth creation, education, personal work and leisure, and political action. Technological innovation will continue to be a factor, but it will never be the only driver of change, and not always the most important. The information society is an essentially social phenomenon: it is about how people live and work both individually and with each other. Therein lies its importance and its unending fascination.

References

Bell, D. (1974) *The coming of a post-industrial society. A venture in social forecasting*, London, Heinemann. For Bell's work, see Duff, A. S. (1998) Daniel Bell's theory of the information society, *Journal of Information Science*, **24** (6), 1998, 373–94.

Black, A. (1998) Information and modernity: the history of information and the eclipse of library history, *Library History*, **14** (1), 39–45.

Cassidy, J. (2002) *Dot.con. The greatest story ever sold*, London, Allen Lane.

Castells, M. (1996) *The rise of the network society*, Oxford, Blackwell.

Castells, M. (1997) *The power of identity*, Oxford, Blackwell.

Castells, M. (1998) *End of millennium*, Oxford, Blackwell.

Dearnley, J. and Feather, J. (2001) *The wired world. An introduction to the theory and practice of the information society*, London, Library Association Publishing.

Feather, J. (2000) *The information society. A study of continuity and change*, 3rd edn, London, Library Association Publishing.

Giddens, A. (1999) *Runaway world: how globalisation is re-shaping our lives*, Cambridge, Profile Books.

Habermas, J. (1989) *The structural transformation of the public sphere [Strukturwandel der Öffenlichkeit]*, London, Polity Press.

Hayes, R. M. (2003) Economics of information. In Feather, J. and Sturges, P. (eds), *International encyclopedia of information and library science*, London, Routledge.

Machlup, F. (1962) *The production and distribution of knowledge in the United States*, Princeton, NJ, Princeton University Press. For Machlup see Dryer, J. S. (ed.) (1978) *Breadth and depth in economics: Fritz Machlup – the man and his ideas*, Boston, MA, D. C. Heath.

Masuda, Y. (1990) *Managing in the information society: releasing synergy Japanese-style*, Oxford, Basil Blackwell.

Meadows, A. J. (ed.) (1987) *The origins of information science*, London, Taylor Graham.

Porat, M. U. (1977) *The information economy: definition and measurement,* Washington, DC, US Department of Commerce.

Vakkari, P. and Cronin, B. (eds) (1992) *Conceptions of library and information science,* London, Taylor Graham.

Winston, B. (1998) *Media, technology and society: a history from the telegraph to the Internet,* London and New York, Routledge.

2
The information society: a secular view

Alistair Black

Introduction

Those of us who are unable to proclaim faith in the sacred or utopian qualities of information, or in the existence of an information society, might be said to profess a *secular* critique of the belief that we have entered a fundamentally new age, one that is centrally defined by the arrival of digital information and communication technologies (ICTs). The word 'secular' is employed here in its dual sense. Firstly, 'that which is concerned with the affairs of this world; that which is temporal; not spiritual or sacred; not concerned with religion or religious belief; not bound by a religious rule'. Secondly, 'that which lasts for, or occurs over, an indefinitely long time; going on from age to age; continuing through long ages'.[1] This second definition provides a useful, yet under-used, methodological route for challenging the information society idea. Adopting a long view of both the information infrastructure and the definition of information facilitates a valuable re-assessment of the information society proposition by questioning its novelty as well as its accepted, popular meaning. An historical perspective challenges the faith of the 'info-enthusiasts'.[2] The 'information society' secularism which this chapter proposes rejects both the blind belief that has been shown in the power of digital ICTs and the various forms of worship in which information society millenarians have engaged.[3]

Challenging the faith: the information society as 'regime of truth'

The dictum that 'knowledge is power' has become a comforting cliché for those who interpret the social effects of recent advances in the technologies of information as ultimately liberating. As one commentator put it in the formative period of the information technology revolution in the early 1980s:

> Information is wealth, and wide and swift access to information is power. That is the credo of information technology. It is a truism ages old, understood long before Francis Bacon defined it in 1597.
>
> (Large, 1982, 3)

It is predicted that the digital information revolution will deliver a social revolution that has the potential of unprecedented emancipation and empowerment. The information society will in essence be a 'knowledge society' in which technologies of unimaginable, yet accessible, power will by their very prolific and democratic nature dissolve disadvantage and engineer egalitarianism.

This enticing vision is based on the recognition of a strictly one-way relationship between knowledge and power, with knowledge serving as the determining force. However, according to the French cultural theorist and historian Michel Foucault, the way power and knowledge interact is much more complex (Gordon, 1980). For Foucault, knowledge is not simply a factor that determines power; it is also a product of power itself. Power, argued Foucault, has the capacity to generate knowledge: 'we cannot exercise power except through the production of truth'.[4] All knowledge is to a degree socially constructed. History has the advantage of revealing areas of knowledge which, according to current 'truth', were in the past patently false, deriving their legitimacy from the fact that powerholders 'made them true'. In this connection one might include the past 'truths', or 'regimes of truth' in Foucault's vocabulary,[5] that the sun revolves around the earth, or that homosexuality is a disease, or that poverty results essentially from individual character.

A prominent 'regime of truth' over the last quarter of a century has been the idea of the information society. Its legitimacy, its sustenance, is drawn from a wide array of interested parties who, albeit perhaps not in any conspirational way, stand to gain social or professional recognition, if not material reward, from establishing the information society as a 'given' phenomenon, as an incontrovertible 'fact'. The information society has become less a superhighway than a 'superhypeway' (Preston, 2001, 9). Librarians appear particularly anxious to celebrate the information society. It has been advised that librarians 'should be in the business of promoting the Information Society' (Hendrix, 1997, 1). Alongside librarians it is possible to detect strong support for the concept from other information professions and from the information industries generally, from software engineers, computer hardware manu-facturers, the media industries, and from the communication, marketing and advertising sectors (collectively referred to by Roszak (1988, 34–61) as the 'data merchants'). Each of these is a stakeholder in the information society proposition. Each contributes to the 'discursive formation', the panoply of interlocking discourses, which underpins the theory of the information society.

In the last quarter of the 20th century the information society proposition attained near-paradigmatic status (Duff, 1995). It has become a commonplace, if not exactly a household, explanation and interpretation of change in the late 20th century. This chapter is located in the critical and increasingly persuasive discourse that the information society proposition is in reality a mirage: a vision built on the shifting sands of the disquietening social change that has characterized recent decades. More specifically, the argument is made here that the myth of the information society is easily exposed by employing an historical perspective on the meaning of information and on the components of what may be described as the 'information infrastructure': the array of institutions, technologies, techniques and mass media which facilitate the collection, storage, organization and transmission of information.[6] Using information as a lens to enhance our long view of Western social, cultural and economic development immediately confronts the proposition put forward, among others, by Drucker (1969) that the new knowledge technologies and the resultant knowledge society have delivered an 'age of discontinuity'.

The reification and deification of information: the spiritual 'form' of information and the secular response

It is ironic that just as we are told that we have entered a knowledge society, fashioned by a belief in the efficacy of reason in the tradition of the Enlightenment project, trust in knowledge itself, in science and in the expert, has come under 'post-modern' attack (Burke, 2000, 1–2; Gillott and Kumar, 1995). It is similarly ironic that although the arrival of an information society is trumpeted in harmony with the worldly instrumentalism of digital ICTs, information retains a mystical, if not sacred, identity.

The over-zealous enthusiasm for the information society idea is part and parcel of the contemporary deification of information. Our tendency to deify information, to view it as a sacred commodity and to wrap it in an intangible mystique, is based, firstly, on the belief that an information-rich 'learning society' acts as an antidote to the material, and in particular to the damaging effects of material*ism* on the 'spirit' (Schumacher, 1973, 18); and secondly, on our perception of information as a 'thing' (the reification of information).[7] Regarding the latter, information is nowadays enthusiastically quantified. Knowledge is neatly disaggregated into data, and: 'As the lumps break down and the bits pile up, words like *quadrillon*, *terabyte* and *megaflop* have become the measure of value' (Brown and Duguid, 2000, 12). Roszak (1988, 24) correctly observes that as information becomes less 'connected with the semantic content of statements', it is increasingly associated with the scientific (as opposed to the semiotic) model of communication theory which is defined by 'a purely quantitative measure of communication exchanges . . . through some mechanical channel'. In the context of this model, although mediated by machines or systems which convey it as tangible 'signals' that can be decoded, information is none the less conceptualized as lacking visibility, as 'stuff' lost in the ether. The ancient meaning of information, on the other hand, centres on 'process', not 'item'. The etymology of 'information' reveals that for most of its history it has been perceived of not as a 'thing', rather as an 'action' or a 'happening'. 'Information' is derived from the Latin words 'informare' (to instruct) and 'informatio' (or idea).[8] As such, it has a long history of being used in the sense of the *receiving* or *giving* of 'new knowledge' about something.[9]

Furthermore, according to Peters (1988), in the late Middle Ages 'information' took on an additional and more profound, near-spiritual meaning, one which emphasized the 'information as process'. In the early Renaissance of the 13th century the reinterpretation of the works of Aristotle by Thomas Aquinas and his contemporaries included a re-appraisal of the meaning of 'information'. Of particular relevance in this respect was Aristotle's thinking on physics. In seeking the causes of physical change in natural bodies, Aristotle identified two main ingredients of change: firstly, matter (or that which persisted through change); and secondly, form (that which appears in the process of change). Through change, said Aristotle, matter acquires form it did not previously possess. For Aristotle (and Thomas Aquinas) neither matter nor form could exist by itself (this was unlike Plato's Forms, 'universal ideas' or 'timeless truths' such as beauty or love, which existed independently of objects). In keeping with Aristotle's idea of 'form', a dog, for example, could be perceived of as a body of matter 'in-formed' by the 'form', or essence, of dog (or 'dogness'). An Aristotelian 'form', therefore, can be defined as 'that which makes an object what it is'. For Aristotle, there existed no separately existing transcendental Platonic 'form'.

Aristotle wrote of the 'formal cause of an object'; material objects being shaped, or 'in-formed', by 'forms' from within. Aquinas applied Aristotle's matter–form relationship directly. He believed all substances were composed of 'form' and matter, and that the soul was the substantial 'form' of the body, even though it was entirely immaterial in its inner structure. Thus, ancient philosophy, as interpreted by medieval thinkers, associated 'information' with the infusion, or the instillation, of form into matter: the shaping of matter by intangible, although not transcendental, 'form'. In the absence of scientific reasoning and knowledge, the idea of the form was a means of explaining how particular matter took on a particular shape: matter 'in-formed' by 'form'.[10]

Putting the intricacies to one side, the essence which can be extracted from this philosophical discussion is a conceptualization of information as a 'process', not a 'thing'. This is similar to the view of information adhered to by thinkers of the early Enlightenment when addressing questions of epistemology. Empiricists argued that the way individuals obtained knowledge was merely through interaction with the real world; through experience and the senses. Our minds are in-formed by environment: intellect shaped by nature. Rationalists, on the other hand, believed in the existence of knowledge 'a priori'. That is to say, the mind at birth is not a blank page, but is populated by innate, native, intuitive powers, thoughts and qualities – such as love, a sense of duty, a linguistic programme for acquiring language, or simply inherited personality traits – by which we are able to make an impression on our environment; by which we are able to in-form the world.

Again, the detail of the philosophical discourse need not delay us. What needs to be stressed is the continuation in the early Enlightenment of the ancient–medieval notion of information as a process; specifically, the process of the mind imprinting itself on reality, or vice versa, according to one's epistemological persuasion. However, where Enlightenment thought did eventually depart from earlier interpretations of information was in the questioning of metaphysical power. The 'in-forming' 'forms' of Aristotle and Thomas Aquinas, formulated as they were in rigid, non-secular belief systems, inevitably evince a mystical explanation of reality. The Enlightenment, on the other hand, stressed the possibilities of progress and of emancipation, of humanity breaking free from tradition, the Church and divine determinism. Central to the Enlightenment project was the belief that humanity could take control of its environment and change it for the better, through the development of rational social and political systems. This secular epistemological revolution announced that knowledge and truth could be discovered by human agency, and not simply revealed by God.

The 18th century saw the emergence of the human, or social, sciences, which constituted, in essence, the secular response to belief in divine revelation. At the heart of the social sciences resided the desire to gather and interpret data about society and the world.[11] Collecting and analysing data on human society and the natural world would reveal universal truths; science would replace divine revelation as the path to knowledge. It is here, in the empiricist tradition of the Enlightenment, that one can detect the roots of the modern meaning of information as 'thing'. Despite the fact that information can still be regarded as part of a process – data, it is said, are facts, and information the meaning that human beings give to these facts by means of organization and analysis (Davis and McCormack, 1979, 19) – in the popular mind, it might be suggested, information is considered to be synonymous with data. Like data, information is deemed, fancifully perhaps, to be scattered about like pebbles on a beach, or floating like gaseous atoms in the atmosphere. Information, conceived as data, might be 'stuff', but it is 'stuff' that is difficult to touch.

Thus, paradoxically, although information is generally seen as a 'thing', it is nonetheless also described as the ultimate intangible. Despite efforts to measure its value and to quantify it, information remains elusive, in the sense that: 'Anything contains information and information may relate to anything' (Ritchie, 1982, 96). Information retains a dimension of mystery as bewildering as that assigned it by Aristotle's 'forms'. It is no surprise, therefore, that those who claim they can come to understand the workings of this near-metaphysical commodity have evolved aspirations of a priesthood-like magnitude. In deifying information, information society enthusiasts have developed a firm faith in the existence and future utopianism of a society that is largely shaped, or informed, by information.

The long view: information societies before the information society

The contemporary approach to the questioning of the information society has in recent years been forceful and convincing (Lyon, 1988; Webster, 1995; Preston, 2001). Challenging the information society idea through contemporary evidence (which includes evidence drawn from 'recent' history) has proved fruitful. Any serious analysis of current society and recent change will reveal that, contrary to past prediction, leisure time has not increased; stress and hurry at work have if anything increased; legions of tele-workers and tele-cottages have failed to materialize; the environment has not benefited from the 'perceived' shift away from industrialism; material and information poverty persist, and in relative terms may be worsening; and labour has been neither intellectualized nor released from monotonous patterns of work. Further, our own 'everyday' experience of living and working tells us, for example, that printed documentation has proliferated and that the imminent arrival of the paperless office is pure myth (Sellen and Harper, 2002).

As valuable as a contemporary approach to questioning the information society idea, however, is the employment of a 'long-term', historical methodology: a secular perspective. Recent social and technological change might be seen 'as no more than the latest part in a continuum that has stretched over many centuries' (Dearnley and Feather, 2001, 131).[12] In a sense, all societies have to a degree, and in various ways, been information societies (Bud-Frierman, 1994, 13); and, as Duff (2000, 171) argues, it is very difficult to prove that modern societies are relatively more information based than other societies. To support this position, evidence can be drawn from: the history of information infrastructure, from a comparison between the key features of the industrial and information revolutions, and from the evolution of modernity and industrial capitalism.

From incunabula to the internet: the past development of the information infrastructure

Although rare, by virtue of its 'pervasive applications potential', the new technology system, the information infrastructure, which underlies the information society is not unprecedented (Preston, 2001, 10). Tracking the past development of the information infrastructure entails the study of both com-munication and cultural history.[13] The institutions, structures and technologies which have shaped the information infrastructure are worthy of considered historical investigation, if only because, as Bawden and Robinson (2000, 56) correctly observe, the examination of earlier communications revolutions may provide lessons for understanding the one currently underway, although it is a sobering thought that even the internet can now be studied historically (Castells, 2001, 9–35).

Human societies have witnessed a number of momentous developments in the history of information transfer and communication, including, fundamentally, the beginnings of speech and the invention of writing. The arrival of printing in the 15th century represented the next great 'cultural change of phase' (Eisenstein, 1983, 275) – although it has been argued that the ground was prepared for this much earlier, by the expansion of commercial society in the Middle Ages, which increased dramatically the demand for a range of informational devices relating to trade and to property.[14] The Enlightenment (more about this later) generated a whole new industry in the form of institutions, techniques and formats for the growth of knowledge and the storage and communication of information: from the encyclopedia, scientific academy, scholarly journal and salon, to 'mathematically' accurate maps, statistical analysis and reading materials provided in coffee houses (Headrick, 2000; Hoare, 1998).

The 18th century witnessed an explosion in the provision of books and other printed materials through libraries. Before about 1700, the typical form of library (religious, educational and civic) was essentially the endowed institution; thereafter, although endowed provision continued, libraries with a commercial funding base (subscription and circulating libraries of various types) began to appear in large numbers, resulting in a marked escalation in, and popularization of, library provision and use (Sturges, 1994, 632–3). Similarly, museums were to come to fulfil an important 'public sphere' role by relinquishing their status as mere 'cabinets of curiosities' and communicating effective information not only via their artefacts but through supporting documentation also (Bennett, 1995).

With regard to the 19th century, it is important to note the mechanization of printing,[15] as well as other mini-information revolutions constituted by the development of the postal system,[16] and the arrival in the second half of the century of mass advertising, the genesis of today's information-rich 'society of signs'.[17] In addition, special mention must be made of perhaps the most significant development in the history of communication since antiquity: namely, the electric telegraph, which for the first time permitted information to be conveyed almost instantaneously across large distances, thereby facilitating, among other things, colonial expansion (Standage, 1998).[18] In the same vein, the invention of the telephone not only bridged space but placed 'real time' communication on a truly popular footing and contributed significantly to the networking of the *modern* city, decades before the notion of the 'network society' emerged (Sterling, 1995; Graham and Marvin, 2001, 50–1). The late 19th century witnessed the start of efforts, in the form of the international movement for bibliographic organization, to track the world's burgeoning public-domain documentation and, theoretically, to provide universal access to it (Rayward, 1994; Muddiman, 1998; Ditmas, 1948).

In the 20th century communication has been dominated by the evolution of the mass media: popular newspapers, radio, film and television. These, it might be argued, alongside certain non-informational innovations such as the car and the jet engine, as well as various non-print informational formats like audio and video tape, have made as much, if not more, of an impact on people's everyday lives as computing, information technology and the internet.

The past repeating itself: waves of history and industrial/information revolution comparisons

Focusing merely on technologies, techniques and formats is a deterministic way of examining the development of information infrastructure and fails to take account of its social (including political, economic and cultural) causes. The information society is presented by its publicists as a grand periodization of history; so, by the same token, responses to it must entail references to, and analysis of, earlier 'ages'. The identification and naming of historical epochs (whether it be the Bronze Age, the Renaissance, or the information society) is fraught with methodological difficulties. The flow of history is seamless. Epochs are not formed naturally; they are not hermetically sealed, one from the other, in terms of a distinctive identity. (The tendency in recent years to confine certain cultural practices to certain decades, the culture of the 1970s, the 1980s, the 1990s and so on, is a questionable trend in this regard.) Nonetheless, without chronological categories, such as those defined by 'wave theories of history', it is difficult to make sense of the historical record, not least in respect of the important modes of thought and social practices which shape informational activity. Appropriate attention should be paid, therefore, to Kumar's (1991) theory that the information society is merely a further wave in the history of utopianism, previous waves corresponding to grand epochs of Western history over the past three centuries: the Enlightenment; the industrial revolution; the era of free trade (although not everywhere) in the late-19th century; and the immediate post-1945 decades of technological capitalism. Given the failed utopianism of these grand epochs, what chance yet another utopian vision: the information society?

A major factor which legitimizes the use of history to question the arguments of the information society proponents is the mobilization of the past by the proponents themselves to support their position. One of the most publicized uses of history to help argue that Western society is on the brink of a fundamental change is Alvin Toffler's (1980) exploration of the 'third wave' of human social development, to which he sees attached a variety of labels: Information Age, Electronic Era, Global Village, Technetronic Age, Post-Industrial Society. Toffler's three-society model has gained wide acceptance (Law, 2000, 323). In accordance with the idea that we are experiencing a fundamental break in history, it has become commonplace to argue, for example, that information is to our age what coal and iron were to the industrial revolution and the plough was to the birth of agriculture 10,000 years ago (*Information for a new age*, 1995, xi).

Rowe and Thompson (1996, 14–20), in highlighting the work of the economic historian Phyllis Deane (1980), have outlined seven main socio-economic features of the industrial revolution:

1 Widespread and systematic application of science and knowledge to pro-duction.
2 Movement of population.
3 Movement of labour between the sectors.
4 The growth of new patterns of work and new units of production.
5 The emergence of new social and occupational classes.
6 Specialization of economic activity for wide markets.
7 Intensive and extensive use of capital resources.

Each of these features, it might be argued, applies as much today, in the current 'information revolution', as it did two centuries ago; specifically:

1 The rise of a 'knowledge society' in which both digital innovation and what Bell (1980, 501) referred to as 'theoretical knowledge' prioritize brain over brawn.
2 The dispersal of population: contrary to the 'concentration' process of industrialization, there has occurred an outward drift of city populations and the emergence of the post-modern, polycentric, informational city (Castells, 1989).
3 The rise of post-industrial occupations and sectors, with the majority of the workforce migrating to the service sector and, moreover, becoming engaged in 'information work' or work rich in 'information skills'.[19]
4 The emergence of flexible modes of working: the virtual organization, teleworking.[20]
5 The professionalization of society: the decline of a traditional working class synonymous with manual labour, and the parallel rise of white-collar classes and numerous professional and managerial strata (Perkin, 1989).
6 The expansion of markets through customization and the niche targeting of demand; the replacement of Fordist production by post-Fordist regimes and 'just-in-time' methods.[21]
7 Extensive capital investment in modern ICTs; by governments, multi-/trans-national corporations and large-scale research organizations.[22]

The identification of similarities between the core characteristics of the industrial revolution and those of the information revolution,[23] albeit that the ways these manifest themselves inevitably differ from one age to the other, can be used to support the idea that we have entered a radically new age, as momentous as the new age ushered in by industrialization. At the same time, pointing up continuities with the past can also serve to undermine the notion of recent revolutionary change.

Addressing the above lists selectively, it might be argued that the real revolution in service occupations, for example, occurred in the 19th century when, between 1861 and 1911, the total number of people employed in manufacturing grew by around 50%, but the number working in areas such as insurance, banking, finance, central and local government, education and medicine (areas currently considered core to the information society) recorded increases anywhere between 200% and 1000% (Feinstein, 1976, Table 131). Staying with the service sector dimension for a moment longer, info-enthusiasts are always pleased to paint a picture of the gradual evolution of service work (especially information-rich service work) to a point where its dominance has delivered an information society. Yet one of the real continuities in this regard, certainly in the 20th century, was the astonishing growth of non-market services, in areas such as education, health, housing and social security. It is these services, funded by public expenditure, which have attracted the wrath of free-market economists and the political Right.[24] However, a distinction between the contribution of marketed and non-marketed services to the information society is rarely made. The debate over their long-term economic value aside, non-market services represent a significant factor in the information society proposition. Appropriate to this discussion's pursuit of continuities, therefore, it should be emphasized that the collectivist ideologies, not entirely vanquished even in the wake of the decline of Keynesian economics, which have given rise to increasing expenditure on public services can boast a long, pre-service economy heritage, rooted as they are in the needs and values of industrial society. Thus, with regard to the service sector aspect of the information society, but most other aspects also, ideological and 'political' issues must be addressed when assessing the validity of the information society claim.

Continuities: industrialism, capitalism, modernity and surveillance

The information society is not a value-free, or purely techno-economic, concept. Selecting again from the list of continuities offered in the previous section, especially points/similarities 6 and 7, it is plausible to assert that the information society, as Moore and Steele (1991, 4) argue, is essentially an evolutionary phase of industrial capitalism, rather than a revolutionary change of gear for human society.

Industrialism

Despite the late-20th century explosion of information (including the visual image, mass media and consumption signification), industrial society continues to inform the core of our consciousness. Notwithstanding our increased consumption of services, the industrially produced commodity remains, as it became in the second half of the 19th century, 'the centrepiece of everyday life, the focal point of all representation, the dead centre of the modern world' (Richards, 1991, 1). Even Toffler (1980, 23) entertained the term 'super-industrial society' as a descriptor of our age. Thus, taking into account, as a result of industrialization, not only the commodification of society but also the birth of 'acquisitive society', or what Perkin (1989) referred to as the rise of 'social emulative spending', it is difficult to disagree with Crouzet (1982, 12) when he writes that 'the nature of this irreversible process is that it has never stopped and still goes on under our eyes'.

Capitalism

What Lash and Urry (1987) have theorized as the rise of 'disorganised capitalism' cannot be understood without reference to digital ICTs. In the context of the performance of late-20th-century capitalism, the information society might be viewed as a 'network for a crumbling pyramid' (Dordick and Wang, 1993, 7). It is no coincidence that the development of 'information society' technologies followed hard on the heels of a marked decline in corporate profits in the late 1960s and early 1970s.[25] Technological advances were thereafter ushered in to restore profits and improve productivity. The Fordist regimes of production that had underpinned economic growth for decades were seen as no longer viable. In their place, to complement the volatility and growing sophistication of consumer demand, and to bring order to the disorganized materialism that was developing, a more flexible and responsive capitalism, facilitated by dynamic ICTs, was envisioned. Post-Fordist capitalism, characterized by increased customization, niche marketing, just-in-time/agile production and a diversified and globalized accumulation of capital, is wholly dependent on the digital advances that have occurred over recent decades.

Both the shift to post-Fordist regimes of production and the technologies that drive them are embedded in Kondratiev wave theory, which argues that over the past two centuries economic growth in the West has experienced long-term waves (complete cycles lasting around fifty 50 to sixty 60 years) of boom and slump.[26] According to the theory, expansion has been driven by a strong supply-side motor, with entrepreneurs jumping on the bandwagons of technological advance and growing profits. This is inevitably followed by economic contraction, as competition relentlessly trims profits until the point is reached where only technological innovation can jump-start the upward cycle. According to the Kondratiev pattern, Western economies are on the verge of a fresh upswing in the economic cycle, based this time on ICTs developed in the 1980s and 1990s.

Hobsbawm (1977, 13) has pointed out that the global triumph of capitalism was the major theme of history in the second half of the 19th century: 'It was the triumph of a society which believed that economic growth rested on competitive private enterprise, on success in buying everything in the cheapest market (including labour) and selling in the dearest.' Irrespective of the advantages or disadvantages capitalism has brought, the information society (so conceived) has done nothing to change the dominance of this form of social organization. The information society of the 'fifth Kondratiev [wave]' does not mark the beginning of a new society; it is, by definition, merely a further phase in the Kondratiev pattern of capitalist development. Essentially a re-packaging of capitalism, the information society is a repeat performance of earlier efforts to re-structure the economic and technological infrastructure for corporate capital. Of relevance here is, firstly, the late Victorian and Edwardian revolution in information management which followed the economic slump of the 1880s and the generally increasing complexity of corporate activities (Black and Brunt, 1999); and, secondly, the early 20th-century revolution in scientific management and the adoption of Taylorism, which Robins and Webster (1999, 95–102) view as the true 'origins' of the information society.

Modernity

The evolution of industrial capitalism is integral to the unfolding of modernity over the past three centuries. The age of modernity which some see as having passed, but others, including Giddens (1991), view as continuing, can be equated to the history of Western societies since the Enlightenment. The Enlightenment, or modern, project has amounted to an intellectual effort to develop objective science and universal morality; it has aimed to use the accumulation of knowledge for social and individual emancipation and progress. Information has been crucial to the enduring vitality of this project.

In many respects, it was during the age of reason and revolution, between roughly 1700 and 1850, that information, as Headrick (2000) argues, 'came of age', whether in terms of the classification of scientific knowledge, the quantification and statistical analysis of human activity and the natural world, the detailed mapping of continents, countries and towns, the gathering of knowledge into encyclopedias, or the development of postal and telegraphic systems.

Information is as central to *modern* society as to the information society. Humanity's great leap forward has not been its investment in digital technology but its 'modern' proclamation of the importance of 'daring to know', which by definition places a premium on informational activity. As such, the information society is not a new society, but the latest stage of the 'modern project', not least, it might be added, because the information society's various elements constitute, at base, in the tradition of the Enlightenment, an 'improvement ideology' (Dordick and Wang, 1993, 8).

Surveillance

The 'modern' belief in reason promised liberation from the dark side of our human natures, but in reality modernity has been characterized as much by control, conflict and repression as by progress, emancipation and enlightenment. The schizoid nature of modernity is most clearly seen in the activities of the nation-state. On the one hand, the state has served as a vehicle for social and individual advance. On the other hand, it has extended and developed considerably the technologies of surveillance, which, in part, define modern societies (Lyon, 1994; Lyon, 2001). The need of the state to gather information on its citizenry is hardly new. It is certainly not an 'information society' development. In fact a strong case can be made, as Stieg (1980) has attempted, for locating the authentic information (surveillance) revolution in the 19th century, in the context of state monitoring mechanisms such as the census (which became nominal in 1841), government investigations (such as parliamentary select committees and royal commissions), and the registration of births, deaths and marriages (1837). The pattern of state surveillance set in the 19th century intensified in the 20th century, and, in terms of its 'controlling' aspect, culminated in the use of punch-card technology to populate and monitor the death camps of Nazi Germany (Black, 2001). Thus, whether prosecuted by the state or by private organizations (those of corporate capital included), the information society as 'surveillance society' commands a long tradition. By virtue of its anchorage in information gathering and written documentation, what Lewis Mumford (1961, 415–21) called the 'tentacular bureaucracy', and what Max Weber theorized as the 'iron cage' of bureacracy,[27] has contributed significantly, if quietly, to that tradition.

Conclusion: a secular rejection of the information society

An etymology of the word 'information' reveals a shift in its meaning over time: from the ancient notion of 'information as process' to, more recently, its reification, or the idea of 'information as item'. This shift has encouraged the deification of information as a resource shaping a fundamentally new society: an information society. However, the hype and expressions of faith that surround the information society concept have been strongly criticized. Those who resist a utopian celebration of information's social potential might be said to have adopted a secular, or aetheistic, attitude to the information society proposition. This 'faithless' perspective is reinforced by the other main meaning of the word 'secular': that which occurs over a long period of time. The lens of modernity – the era of Western thought and 'progress' (including the growth of industrial capitalism) which has flowed from the Enlightenment – can be employed to view the information society not as an historical discontinuity but as an evolutionary phenomenon, one that is informed by the development of the information infrastructure over the centuries and by an historic utilization of information as a key operational resource by modern state and corporate bureaucratic organizations. The information society cannot be conceptualized as a post-industrial, post-modern phenomenon, for its essences – scientific progress and individual and social emancipation among them – are surely rooted in the modern societies which have flowed, over the past three centuries, from industrialism, capitalism and the Enlightenment project.

Notes

1   These definitions are drawn from *The Random House dictionary of the English language* (1987) and *The concise Oxford dictionary of current English* (1995).

2 A term used by Brown and Duguid (2000).

3 It could be argued that the information professions, including the library profession, engage in 'information society' millenarianism and in the worship of new ICTs as a means to identity formation at a time of unsettling professional change.

4 Quoted in Ramazanoglu (1993, 19).

5 For a discussion of Foucault's notions of discourse and 'regime of truth', see Hall (1992).

6 'Information infrastructure', comprising the print industry, telephony, radio, television, the database industry and libraries, is a term used by Rubin (1998, 1–18). See, also, the use of the term by Borgman (2000) and Rayward (2001).

7 For a perspective on the 'thingification' of information, see Chapter 5 (Information-as-thing) of Buckland (1991).

8 'Information' was used in English from the 14th century, but gained its current spelling only in the 16th century (Bawden, 2001, 93).

9 An 18th-century dictionary of etymology gave one definition of 'information' as 'the act of informing or actuating': see Bailey (1755).

10 These various points have been drawn from: Aristotle (1967); Forms (1976); Urmson and Rée (1991, 22); and Spade (1994, 88–92). Interestingly, an early dictionary by Ash (1775) gave one definition of 'information' as 'the act of animating'.

11 See, for example, Englander and O'Day (1995).

12 The existence of a continuum is also the main thrust behind Feather (2000).

13 Examples of communication history include: Marvin (1988) and Gardner and Shortelle (1997).

14 Clanchy (1993) argues that the period between the Norman conquest and the end of the 13th century witnessed the development of literate ways of thinking and doing business. From Anglo-Saxon England about 2000 charters and writs exist; but from 13th-century England tens of thousands of such documents survive. This was the real beginning of the story of literate communication. Further, as Tompson (1979, 40–2) suggests, the 16th century produced the next spurt in documentation, in the form of parish registration and increased written evidence in court proceedings. This was followed by increased tax documentation

in the 18th century. Guy (1988, 11–12) explains how, under Edward IV and Henry VII, the King's Council (later the Privy Council) became an authentic, bureaucratic governing institution, and how under Elizabeth I the Privy Council's bureaucratic work and documentary output escalated markedly.

15 Partly as a result of this, annual book titles quadrupled between 1840 and 1903: Eliot (1994). Feather (1988, 129–79) explains how improved literacy and increased demand for the written word and education fed through into the growth of publishing and the mechanization of book production.

16 Annual letter deliveries per capita increased from four to 73 between 1839 and 1911 (Perry, 1992, 205).

17 Richards (1991) argues that the growth of mass advertising in the late 19th and early 20th centuries laid the foundation for the semiotic system which has come to govern our culture. For a discussion of the emergence of a 'society of signs', see Harris (1996).

18 With regard to imperial expansion, Richards (1993) explains how British colonial rule led to the accumulation in various institutions – such as the British Museum – of vast amounts of information from far-flung corners of the Empire.

19 In this regard, the work of both Machlup and Porat is neatly described by Dearnley and Feather (2001, 11–14).

20 For a succinct definition of telework, see van Dijk (1999, 170–1).

21 For a description of 'just-in-time' methods, see Mehra (1990, 30–8). See also Murray (1988) for a digestible account of the post-Fordist mode of production.

22 With regard to the multinational corporation, one of its earliest analysts (Tugendhat, 1973, 31) has noted the importance that investment in telephone, telex, telegraph and computers made to its proliferation in the mid-20th century.

23 See Castells (1996, 34–40), for further comparisons.

24 The classic attack on the effectiveness of non-market services was mounted by Bacon and Eltis (1976).

25 For a discussion of the profits crisis, see Gamble and Walton (1976, 137–44). Frank (1980, 33) informs us that in the UK the net 'rate of profit' fell from 3.4% in 1964, to 1.4% in 1970, to 0.9% in 1975. A

similar decline was experienced in the USA.

26   The theory is discussed by Massey (1988, 82–4), and Freeman (1984). The essence of the theory is that boom periods commenced in the 1780s, 1850s, 1890s and 1940s, driven by such radical innovations as, respectively: mass-production textile machinery and steam power; the railways; electricity and the internal combustion engine; and early computing. The work of Kondratiev, a Russian economist of the early 20th century, preceded the post-1945 economic boom and that predicted (by some) for the early 21st century.

27   See Albrow (1970), especially Chapter 3, and Lyon (1994, 31).

References

Albrow, M. (1970) *Bureaucracy*, London, Pall Mall Press.

Aristotle (1967) In *Encyclopedia of philosophy*, New York, Collier-Macmillan.

Ash, J. (1775) *The new and complete dictionary of the English language*, London, Edward and Charles Dilly.

Bacon, R. and Eltis, W. (1976) *Britain's economic problem: too few producers*, London, Macmillan Press.

Bailey, N. (1755) *A new universal etymological English dictionary*, London, T. Osborne and J. Shipton.

Bawden, D. (2001) The shifting terminologies of information, *Aslib Proceedings*, **55** (3), (March), 93–8.

Bawden, D. and Robinson, L. (2000) A distant mirror? The internet and the printing press, *Aslib Proceedings*, **52** (2), (February), 51–7.

Bell, D. (1980) The social framework of the information society. In Forester, T. (ed.), *The microelectronics revolution: the complete guide to the new technology and its impact on society*, Oxford, Basil Blackwell, 500–49.

Beniger. R. (1986) *The control revolution: technological and economic origins of the information society*, Cambridge, MA, Harvard University Press.

Bennet, T. (1995) *The birth of the museum: history, theory, politics*, London, Routledge.

Black, A. and Brunt, R. (1999) Information management in business, libraries and British military intelligence: towards a history of information management, *Journal of Documentation*, **55** (4), 361–74.

Black, E. (2001) *IBM and the Holocaust: the strategic alliance between Nazi*

Germany and America's most powerful corporation, London, Little Brown.

Borgman, C. L. (2000) *From Gutenberg to the global information infrastructure*, Cambridge, MA, MIT Press.

Brown, J. S. and Duguid, P. (2000) *The social life of information*, Boston, MA, Harvard Business School Press.

Buckland, M. (1991) *Information and information systems*, New York, Greenwood Press.

Bud-Frierman, L. (1994) Information acumen. In Bud-Frierman, L. (ed.), *Information acumen: the understanding and use of knowledge in modern business*, London, Routledge, 1994.

Burke, P. (2000) *A social history of knowledge: from Gutenberg to Diderot*, Cambridge, Polity Press.

Castells, M. (1989) *The informational city*, Oxford, Blackwell.

Castells, M. (1996) *The information age: economy, society and culture*, vol. 1, The rise of the network society, Oxford, Blackwell.

Castells, M. (2001) *The internet galaxy: reflections on the internet*, Oxford, Oxford University Press.

Clanchy, M. T. (1993) *From memory to written record: England 1066–1307*, Oxford, Blackwell.

The concise Oxford dictionary of current English (1995) Oxford, Clarendon Press.

Crouzet, F. (1982) *The Victorian economy*, London, Methuen.

Davis, W. S. and McCormack, A. (1979) *The information age*, Reading, MA, Addison-Wesley Publishing.

Deane, P. (1980) *The first industrial revolution*, Cambridge, Cambridge University Press.

Dearnley, J. and Feather, J. (2001) *The wired world: an introduction to the theory and practice of the information society*, London, Library Association Publishing.

Ditmas, E. M. R. (1948) Co-ordination of information: a survey of some schemes put forward in the last fifty years, *Journal of Documentation*, **3** (4), (March), 209–21.

Dordick, H. S. and Wang, G. (1993) *The information society: a crumbling view*, London, Sage.

Drucker, P. F. (1969) *The age of discontinuity: guidelines to our changing society*, London, Heinemann.

Duff, A. (1995) The information society as paradigm: a bibliometric inquiry,

Journal of Information Science, **21** (5), 402–7.

Duff, A. (2000) *Information society studies*, London, Routledge.

Eisenstein, E. (1983) *The printing revolution in early modern Europe*, Cambridge, Cambridge University Press.

Eliot, S. (1994) *Some patterns and trends in British publishing 1800–1919*, London, Bibliographical Society.

Englander, D. and O'Day, R. (eds) (1995) *Retrieved riches: social investigation in Britain 1840–1914*, Aldershot, Scolar Press.

Feather, J. (1988) *A history of British publishing*, London, Croom Helm.

Feather, J. (2000) *The information society: a study in continuity and change*, 3rd edn, London, Library Association Publishing.

Feinstein, C. H. (1976) *Statistical tables of national income, expenditure and output of the UK 1855-1965*, Cambridge, Cambridge University Press.

Forms (1976) In Lacey, A. R. (ed.), *A dictionary of philosophy*, London, Routledge and Kegan Paul, 1976.

Frank, A. G. (1980) *Crisis: in the world economy*, London, Heinemann Educational Books.

Freeman, C. (1984) Keynes or Kondratiev? How can we get back to full employment? In Marstrand, P. (ed.), *New technology and the future of work and skills*, London, Frances Pinter, 103–23.

Gamble, A. and Walton, P. (1976) *Capitalism in crisis: inflation and the state*, London, Macmillan.

Gardner, R. and Shortelle, D. (eds) (1997) *From talking drums to the internet: an encyclopedia of communications technology*, Santa Barbara, CA, ABC-CLIO, 1997.

Giddens, A. (1991) *Modernity and self-identity*, Cambridge, Polity Press.

Gillott, J. and Kumar, M. (1995) *Science and the retreat from reason*, London, Merlin Press.

Gordon, C. (ed.) (1980) *Michel Foucault: power/knowledge*, London, Harvester, Wheatsheaf.

Graham, S. and Marvin, S. (2001), *Splintering urbanism: networked infrastructures, technological mobilities and the urban condition*, London, Routledge.

Guy, J. (1988) *Tudor England*, Oxford, Oxford University Press.

Hall, S. (1992) The west and the rest: discourse and power. In Hall, S. and Gieben, B. (eds), *Formations of modernity*, Cambridge, Polity Press.

Harris, D. (1996) *A society of signs*, London, Routledge.

Headrick, D. R. (2000) *When information came of age: technologies of knowledge in the age of reason and revolution*, Oxford, Oxford University Press, 2000.

Hendrix, F. (1997) Public libraries and the information superhighway, *Public Library Journal*, **12** (1), 1–5.

Hoare, P. (1998) The development of the European information society, *Library Review*, **47**, (7&8), 377–82.

Hobsbawm, E. (1977) *The age of capital 1848–1875*, London, Abacus.

Information for a new age: re-defining the librarian (1995) Englewood, CO, Libraries Unlimited.

Kumar, K. (1991) *Prophecy and progress: the sociology of industrial and post-industrial society*, London, Penguin.

Large, P. (1982) Brave new world. In *Brave new world: living with IT*, London, Macdonald and Co., 3–20.

Lash, S. and Urry, J. (1987) *The end of organised capitalism*, Oxford, Polity Press.

Law, D. (2000) Information policy for a new millennium, *Library Review*, **49** (7), 322–30.

Lyon, D. (1988) *The information society: issues and illusions*, Cambridge, Polity Press.

Lyon, D. (1994) *The electronic eye: the rise of surveillance society*, Cambridge, Polity Press and Basil Blackwell.

Lyon, D. (2001) *Surveillance society: monitoring everyday life*, Buckingham, Open University Press.

Marvin, C. (1988) *When old technologies were new: thinking about electric communication in the late-nineteenth century*, Oxford, Oxford University Press.

Massey, D. (1988) What's happening to UK manufacturing. In Allen, J. and Massey, D. (eds), *The economy in question*, London, Sage.

Mehra, S. (1990) The transferability of just-in-time concepts to American small businesses, *Interfaces*, **20** (2), (March–April), 30–8.

Moore, N. and Steele, J., (1991) *Information intensive Britain*, London, Policy Studies Institute.

Muddiman, D. (1998) The universal library as modern utopia: the information society of H. G. Wells, *Library History*, **14**, (November), 85–101.

Mumford, L. (1961) *The city in history: its origins, its transformations and its prospects*, London, Secker and Warburg.

Murray, R. (1988) Life after Henry, *Marxism Today*, **32** (10), (October), 8–13.

Perkin, H. (1969) *The origins of modern English society, 1780–1880*, London, Routledge and Kegan Paul.

Perkin, H. (1989) *The rise of professional society: England since 1880*, London, Routledge.

Perry, C. R. (1992) *The Victorian Post Office: the growth of a bureaucracy*, London, Royal Historical Society.

Peters, J. D. (1988) Information: notes towards a critical history, *Journal of Communication Inquiry*, **12** (2), 9–23.

Preston, P. (2001) *Reshaping communications*, London, Sage.

Ramazanoglu, C. (1993) Introduction. In Ramazanoglu, C. (ed.), *Up against Foucault*, London, Routledge.

The Random House dictionary of the English language (1987) New York, Random House.

Rayward, B. (1994) Some schemes for restructuring and mobilising information in documents: a historical perspective, *Information Processing and Management*, **30**, 163–75.

Rayward, B. (2001) 'Seminar on historical perspectives on information infrastructure', delivered at the University of Illinois. Available at: http://leep.lis.uiuc.edu/fall01/lis450hpi/index.html.

Richards, T. (1991) *The commodity culture of Victorian England: advertising and spectacle 1851–1914*, London, Verso.

Richards, T. (1993) *The imperial archive*, London, Verso.

Ritchie, S. (ed.) (1982) *Modern library practice*, Buckden, ELM Publications.

Robins, K. and Webster, F. (1999) *Times of the technoculture: from the information society to the virtual life*, London, Routledge.

Roszak, T. (1988) *The cult of information: the folklore of computers and the true art of thinking*, London, Paladin Grafton.

Rowe, C. and Thompson, J. (1996) *People and chips: the human implications of information technology*, 3rd edn, London, McGraw-Hill.

Rubin, R. E. (1998) *Foundations of library and information science*, New York and London, Neal-Schuman.

Schumacher, E. F. (1973) *Small is beautiful: a study of economics as if people mattered*, London, Blond Briggs.

Sellen, A. J. and Harper, R. (2002) *The myth of the paperless office*, Cambridge, MA, MIT Press.

Spade, P. V. (1994) Medieval philosophy. In Kenny, A. (ed.), *The Oxford illustrated history of Western philosophy*, Oxford, Oxford University Press, 88–92.

Standage, T. (1998) *The Victorian internet: the remarkable story of the telegraph and the nineteenth century's pioneers*, London, Weidenfeld and Nicolson.

Sterling, B. (1995) The hacker crackdown: evolution of the US telephone network. In Heap, N. et al. (eds), *Information technology and society: a reader*, London, Sage and the Open University Press.

Stieg, M. F. (1980) The nineteenth-century information revolution, *Journal of Library History, Philosophy and Comparative Librarianship*, **15** (1), (Winter), 22–52.

Sturges, P. (1994) United Kingdom, modern. In Wiegand, W. A. and Davis, D. G. (eds), *Encyclopedia of library history*, New York, Garland, 631–9.

Toffler, A. (1980) *The third wave*, London, Pan.

Tompson, R. (1979) *The Charity Commission and the age of reform*, London, Routledge and Kegan Paul.

Tugendhat, C. (1973) *The multinationals*, Harmondsworth, Penguin.

Urmson, J. O. and Rée, J. (eds) (1991) *The concise encyclopedia of Western philosophy*, London, Unwin Hyman.

van Dijk, J. (1999) *The network society: social aspects of new media*, London, Sage.

Webster, F. (1995) *Theories of the information society*, London, Routledge.

3
World gone wrong? Alternative conceptions of the information society

Dave Muddiman

Introduction

Ever since its inauguration in the 1970s as a label for contemporary social change, the notion of the information society has provoked considerable scepticism and censure. Its popularity in information technology (IT), business and management circles has been countered by the criticism of a good number of serious social commentators. Social scientists have pointed to its inadequacy as an analytical concept: Nicholas Garnham, for example, recently claiming that 'it fails as theory because it is internally incoherent and unsupported by evidence' and that 'its popularity within policy discourse can only be understood ideologically' (Garnham, 2000, 139). Historians have observed that the information 'age' is nothing new; information having been a key feature of development in societies as diverse as ancient Sumeria and 19th-century Britain (Hobart and Schiffman, 1998; Beniger, 1986). The widely read information sociologist Frank Webster perhaps goes furthest of all, enquiring bemusedly *'what* information society?'; and observing that although information is clearly important in contemporary life it is no more pervasive than other phenomena such as cars or electricity (Webster, 1994). Perhaps as a result, numerous commentators have engaged in a search for alternative descriptors which might better capture the character of the age: the network society (Castells, 1996), surveillance society (Lyon, 2001), risk society (Beck, 1992), the global age (Albrow, 1996), digital capitalism (Schiller, 1999), postmodernity (Harvey, 1990; Bauman, 1992), and so on.

Undoubtedly, some of this dissatisfaction with the information society concept can be attributed to its embeddedness in the popular mythologies and assumptions of the modern, Western, capitalist world. Chief among these discourses are *technological determinism*, the belief that social change is fundamentally driven by technical development; and *utopianism*, the assumption of progress and improvement towards the ultimate goal of an 'ideal' society. Protagonists of the information society invariably bring these two myths together, arguing that the revolutionary processing power of computers linked in a 'global brain' holds out the promise of unlimited knowledge accessible to all. Such myths are reflected not only in the IT hype of industry moguls like Bill Gates (Gates, 1995), but increasingly in the policy discourse of politicians such as Tony Blair. In the preface to the UK information policy statement *Our information age*, for example, Blair claims that 'information is the key to the modern age'; that 'the potential of the new networks is breathtaking' and that 'the new age of information offers possibilities for the future limited only by the boundaries of our imaginations' (UK. Central Office of Information, 1998, 1).

However, as the tragic events of 11 September 2001 and their aftermath perhaps suggest, such rose-tinted utopianism clearly misrepresents the disjuncture and fragmentation which pervades the contemporary world. It is, of course, clear that the world is undergoing unprecedented change, and that this is to some degree enabled by the rapid development of information, communication and network technologies (ICTs). However, it is by no means clear that the world will be transformed in the direction of enlightenment, democracy and prosperity. On the contrary, exploitation, exclusion, eco-vandalism and authoritarianism continue to pervade the planet: enabled, in most cases, by the technological infrastructure of the information society. Indeed, some commentators suggest that the development of ICT networks and systems is in the final analysis driven by the interests of economic and political forces which perpetuate inequality and division and has little to do with reshaping a world gone wrong (Lyon, 2001; Schiller, 1999).

Orthodox accounts of the transition to an 'information' society, it is argued here, do little to explain this state of affairs. Instead, this chapter focuses on those theories of society which attempt to examine the underpinning dynamics of societal change and which explore the complexity and fragmentation of the contemporary information scene. In the first section of the chapter I thus review *neo-Marxist* approaches to contemporary change and argue that conceptions of a 'restructured' or 'informational' capitalism offer by far the most convincing explanation of current economic, political and occupational trends. I then go on to suggest that such analysis needs to be complemented by *postmodern* perspectives on knowledge, education and culture in order to more fully understand the current shifts in communication, identity and ideas. Taken together, I argue, these theories offer a much more complete and convincing account of our world (both material and informational) than the discourse of the information age.

'All that is solid': the information society and the restructuring of capitalism

Protagonists of the information society typically describe it as a world in which previous economic and social systems have been swept away. For Drucker (1993), we live in 'post-capitalist society' and according to Tom Stonier (1983, 12) 'a country's store of information is now its principal asset, its greatest source of wealth'. Such knowledge-based societies, according to the prophets of futurology and management consultancy, hold out the promise of ever rising standards of living, fulfilling 'knowledge-based' employment, educational advance and social inclusion. Some like Francis Fukuyama (1992) have even (ill-advisedly) linked this vision with the concept of the 'end of history' and the arrival of a new age of global harmony.

Neo-Marxists unsurprisingly reject these formulations. Utilizing Marxist concepts and methods of analysis (although for the most part rejecting the classical Marxist political project), they suggest that capitalism is still the dominant shaper of the contemporary world. They argue that the new patterns of social relations which have emerged over the last 30 years or so have been basically determined by the continuance and expansion of market economics rather than by technological change or by any new regime of 'information'. Summarizing this approach, Webster (2000) points out that a number of key features of this market system have intensified in this period. These include: the private rather than the public supply of services; private ownership of property (including 'ownership' of information through copyright, etc.); work for wage labour; provision of services, goods and information according to ability to pay; and the increasing validation of the idea of competition as the main way of organizing economic and social life. All this represents, for Webster, an *expansion* of capitalism and its penetration of an ever wider and deeper range of human affairs, including fields such as personal and social services; volunteering and crucially, knowledge and information. He likens this process to the 'enclosure' of common land in 18th-century England whereby communal methods of farming were superseded by the agriculture of the market.

Information societies thus represent a restructured, rather than a transformed, social order. Marx and Engels themselves had expected this constant restructuring of capitalism: in an oft-quoted passage from the *Communist manifesto* ([1848] 1983, 17) they argued that:

> the bourgeoisie cannot exist without [the] . . . constant revolutionising of production, uninterrupted disturbance of all social conditions, everlasting uncertainty and agitation . . . all fixed fast frozen relations are swept away . . . all that is solid melts into air.

At the turn of the millennium, neo-Marxists typically observe, such change adds up to a 'late'; 'disorganized'; 'informational'; 'cybernetic' or 'digital' capitalism. In economic terms this is characterized by the development of worldwide communication networks which enable the reach of the market to all corners of the globe (Schiller, 1999). It is linked to the rise of the transnational corporation as the dominant form of industrial organization, its power now mobile and flexible through the networks it controls. In the productive enterprise itself it is marked by a move away from centres and methods of 'mass' production and a shift to 'post-Fordist' systems marked by 'flexible' working methods, small-scale batch production, outsourcing, sub-contracting and 'just-in-time' delivery methods (Amin, 1994) . Enabled by technologies such as computer-aided design, such networked enterprises have created new markets for goods with a high design or 'informational' rather than functional value (Lash and Urry, 1994). In consequence, a global consumer marketplace fuelled by an increasing obsession with signs and style (as opposed to utility) has mushroomed and is, at least for the time being, guaranteeing the popularity and the survival of the system it supports.

In the workplace it is commonplace to claim that these shifts are transforming industrial relations, management styles and the nature of work itself. Analysts such as Castells (1996) point to the emergence of the networked rather than hierarchical enterprises where workers adopt flexible, multiskilled and 'knowledge-based' roles. Professions are displaced by portfolio careers shaped by an ability to 'self programme' or adapt to change; Handy (1995) envisages a 20:80 society where only 20% or 'core' workers are employed in stable jobs by long-standing companies and organizations. Neo-Marxists are extremely sceptical of these claims. Empirical evidence, they point out, does indeed point to the growing instability of employment, but much of this affects low-grade work and is consistent with the Marxist idea of a pliable 'reserve army of labour' which responds to economic boom and recession (Warhurst and Thompson, 1998). The significance of 'information' and 'knowledge' work, neo-Marxists claim, is also much overstated: much of this, they observe, is retail, personal service or financial work that has been mislabelled and the demand for some 'knowledge specialists' (like librarians) can be argued to have actually declined. Within workplaces researchers identify increasing regulation of labour and intensification of work as key contemporary trends: little is heard of the 'leisure society' now. Techniques such as just in time, total quality management, benchmarking and customer care are seen as attempts to systematize and routinize *service* employment, bringing to it many of the techniques and ideas of the Taylorism of the industrial age (Robins and Webster, 1999, 89–110). New concepts such as 'knowledge management' can be read as attempts by organizations to better 'capture' the tacit expertise of employees in order to mobilize it for competitive advantage. 'Winning hearts' techniques, such as neuro-linguistic programming, might be seen as a crude attempt to inculcate the values and ideologies of the market and to influence the minds (and whole experience) of individual employees (Thompson, Warhurst and Callaghan, 2000).

The Schumpeterian workface state (SWS)

In response to these shifts in the social relations of the contemporary workplace it is clear that post-industrial capital requires a new kind of workforce, one not simply skilled in the mechanics of ICT, but one which is flexible, hard-working, entrepreneurial, and (up to a point) well educated. In the view of some neo-Marxist theorists, these labour market needs have resulted in significant changes in the nature of the nation-state, and the way in which it regulates social life. Hence the mid-20th century *Keynesian welfare state*, which attempted to compensate for the dysfunctions of the market through demand management, full employment and the provision of a welfare state for all, is, it is claimed, being systematically replaced by a *Schumpeterian workfare state* (SWS). This kind of state (so called because of its pursual of the supply side economics advocated by the Austrian economist Joseph Schumepter, 1883–1950) focuses its energies on meeting the conditions required for global capitalism to thrive (Jessop, 1994; 2000). It prioritizes social order, economic competitiveness through low taxation, and an education system which produces a flexible, well-trained 'self programmable' workforce. Partly because of these priorities, it presides over a shrinkage of the publicly funded Keynesian welfare state through privatization, cuts in expenditure and 'partnership' arrangements with business, the voluntary sector and sometimes local communities themselves. ICTs often figure prominently in the transition to the SWS: in the UK the Blair government's current plans for 'e-government', for example, envisage a shift to a 'networked' welfare state with an emphasis on electronic 'self-help' and an array of linked providers and consumers.

Two areas in particular might serve to illustrate contrasting facets of the SWS. In many advanced economies, educational systems have progressively abandoned a liberal, humanistic model in favour of 'new vocationalist' educational goals. Such reformed systems typically prioritize the teaching of competencies and skills (especially those linked to ICTs); they are closely linked with the world of commerce and industry; and they are committed to widening participation and 'lifelong learning'. In addition, they inculcate values of self reliance; entrepreneurialism and teamwork (Robins and Webster, 1999, 168–218) . In the UK such ideas are now at the centre of plans for a 'learning age': an expansion of applied learning designed to produce a workforce able to compete in an information economy. They have penetrated not only vocational and higher education, but also schools themselves where there are increasing links with business and commerce, new managerial forms of governance and an increasing exposure of children to the commercial world through adoption of technologies like the internet (Selwyn, 1999). In specific terms, such new educational priorities have undoubtedly changed the orientation of a large number of educational curricula and programmes of study – including those, for example, in the field of library and information studies itself (Muddiman, 1994).

Although the emerging SWS has in this way presided over an expansion of education for work, many other public services have typically been neglected, run down, or transferred to the private sector. In the UK information sphere this process has resulted in a 'withering of public access' through the sale of public systems like telephones and the expansion of many new media and communication channels along commercial lines (Haywood, 1989; Webster, 1995, 101–34). In contrast traditional guarantors of public access to information like public libraries have been starved of funding for innovation and instead urged to commercialize and marketize their operations through private sector partnerships (Black and Muddiman, 1997, 93–115). Even the creation of a 'people's network' through the wiring up of the UK public library system for internet access has proved problematic. Funded by non-mainstream (and finite) lottery funding its progress is patchy, uneven, and at the time of writing only about half complete (Dutch and Muddiman, 2001). Beyond its initial creation, the future expansion and development of the network is uncertain.

Social exclusion

Institutions like the public library, neo-Marxists contend, typify the difficulties experienced by state welfare organizations under the SWS. Partly as a result of this shrinkage of the 'social wage', advanced capitalist societies, wealthy though they may seem, are actually *more unequal* than their predecessors. They are characterized, above all, by social exclusion: the disconnection of large segments of their population from the norms and opportunities of mainstream life (Young, 1999). Such exclusion is underpinned by the persistence in these societies of social divisions linked to poverty, class, gender, race and disability. Some neo-Marxists argue that these divisions have intensified in post-industrial capitalism, fuelled by the instability of flexible labour markets and the decline of social welfare. Moreover, social exclusion is manifesting itself in a multiplying array of indicators: in the UK, for example, not only has the gap between rich and poor widened dramatically since the 1970s, but poor housing, poor health, high crime, the spiralling use of drugs and a spatial concentration of deprivation (resulting in 'zones' of exclusion) are all now familiar features of contemporary life (Walker and Walker, 1997). Exclusion also has its 'informational' dimensions, apparent in differential access to and use of ICTs and institutions like libraries (UK. DTI, 2000; Muddiman et al., 2000). This 'digital divide' (like social exclusion as a whole) has increasingly attracted the attention of policymakers, concerned about social breakdown and 'cohesion' and keen to build a 'socially inclusive Information Society' (National Working Party on Social Inclusion, 1997). However, in line with the general orientation of the SWS, initiatives in the UK have largely revolved around 'workfare' solutions to the problem focusing on employability, ICT literacy and skills. Such solutions place a heavy emphasis on individual responsibility for a response to exclusion and do little to address 'exclusion as a domain'. The goal of creating a 'social order which excludes exclusion' remains as (and arguably more) distant as ever (Byrne, 1999, 78).

This domain of exclusion is, of course, the overriding feature of advanced, or informational, capitalism. Its global dimensions magnify many times the everyday inequalities found in the UK: the information society of the West thrives, neo-Marxists observe, on the back of the industrial sweat and grinding poverty of much of the Third World (Sivanandan, 1998). It may well be, as the theorists of 'globalization' contend, that under the impetus of the internet and global networking the world is evolving into a single place with system-like properties (Albrow, 1996). But such developments do little to make the world a gentler, kinder place: indeed they kindle conflict because of their threats to national autonomy, their diffusion by transnational corporations of the market values of the USA, and their tendency to engender 'rising inequality and exclusion throughout the world' (Castells, 1998, 70). Digital development for Third-World populations is in consequence sometimes painfully slow: between 1997 and 2000, for example, Africa's share of the world's internet connections actually *declined* from 0.9% to a pitiful 0.6% (Castells, 2001, 261). In most 'less developed' regions of the world ICT use is confined to key urban centres, globalized business activities and social elites; and even in states like South Africa, where internet use is growing very fast, only 11% of black households have access to a telephone and 2.1 million households have no telephone within five kilometres' distance (Castells, 2001, 262). For people such as these, talk of an information society is a distant, unreachable irrelevance. Advanced capitalism, on the other hand, brings with it the daily afflictions of a market system, inequality, powerlessness and poverty, that are only too real.

'Melts into air': postmodernity, hypermodernity and beyond

Theories of the restructuring of capitalism provide, in many respects, a convincing, all encompassing, analysis of the material realities of the contem-

49

porary world. They highlight the continuance of market economics, its perpetuation of social division, and its colonization of ever expanding domains of human experience, including 'information' and knowledge itself. For postmodernists, however, such 'grand theory' seriously oversimplifies our lived experience at the turn of millennium, as well as understating the extent of change within capitalism itself (Kumar, 1995, 63–5). The contemporary age is not simply one of 'late capitalism'. It is an era of speed, of surface and of complexity; of 'life fragmented into a series of meaningless spectacles . . . a world which looks suspiciously like a 20 channel satellite TV with a madman holding the remote control' (Bauman, 1994, 24). It is a 'world gone wrong' where states, communities and individuals are unstable, multiple and diffuse and where material reality is obscured by signs and media babble. It is a society, so the hypothesis runs, that is *postmodern*: a world where, in a cultural and experiential sense at least, we are seeing the beginning of the end of the modern age.

This shift towards the 'postmodern condition', it is argued, marks a major fracturing of the process of modernization that we so take for granted. It undermines the 'project' of modernity, the development of society on the basis of scientific and bureaucratic rationality and principles of humanism, citizenship and rights, which can be traced back to the European Enlightenment and the scientific revolution of the 18th century (Harvey, 1990, 10–38). Attempts to construct such societies, postmodernists claim, have run their course. 'Grand narratives' of human improvement like scientific socialism have ended in failure. The technical and instrumental rationality of modern science threatens the planet. Modernity has been unmasked, at least in part, as a discourse of exclusion and domination: of women, of non-Europeans and of Nature herself. In its place, according to commentators like Lyotard (1986), we have only a series of 'discourses' or 'language games' in which values and ideas have become interest based, particular, and rooted in desires. A multiplicity of new codes and signs thus pepper our experience in the postmodern world: the consumer-fuelled logos of corporate capitalism (Klein, 2000), the menacing discourses of sanitized militarism (Virilio, 2000), and the strange alien symbols of the dispossessed Other. In spite of the best efforts of some, such 'language games' no longer offer us a stable, coherent or consistent view of the world.

Simulation

In everyday terms, of course, most of us experience this cascade of signs and discourses through the burgeoning electronic media which dominate both our homes and our work. Early postmodern theorists such as Jean Baudrillard tended to highlight the way in which the mid-century mass media constructed such *simulations*: artificial hyperrealities more real than reality itself. 'TV is the world', declared Baudrillard in 1988, claiming for example, that Disneyland was the real America and that computer and media simulations constituted the real Gulf War (Baudrillard, 1988; 1991). More latterly, analysts such as Mark Poster have pointed to the emergence of a 'second media age' of interactive communication which increases exponentially the potential for simulation. A central feature of this age, of course, is the emergence of cyberspace: the convergence of computer processing power; multimedia and networking technologies to enable the fabrication of 'virtual worlds'. These worlds are no longer the stuff of science fiction: 'real' or not they are genuine places where people meet, communicate, learn , buy and sell. They suggest an immense potential for fantasy, self discovery and self construction and the 'multiplication' of reality itself (Poster, 1995, 94). At the very least, they promise a quantum change in the way many of us experience the world.

Postmodern cyberspace, it can perhaps thus be argued, is already in the process of undermining our sense of possessing a stable, individual identity located firmly in the material word. Ever increasing numbers of internet users and computer console addicts deconstruct, reconstruct and play with their identities through chat rooms, gaming and other multi-user facilities (Jordan, 1999, 59-99). Howard Rheingold points to the emergence of 'virtual communities' in which internet groups create new forms of social interaction based on both real and imaginary persona: a counterbalance, perhaps, to the decline of material community and the alienation and isolation of modern life (Rheingold, 1994). Some see a potential for liberation, and the celebration of difference, in all of this, feminist writers like Donna Harraway (1991) claiming, for example, that 'cyborg' identities promise an escape from, and challenge to the dualism and domination of gender. Others, more pessimistically, argue that such fractured and 'posthuman' social psychology reflects an accelerating depthlessness and schizophrenia in the human condition, and that virtual communities and the virtual life represent, in the end, a retreat from moral engagement and the problems of the 'world we live in' (Robins, 1995).

Postmodern society, however, does not exclusively exist in the domain of simulation, cyberspace or the virtual world. Indeed, for theorists of postmodernity, the postmodern turn in ideas has real, material consequences: postmodern society *is* (contra Robins) the world we live in. For example, urban geographers like David Harvey and Ed Soja have highlighted the impact of postmodern thinking on physical space through the 'deconstruction' of the modern cities like Los Angeles into a 'confusing collage of signs' (Soja, 1989, 245). More recently, the proliferation of telecommunication networks has accelerated this urban fragmentation; new niche network infrastructures result in the gradual collapse of planned, universal services like healthcare, telephones or public libraries. Cities become 'splintered' into zones increasingly segmented by affluence, identity and access (Graham and Marvin, 2001). Such trends, for observers like David Lyon, further confirm the truism that 'if postmodernity means anything, it means consumer society' (Lyon, 1994, 68). Postmodern capitalism fuses the material world and the world of signs – the acquisition and display of its artefacts preoccupies the life of its people; shopping malls are its new cathedrals. Increasingly, it fuels the development of 'economies of signs and space' where fashion and image, speed and flexibility dictate supply and demand (Lash and Urry, 1994). Postmodernity is thus the 'cultural logic of late capitalism', its forms and simulations a characteristic embodiment of the ways in which the market system shapes our way of life.

Surveillance society

Postmodern techniques and ideas are also increasingly apparent in the mechanisms of governance and control adopted by advanced workfare states. Postmodern society is, from this perspective, surveillance society (Lyon, 2001): a world of interconnected databases and image banks, of 'capture', 'tracking', profiling and predicting. Such techniques, according to Poster (1990), constitute a 'superpanopticon', an invisible network of 'soft' surveillance, where disaggregated bits of information are sorted, correlated and reconstituted. As objects of such surveillance (unlike the victims of Bentham's original Panopticon), we experience it predominantly at a distance. Moreover, it fragments and distorts our identities, categorizing and reconstituting us in one-dimensional terms as consumers, criminals, insurance risks, targets for junk mail and so on. It reduces *us* to simulations (Bogard, 1996). In spite of this, the data of soft surveillance is widely regarded as 'hard' or 'evidence based' and typically used to find managerial solutions to social problems, to determine commercial strategy, or to devise structures and systems of spatial and social control. Postmodern modes of governance and politics thus claim to adopt 'value-free' remedies to the ills of the contemporary world based on the availability and careful analysis of information. In view of the superficial, degraded and sometimes distorted status of the data on which they often rely, it is hardly surprising that the effectiveness of these managerial techniques is frequently called into question (Beck, 1992; Pollitt, 1993).

The changing nature of information

Postmodern societies are thus perhaps not as 'information rich' as they seem. Indeed, according to J.-F. Lyotard the changing nature of information and knowledge (as opposed to its increasing availability) is the most fundamental feature of postmodern society. Knowledge is not unproblematically more abundant or accessible (as many protagonists of the information society claim) but 'the status of knowledge is altered as societies enter the postmodern and post-industrial age' (Lyotard, 1986, 1). Knowledge becomes detached from its human context and reconceptualized as an 'informational commodity indispensable to productive power'. Its worth is no longer linked to the 'grand narratives', truth, progress; education, but instead it is valued for it 'performativity' - its capacity to improve the performance of the particular system or sub-system it serves. Knowledge is thus increasingly reified (objectivized) and legitimized as property or commodity; the concept of knowledge as a 'public' entity is undermined (Lyotard, 1986, 3–5). The burgeoning disciplines of information law and information management (IM) support this enterprise, the former establishing the regulation and control of a knowledge market (May, 1998), the latter concerned with the utilization of this new informational commodity to maximum effect.

Information management, and more latterly knowledge management (KM), have arguably had a significant impact already upon the information and library professions, representing what many observers claim to be the future salvation of information work (McInerney and LeFevre, 2000; Koenig, 2000). Their professional significance is considered elsewhere in this book; here it is nevertheless important to observe their centrality in the construction of new forms of postmodern knowledge. KM, in particular, constitutes a set of techniques through which both personal and public knowledge can be re-engineered into an *organizational* resource for competitive advantage. KM is becoming, argues Michael Koenig (2000, 184), indispensable to the networked enterprise, its technologies and techniques the key to 'capturing a company's corporate expertise' and creating a 'faster learning organisation'. These processes, we might observe, accelerate the *marketization* of knowledge, its tendency to become organizational capital as opposed to individual intelligence or public discourse. Such trends, of course, also explicitly link the postmodern conception of knowledge with the informational capitalism that neo-Marxists describe. Information and knowledge management is, in the end, the means by which the market is capturing, privatizing and 'enclosing' the domain of knowledge (Webster, 2000, 72). Postmodern knowledge, and its management and manipulation, is thus, in the end, not simply a reflection of the culture of late capitalism. It is fast becoming its property and its currency.

Conclusion

Theories of postmodernity and theories of capitalist restructuring both present wide-ranging, empirically grounded and critical accounts of recent economic and social change. While it is the case that neither alone provides a complete, all encompassing theory of the contemporary world, both, I would argue, depict elements of the divided and fragmented universe of the new millennium with more veracity than technologically determinist and utopian accounts of the 'information' society. I would claim further that postmodernity and 'informational' capitalism can be seen as complementary theoretical constructs. Unlike those Marxists who dismiss the postmodern as unreal and superficial (for example Callinicos, 1989), I would suggest, on the contrary, that postmodern perspectives illuminate many of the key features (both cultural and material) of the contemporary techno-economic system. As long as we consider it critically, the idea of *postmodern capitalism*, in my view, captures both the cultural complexity and the fundamental substance of the contemporary age.

Such perspectives, of course, are in the main absent from the professional discourse of fields such as information and library science publications such as this (see, for example, Raitt, 1997). Instead, librarians and other information professionals have by and large embraced the discourse of the information age, hoping optimistically that libraries will become the 'hearts and minds of the Information Society' (Batt, 1997). However, as this chapter has suggested, an awareness of the realities of postmodern capitalism can do much to explain many of the current uncertainties of the information and library scene. Restructured 'informational' capitalism has fractured many of the links of the profession with public service, and the values associated with mid-20th century Keynesian welfare states. Postmodern conceptions of knowledge challenge and undermine ethical commitments to freedom of information, universal literacy and enlightenment. To survive, the information professional must now seemingly enter a Faustian bargain, adopt the technologies, techniques and tactics of informational capitalism, and become a knowledge manager, information consultant or learning skills adviser. For the few, it might be possible to retain a commitment to a just information society; for most, however, working life will be shaped by the ethically silent concerns of performance, productivity and profit.

It is tempting, perhaps, to suggest that the libraries of the 21st century should retreat from this world gone wrong; that they should distance themselves from postmodern capitalism and function, like libraries of medieval monasteries, as beacons of knowledge in a dark age. But for information and library services which grapple on a daily basis with the human consequences of techno-economic change, such retreat is not an option. As Castells (2001, 282) declares: 'at this time, and in this place, you will have to deal with the network society', there is no alternative to engagement. However, such engagement would be well served, we can perhaps conclude, by firstly unmasking the information society as the myth and ideology it surely is. Perhaps then the information and library community can challenge the inequalities, injustices and chaos of postmodern capitalism by building new pathways to knowledgeability based on values of social justice; universal literacy and the right to know. At least if we can begin to see the world clearly for what it is, we might be able to change it.

References

Albrow, M. (1996) *The global age*, Cambridge, Polity Press.

Amin, A. (ed.) (1994) *Post-Fordism. A reader*, Oxford, Blackwell.

Batt, C. (1997) The heart and brain of the information society: public libraries in the 21st century. In Raitt, D. (ed.), *Libraries for the new millennium: implications for managers*, London, Library Association Publishing.

Baudrillard, J. (1988) *America*, London, Verso.

Baudrillard, J. (1991) *La guerre du golfe n'a pas eu lieu*, Paris, Galilee.

Bauman, Z. (1992) *Intimations of postmodernity*, London, Routledge.

Bauman, Z. (1994) Deceiving the twentieth century, *New Statesman and Society*, (1 April), 24–5.

Beck, U. (1992) *Risk society: towards a new modernity*, London, Sage.

Beniger, J. (1986) *The control revolution: technical and economic origins of the information society*, Cambridge, MA, Harvard University Press.

Black, A. and Muddiman, D. (1997) *Understanding community librarianship: the public library in postmodern Britain*, Aldershot, Avebury.

Bogard, W. (1996) *The simulation of surveillance: hypercontrol in telematic societies*, Cambridge, Cambridge University Press.

Byrne, D. (1999) *Social exclusion*, Buckingham, Open University Press.

Callinicos, A. (1989) *Against postmodernism: a Marxist critique*, Cambridge, Polity Press.

Castells, M. (1996) *The rise of the network society*, Oxford, Blackwell.

Castells, M. (1998) *The end of millennium*, Oxford, Blackwell.

Castells, M. (2001), *The internet galaxy: reflections on the internet*, Oxford, Oxford University Press.

Drucker, P. (1993) *Post capitalist society*, New York, HarperCollins.

Dutch, M. and Muddiman, D. (2001) The public library, social exclusion and the information society in the United Kingdom, *Libri*, **51** (4), 200–19.

Fukuyama, F. (1992) *The end of history and the last man*, London, Hamish Hamilton.

Garnham, N. (2000) Information society as theory or ideology: a critical perspective on technology, education and employment in the new information age, *Information, Communication and Society*, **3** (2), 139–52 .

Gates, B. (1995) *The road ahead*, London, Viking.

Graham, S. and Marvin, S. (2001) *Splintering urbanism: networked infrastructures, technological mobilities and the urban condition*, London, Routledge.

Handy, C. (1995) *The future of work*, London, W. H. Smith.

Harraway, D. (1991) *Simians, cyborgs and women: the reinvention of nature*, London, Free Association Books.

Harvey, D. (1990) *The condition of postmodernity*, Oxford, Blackwell.

Haywood, T. (1989) *The withering of public access*, London, Library Association Publishing.

Hobart, M. and Schiffman, Z. (1998) *Information ages: literacy, numeracy and the computer revolution*, Baltimore, Johns Hopkins University Press.

Jessop, B. (1994) The transition to post-Fordism and the Schumpeterian workfare state. In Burrows, R. and Loader, B. (eds), *Towards a post-Fordist welfare state?*, London, Routledge.

Jessop, B. (2000) The changing governance of welfare: recent trends in its primary functions, scale and modes of co-ordination. In Manning, N. and Shaw, I. (eds), *New risks, new welfare: signposts for social policy*, Oxford, Blackwell.

Jordan, T.(1999) *Cyberpower: the culture and politics of cyberspace and the internet*, London, Routledge.

Klein, N. (2000) *No logo*, London, Flamingo.

Koenig, M. (2000) Information driven management – the new, but little perceived business zeitgeist, *Libri*, **50**, 174–90.

Kumar, K. (1995) *From post-industrial to postmodern society: new theories of the contemporary world*, Oxford, Blackwell.

Lash, S. and Urry, J. (1994) *Economies of signs and space*, London, Sage.

Lyon, D. (1994) *Postmodernity*, Buckingham, Open University Press.

Lyon, D. (2001) *Surveillance society: monitoring everyday life*, Buckingham, Open University Press.

Lyotard, J.-F. (1986) *The postmodern condition: a report on knowledge*, Manchester, Manchester University Press.

Marx, K. and Engels, F. [1848] (1983) *Manifesto of the communist party*, centenary edn, London, Lawrence and Wishart.

May, C. (1998) Capital, knowledge and ownership: the information society and intellectual property, *Information Communication and Society*, **1** (3), 246–69.

McInerney, C. and LeFevre, D. (2000) Knowledge managers: history and challenges. In Prichard, C. et al. (eds), *Managing knowledge: critical investigations of work and learning*, London, Macmillan.

Muddiman, D. (1994) Innovation or instrumental drift? The new vocationalism and information and library education in the United Kingdom, *Education for Information*, **12**, 259–70.

Muddiman, D. et al. (2000) *Open to all? The public library and social exclusion*,

Library and Information Commission Research Reports 84, 85, 86, London, Resource – The Council for Museums, Archives and Libraries.

National Working Party on Social Inclusion (1997) *The net result: social inclusion in the information society*, London, IBM/Community Development Foundation.

Pollitt, C. (1993) *Managerialism and the public services*, Oxford, Blackwell.

Poster, M. (1990) *The mode of information: poststructuralism and social context*, Cambridge, Polity Press.

Poster, M. (1995) Postmodern virtualities. In Featherstone, M. and Burrows, R. (eds), *Cyberspace, cyberbodies, cyberpunk*, London, Sage.

Raitt, D. (ed.) (1997) *Libraries for the new millennium: implications for managers*, London, Library Association Publishing.

Rheingold, H. (1994) *The virtual community: surfing the internet*, London, Minerva.

Robins, K. (1995) Cyberspace and the world we live in. In Featherstone, M. and Burrows, R. (eds), *Cyberspace, cyberbodies, cyberpunk*, London, Sage.

Robins, K. and Webster, F. (1999) *Times of the technoculture: from the information society to the virtual life*, London, Routledge.

Schiller, D. (1999) *Digital capitalism: networking the global market system*, Cambridge, MA, MIT Press.

Selwyn, N. (1999) Schooling the information society?, *Information Communication and Society*, **2** (2), 156–73.

Sivanandan, A. (1998) Globalism and the left, *Race and Class*, **40**, 5–20.

Soja, E. (1989) *Postmodern geographies: the reassertion of space in critical social theory*, London, Verso.

Stonier, T. (1983) *The wealth of information: a profile of the post-industrial economy*, London, Thames Methuen.

Thompson, P., Warhurst, C. and Callaghan, G. (2000) Human capital or capitalising on humanity: knowledge, skills and competencies in interactive service work. In Prichard, C. et al. (eds), *Managing knowledge: critical investigations of work and learning*, Macmillan, London.

UK. Central Office of Information (1998) *Our information age: the government's vision*, London, COI.

UK. Department of Trade and Industry (2000) *Closing the digital divide: information and communication technologies in deprived areas: a report by Policy Action Team 15*, London, DTI.

Virilio, P. (2000) *The information bomb (La bombe informatique)*, English edn, London, Verso.

Walker, A. and Walker, C. (eds) (1997) *Britain divided: the growth of social exclusion in the 1980s and 1990s*, London, CPAG.

Warhurst, C. and Thompson, P. (1998) Hearts, hands and minds: changing work and workers at the end of the century. In Thompson, P. and Warhurst, C. (eds), *Workplaces of the future*, London, Macmillan.

Webster F. (1994) What information society?, *The Information Society*, **10**, 1–23.

Webster, F. (1995) *Theories of the information society*, London, Routledge.

Webster, F. (2000) Information, capitalism and uncertainty, *Information, Communication and Society*, **3** (1), 69–90.

Young, J. (1999) *The exclusive society*, London, Sage.

Part 2
The information society and daily life

4

Policy push, personal pull: trying to make sense of the journey towards the information society

Chris Batt

Introduction

Picture the scene: 2020, a warm summer evening, somewhere in England. For two weeks the premium movie channels have been blasting the airwaves with ads for the premiere of the latest blockbuster from Kenneth Branagh, the grand old man of British film. Running in prime time on all 50 pay-to-view movie channels, showing three times during the evening and priced at 250 euro per broadband feed. Local-end (home) video recording is disabled and nobody is going anywhere.

The British immersive film industry leads the world, and consequently families across the face of the planet, in gardens, in igloos, even in houses, are planning to join this dying custom of the single launch of a movie. In English gardens, video sheets are unrolled and hung from trees, walls and sheds while personal surround sound systems tune themselves to the media command centres that sit on the local end of the broadband feed. It is a convivial event, with families and friends together watching the big show, where they want to. Personal sound systems do not destroy the tranquillity for those not watching, while talking is still possible. Gone are the cinemas where people sat in silent rows unable to move around or react as they wished. The utility of those dark impersonal buildings does not now run to movies! With extended family and friends watching – the grown-ups in gardens, the kids in bedrooms – the 250 euro price of the feed is cheap for what will be an entertaining and happy evening.

The film begins. An exciting adventure set in a bygone age, *A winter's tale* is steeped in Shakespearian characters and settings that are as close to the mythical age as possible. The latest post-production techniques are better than reality: 'If you've tried reality, now go virtual and try the real thing', 'If you wanna get real, get virtual' may have become slogans to forget, but without doubt the virtual effects and the attention to authenticity make it hard to believe that the watchers are not part of the action.

They are spellbound, they gasp, they talk, they share. From time to time they press buttons on their 'personal remotes' to mark a particular moment, image or setting. For all movies, indeed all broadcast media are no longer simple, linear, flat events that happen and then are over. The film, the natural history programme, the cultural epic are in a real sense merely the tip of an information iceberg that offers pathways and voyages into the world that they describe. The immersion may not be a part of the event, but diving into the body of the iceberg (if that is possible?) is a natural follow on.

The act of creation has become more than the visible product. The medium of broadcast, of shared viewing, while still commanding global attention, is equally a metaphor for the richness beyond. New technologies and old skills have come together to make the power of film and television a doorway into culture, into history and into the future.

The movie is over, the video sheets now dissolving into the myriad local, national and international channels that make up the medium. Parties are starting, but some people are already reviewing the data they have gathered during the film using their personal remotes. Each press has 'tagged' a route into the iceberg. Context relevant and designed to fit the profile of the user, the route may be to places, images, objects, more movies about the events depicted, about Shakespeare, about literature and even how to escape from bears. The legacy of *A winter's tale* is at once opinion about performances, camera angles, interpretation and the millions of people inspired to search further beneath the surface of what they have seen. Technology has made viewing at the same time more gregarious and a personal lifetime's journey into the richness of our societies and cultures. It has done something even more dramatic. Network technology has enabled everyone (or at least everyone who has access to the networked resources) to become an equal contributor to a global forum of debate, challenge, argument and empowerment. It continues to transform how people see themselves within the context of others. The network is at once a delivery mechanism for entertainment, for learning, for shopping, for information and at the same time a common ground for the two-way exchange of ideas unfettered by the will of the media mogul, the power of any single government to control its citizens or by international treaty. Quite literally, the biggest 'free for all' in history.

What is the meaning of all this? What should we understand by it? What challenge does it present for the future of our cultural and learning institutions? Of course, it presents just one of many possible futures. One in which there are things that we can recognize, some things that we could almost do now, and some things that today are impossible. Technological possibilities are always fun, but my interest here is in the social and policy environment that will now and in the future predict what direction our future might take. To do that we have to identify some key indicators that might give us clues, about which we can ask meaningful, if leading, questions.

There is global interest in the information society, and for good reason. Never before within the fabric of the developed societies has there been so visible a shared hope of what an information society might do; never before within the developing world has there been so obviously the hope that the emerging technological networking of information (telephony, internet, etc.) will produce a steep change in the ability of those countries to educate coming generations, to compete in world markets and to become part of a global community. What will be the factors that might bring these things about, assuming we could define such hopes in tangible form? This question is at the heart of what follows, although the reader is cautioned in advance that there are no simple patterns or conclusions to be drawn. My purpose is to place some features on a still-unexplored landscape and to indicate how they may relate and interact with each other.

This chapter will examine four areas of influence that must affect the chances of us sharing that global premiere of *A winter's tale*. They are:

- common features of the information society
- technological change
- public policy, private practice
- social transformation.

It will then conclude with some thoughts on the impact of various mixes of these phenomena as they might interplay and combine together.

65

Common features of the information society

Scrape away the gloss many present as their vision of the information society and we find uncertainty and generalization. Terms such as knowledge society, learning society, even wisdom society are used with no more clarity than concepts such as 'free society' or 'empowered citizen' – we sense the implication without clear meaning. Grasping for that meaning more often than not produces the effect of sand through fingers. That has not stopped a global industry of books, journals, policies and polemic telling us what will be and what needs to be done.

Nevertheless, we will need to find benchmarks that can define our arrival in or approach to an information society; otherwise we are lost before we start. I want to offer a 'triangle of factors' that will act as indicators towards the information society; they are information, connectivity and social capital.

Information

Many would argue that we have too much information already and that the internet presents the ultimate in overload nightmares; to paraphrase Oscar Wilde, 'we have information on everything, but know the meaning of nothing'. Nevertheless there is an emerging consensus that of all the factors, and there are more than the three examined here, the nature, the presentation and relevance of the content on the networks will be the 'killer app'. The concept of content rather than information is becoming a widely used descriptor for web-based information since it implies more than the word information. It suggests a product, with structure, that can be trusted, that is integrated into the nature of the network and is focused on the end-user. Currently this may seem a fine distinction to make, but it is significant in defining a change from the heterodox mass of information that today is the source of our knowledge – books, reports, the web, broadcast media, mediation, advice services, word of mouth – to the more coherent, integrated, flowing and user-focused environment that the web will have to become if everyone is to benefit.

As a measure of change, therefore, we might expect to see sustained increase in digital content as 'coherent information', the exploitation of connectedness to create journeys linking different sources and places, drawing from online encyclopedias, museums, multimedia and people's memories to deliver to one location a personalized experience that is much more than the haphazard location of random bits of information. Content will drive learning, create new life skills, support daily life and personal development and enable everyone to achieve more and understand others better. These may sound noble sentiments for something as apparently simple as packaged information, but the medium that content inhabits is itself a powerful force for change.

Connectivity

There can be no doubt that the most dramatic manifestation of connectivity is the new fluidity of information flowing from one place to another, from one place to everywhere. The world wide web, e-mail and the mobile phone sum up for better or for worse the swirling ocean of information exchange that now takes place around us. To judge this good or bad is to miss the obvious point that these phenomena are in what they do little different from much of our present behaviours. So far, the primary effects of the web, e-mail and mobile phones are of scale and speed rather than of difference from the past. They allow more people to do more things, more cheaply than they could do before.

And yet, of course, it is not that simple. The fact that these new forms of communication have proved so spectacularly popular, with hundreds of millions of e-mails and small text messages (SMS) a month in the UK alone, has created new commercial opportunity and while the majority of high flying dot coms turned out to have all the aerodynamics of a bunch of keys, there are new service industries emerging to support and develop these new markets. Mobile and fixed telephone companies (telcos) may not be having the best of times as the business models of these new consumer technologies are tested, but we see in this information-rich market a reflection of the sustained move away from industrial production that so many developed countries have shared over the past 40 or more years. A move away from the production of real, tangible things like cars, ships, aeroplanes. Now other countries can do that better, more reliably and more cheaply.

Along that continuum that has moved us from an industrial society towards an information society through what Daniel Bell (1974) always called the post-industrial society there are other features to show the shift towards the creation and exploitation of networked content rather than the fabrication of physical objects; financial services in a global market is the most obvious example, although the news media, espionage and the call centre phenomenon are others that come immediately to mind. All of these activities depend on the interconnection of systems to gather, manipulate and re-form information to meet particular ends. Thus connectivity is creating new ways of doing old things, such as personal banking by phone or online, and new opportunities for service delivery: the 'content' referred to above. Examples of such networked products include:

- *E-books*, which may change the nature of authorship as that connectivity of media (image, sound, text) will enable 'creators' to turn linear storylines into infinite experiences.
- *Distributed services* such as Napster where network connectivity enabled a global database of music files to be shared. While ahead of copyright law, Napster demonstrates that new forms of distributed exchange will be possible.
- *E-commerce.* This has not yet challenged the High Street, but the personalization of service that is possible in this coherent environment suggests that in the future there will be many niche markets where people will prefer to purchase across a network. Amazon.com and other online bookshops already offer e-mailed personal recommendations based on previous purchases and the chance to see what other books people who bought your particular choice have selected.
- *The disconnection of product or service from place*, which is making it possible for institutions that previously depended on physical visits, to reach out to new audiences and to support their existing users in new ways. Museums, libraries and other cultural institutions now put information about their services on the web, give access to their catalogues and are now beginning to work together to create new experiences that could not exist in a single institution. This offers a rare win/win situation where the creation of and access to new cultural content will change how individuals and communities behave and at the same time will encourage the emergence of private sector interest as critical mass becomes achievable.

Whether such developments are good, bad or socially neutral is impossible to decide. The fact that I must wait 15 minutes listening to canned music before being able to book an airline ticket may be frustrating, but the booking can be done at any time of day or night and avoids the need to visit travel agents and queue behind others equivocating over holiday choices.

Social capital

The third characteristic is social capital, the capability of people to support, develop and take advantage of networking and networked information. Where in the past the terms 'librarian' and 'information worker' suggested connotations of libraries of one form or another, it is now no leap of the imagination to consider that many people working in service industries such as finance, insurance and travel are first of all information workers. They use databases, understand the need for accuracy, reliability and timeliness, and base their decisions on the data that are presented to them, usually on a computer screen. Information is the bread and butter, the food of progress. Recognizing the need for a competent workforce capable of developing and using these systems in new and imaginative ways has been high on the government agenda for some years and while at present there is a downturn in demand in some service industries, the longer term will demand a workforce that is well trained, understands the nature of information as raw material for creating content and can work in an environment where re-training and professional development are the norm. Not everything will last for long since new systems linked with global competition will guarantee the survival of only the very fittest.

It is already evident that the move towards an information society where networking underpins daily activity does not bring with it in the short or in the medium term an encompassing automation of all process and services. Effective and skilled workers are going to be more important than ever, dealing with the human problems that do not fit easily into the order of automation. System complexity will bring greater sophistication to wide ranges of need, expressed in diverse ways, but not for some time yet. The role of the human mediator will be a secure job for a good few years to come. And there will be a growing demand for creators of content and all the ancillary skills that will be called for: in hardware and software design and support, market research, psychology, pedagogy, and so on.

Of course, having a workforce that is adequate and competent is only one part of the social capital dimension, and probably the easier part. It is quite apparent that significant numbers of citizens use the networked services that

69

are available to them. Digital television as a key to more channels and services is approaching 50% penetration in UK homes while over 40% of the population has access to the internet. Online shopping is a small but growing market, as are online banking and the wide use of telephone-based services. All these are changed patterns of behaviour, but today, for every citizen who is at least mildly interested in the web, there is at least one other who through lack of incentive, money, ability, motivation, or opportunity is not. Information competency – the ability to judge what information is needed to support a decision or action, use all available channels and be inquisitive – remains a rare skill. Progress stems not simply from making more useful information available on the web, although that will help. It depends on demonstrating to every citizen that information (including digital content) should be a staple for living and that it is easy to get. The social capital to underpin the information society is therefore not just workers with the right skills, it is a population who understands that information will help at every turn, that it is easy to obtain, can widen the view of the community and the wider world and help one to understand others. Moreover, that the traditional sources of information (TV, newspaper or someone in the pub) are generally partial and unreliable, until substantiated by other sources. Such observations, I believe, underline the importance of intervention for the public good, both to increase the skills base and to protect citizens from the control of powerful minorities.

The purpose of this section has been to offer some impressions of those factors that will form the basis for benchmarking the maturing of the information society. For sure, there will be many more and change won't stop when the benchmark indicator lights show solid green on the progress board. Quite what a post-information society would look like is even more uncertain than the appearance of the information society that is the topic of this book. Will it carry us towards a global community of information societies, or a single integrated, globalized network of information users? Who knows? Yet there are some interesting thoughts that emerge from comparison with the shift out of our industrialized past. Will our information industries move elsewhere, the Pacific Rim, Siberia, the Moon? Will the legacy of the information age be people who are more sophisticated in their use of information, just as we accept and use industrial products from across the world, and use such products to cross the world ourselves in a short time and with little effort? All of that is for the future, but we do well to remember that an information society will be no more an 'end state' than were the Renaissance or the hula hoop.

Technological change

While there is no intention to wax lyrical on all the wonders of technology for its own sake, it is essential to establish some of the trends that are likely to emerge in the medium term for it will be the continued massification of digital technology that enables us to foresee a future where so much content can be presented to so many. Of course, we might hypothecate a non-technological society richer in information than ours and with the skills to use it, but that would be an *informing* society for some rather than one where through the connectivity of networking, all will be connected together in two-way/many-way interactions. It is precisely the ability to connect everyone and offer equality of opportunity to explore and exploit that has never been seen before.

How far can we be confident about the technological developments that are described at the beginning of the chapter? Starting with general factors, we are likely to see a continuing increase in the power and capacity of consumer PCs and servers so that more sophisticated products will emerge. The 'holy grail' of universal broadband connectivity that is testing government policy in many developed countries may well be achieved, but it will take time since there are currently no practical business models (or technologies) to justify providing broadband to remote communities in ways that are self-sustaining. That may continue to be true even when there exist broadband 'killer apps' that encourage big consumer markets, immersive, online kids' games for example, and where the pricing of broadband connections to the home does not make it a luxury item. Certainly, if the future were to offer that vision of the global premiere, then the problems of broadband roll-out will have to be addressed sooner rather than later. And that will mean a lead being taken by government since the private sector is currently in no fit state to bear the risks that are involved. Universal access to broadband is not a technological uncertainty since the methods and resources needed to achieve it are well known, but overcoming such economic barriers will be an essential feature of convivial experiences such as the premiere of *A winter's tale*.

Integration

The next essential trend will be the convergence of technologies and systems into 'integrated end-user solutions'. Already the majority of us inhabit environments controlled by the microprocessor – in the car, the fridge, the washing machine, hi-fi, PC, TV, video/DVD player, camera and so on. However, the actual division of technological labour in our homes is very much what it has been for many years. What I mean by this is that particular activities are still generally defined by particular physical spaces: the hi-fi is in the front room, the PC in the den, the TV and associated equipment (satellite dish, DVD player, surround sound) is somewhere else. If in the future delivery mechanisms for information and communication are to play larger parts in our everyday lives, then there will need to be far more integration of design and flexibility in use. Our traditional behaviours at home are probably defined by the restricted space that most people used to have and the limited choice of things to do in those spaces. We have been through a generation that has seen the redefinition of the home environment so that the bedroom (especially for children) has become a living space, just as has the garden, subject to the weather (although the 'conservatory movement' has enabled greater use of garden-like spaces).

With more channels for rich content and thus more choices in the future the need to draw all of the technical devices into an integrated solution will become essential. Those devices need not be distributed around the house and/or the garden, but gathered into one place so long as it is possible to deliver what is required to the individual or group of people with suitable means of interaction. The digital roll-up screen that can talk to the central command unit is one possibility, along with the ability to deliver 'shaped' sound to the individual so that their experience does not intrude significantly on those close by.

If convergence of technologies into 'integrated consumer channels' is a necessary requirement then we must recognize that the same is true of the control of those channels for the convenience of the user. Today we sit with devices to control VCRs, DVDs, TVs, we have Palmtop computers and we have sophisticated washing machines. We also have personal computers that, if they have travelled a long way in the past ten years, cannot by any stretch of the imagination be said to offer foolproof and simple methods of operation. Windows is great if you have nothing better to do, but how many people have the time and incentive to use their Desktop to full advantage or push their word-processor software to the limit of performance? Very few is my guess. Imagine what life would be like if you had to boot up Windows before you could drive your car: by now we would all be walking everywhere. The reality is that the majority of people will want to do a few simple, straightforward things again and again: send e-mails, listen to chosen radio stations, watch things, surf along well-trodden paths and so on, doing it with ease at the click of a button, the nod of the head, where and when.

Content

The final technologically related trend is almost certainly the most significant in the context of mass consumer markets (and probably for all markets). In-depth discussion of the future integration, scope and economics of networked content, the information, services, entertainment, must be beyond this chapter since there is so much to be explored, so many questions to be aired. However, we cannot ignore the fact that it will be the content of the networked services that creates mass-market interest. If there is enough of it and if it is attractive to large audiences then business models for sustainability will emerge, as has been the case with the growth of pay television. What is different about the content on digital networks, as for example the world wide web, is the rich interconnectedness bringing resources together from many and diverse sources. Until now the network that we call the internet has been no more than simple protocols and connections that have kept cleverness and control at the edges, the servers that provide the content and the end-user machines. Across the network, anything can go anywhere without let or hindrance. The world wide web enables different content servers to interact and present themselves in more attractive and fluid ways for the end-user. There is currently little chance of control or intervention in the system.

Connection

There are going to have to be some big decisions made by governments in the next few years about the extent to which web-like services should be made widely available to everyone, as a primary means of delivering information and experience in the domestic, workplace and educational settings in symbiotic relationship with the broadcast media. We already inhabit virtual worlds through television, very much a metaphor for the 'real', and it is within the context of broadcast media that we are beginning to see convergence of linear programming and that interconnectedness that is the internet. The BBC's website is an emerging example of this with extensive information resources on the web to support and enrich the traditional broadcast medium.

Such connectedness could be a very powerful driver for the encouragement of an informed and inquisitive society. It would be a key mechanism for learning for life since if it were possible to offer the utility described above when watching *A winter's tale*, to bookmark items and events for later investigation, the incentive to question and explore would be greatly encouraged.

Implicit in such techniques must be the brokering of new relationships between public and private, public and public, between movie production and the small screen, between old industries and new markets, powerful forces that governments will need to manage. Current discussions within the public sector (in the UK and across Europe) on the creation of a common information environment for all digital resources are early steps towards the convergence on content focusing on the end-user. In that future the first priority for that end-user will be the digital object, the piece of information, rather than a particular website or database. We will need new interfaces, new middleware to manage the integration, and rigorous standards for the design and linking of those digital objects and other resources. Sustained effort will be needed to plan how integration will match the needs of both the naive and the specialist user.

Technology can enable or disable an inclusive information society meaningful to all. Whether or not you tend towards utopia rather than dystopia may depend on how reliable your PC has been in recent days, but the fact remains that with vision and effort the technologies and services we already have could do much to improve the lives of every citizen. However, the real measure of a technology's success will be its invisibility. If the physical bits continue to dominate as they do at present, most people will never get to the content that may be there for the finding. Facility of use, access to content and the integration of systems will have to be paramount.

Public policy, private practice

If assessing the impact of technology over an extended period is problematic, at best trying to project the past into the future, extending that assessment into the fields of public policy and the market economy rapidly begins to look foolhardy. There are, of course, some features that we can observe from the past five years that may help us in the short to medium term. Most obvious is the level of commitment of the present UK government to the wide adoption of ICT, networking and broadband technology, a commitment that has been backed up by significant investment to create public networking resources (National Grid for Learning, the People's Network, UK Online) that are intended to give the whole population easy access to the technology and the support necessary to make them competent in their use. While such interventions are to be seen across Europe, indeed in many parts of the world, the UK was an early entrant and has sustained a level of investment still the envy of many countries. It is evident even from casual observation that without the investment of public funds the progress made during recent years would have been negligible.

There are two questions that arise from this observation. First, what is the probability of sustained government investment being maintained into the medium and long term; and second, what balance might emerge between public and private investment? Will a viable market for networking and networked resources develop and will the government remain committed to pushing the UK forward to achieve the target of being the leading knowledge economy within the next five years?

Lessig (2001) in his recent study *The future of ideas* presents the internet as an example of a 'commons', a space freely available to all to use as they wish, without control from the private or the public sector. He argues that unless the present structure of the internet is sustained and defended, the very nature of its accessibility, its neutrality, its role in innovation and the development of ideas will be lost. This ubiquitous freedom which is assumed in so many models of the information society could be killed as quickly as it has flourished. Yet while at heart we might all wish to see a sea of digital content flowers blooming on our web of the future, to be picked and cross-pollinated by anyone and everyone on the face of the planet, is that likely? Will governments and/or the media moguls of whatever form allow that to happen?

On the journey towards the information society we are travelling through a landscape that is unlike other mixes of public policy and private sector interest. There is no commercial market for digital content creation since demand has yet to be established within a mass market and the significant investment that is currently being made is on behalf of the government to support the core policies of learning and education: visible in the higher education's Distributed National Electronic Resource, the schools' National Grid for Learning and Curriculum Online, and lifelong learning's New Opportunities Fund Digitisation Programme, Culture Online and LearnDirect. There is big money being sunk to create online learning resources, just as the government has made a strong policy and financial commitment to offer universal access to the technological resources to every citizen. The technology and the skills are the means, a learning society is the end. The policy platform suggests that this investment will be the means to build a strong knowledge economy within the UK, where the population will have better information and better skills in the use of the technologies, and therefore be able to make more productive decisions about their lives, thus contributing to a society that competes effectively in a global market for information, services and knowledge. To achieve this the Government must foster a viable market economy that is innovative and competitive on the world stage.

It is at this point where the uncertainties and unusual nature of the landscape start to become visible. What evidence we do have about the market delivering networks and networked services shows that they are young and very delicate blooms. The dot.com boom came too early, without the critical mass of consumers with the mindset to consume digitally. New business models will emerge as more people take up the web and use it regularly. Examples such as e-banking, bookselling, music exchange and cultural resources were cited as early entries to test new models. But how far will it be possible to maintain clear blue water between the interests of the large media companies and the freedom from direct control that makes the internet what it is today? Our scenario paints a picture of the integration of two virtual spaces, broadcast media and the web, taking the strengths of both without injecting any of the practical concerns that are visible across the globe about the influence that a few large organizations can have over the media that we all experience, wherever we are. The current uncertainties in the UK over the future roll-out of digital television (a key component in the integration of broadcast media and the web) underline this dilemma. If the supply of dTV becomes focused within the control of a small groups of large media companies, what chance then to protect the 'commons' that is the web today?

The past few years have seen dramatic changes in policy towards information within the public sector. What was once more often a tool of demand management, to be queued for and hunted down, is becoming a commodity that is packaged with the end-user in mind. Services such the government's portal UK Online (ukonline.gov.uk) and the health advisory service NHS Direct Online are two powerful examples of those changes, where for the first time people can get access to information and advice in ways directly meaningful to them when and where they want to. If sustained, as I am sure they will be, they will influence how all public services develop nationally and locally. Over time, such services could change the attitudes and expectations of the majority of the UK's citizens and would therefore foster how the commercial market grows. That in itself will not be a neutral effect. As change takes place it will be essential to maintain a careful watch on the extent to which commercial decisions affect the balance between freedom of choice and near-monopoly supply that is becoming apparent in UK television services. If the end-to-end supply of service dominates, then the supplier may find it useful to manage demand and accessibility. For example, if the key delivery channel for content, TV, web, or other, is broadband and the broadband network is in the hands of one or two suppliers, they might decide that constraints be put on bandwidth or the supply of video feeds to maximize income, filter all services or create a walled environment that stopped users gaining access to the rich diversity that is the current web.

The questions that were posed earlier in this section about the scale and extent over time of government investment and the lasting balance between public and private, have not been answered in any firm way. Nor could they be at this stage. In my view this stage of the journey towards an information society requires action to do things, to experiment and to begin a process of change. Governments, in reacting in the way that the UK government has reacted, are doing exactly what they must to begin the process of change. That does not excuse the need to hypothesize about the future, to assess what the risks and opportunities are in the light of experience, or indeed to change tack if it is clear that new problems or dangers are to be faced.

While individual governments will have different approaches to information society policy and the definition of relationships between public policy and markets, both the media and the web are now global phenomena with influence beyond individual sovereign states. In such conditions the relationships between countries and their ability to work together in blocs and globally will be the main agent for managing what the future information society will be like. Yet the decisions and priorities that are set in public policy will require finesse to ensure that the freedom and neutrality of the internet that today offers so much to enable innovation and the empowerment of the individual is not destroyed by too much intervention either in the public interest or the interests of a small number of multinational corporations.

Social transformation

Paradoxes and uncertainties have always abounded when exploring future possibilities. Once one breaks out of the straitjacket that is the worldview of the now, there can be few secure landmarks to guide; this is the nature of prognostication. Sometimes it is possible to assess the balance of probability with more confidence – when global tension is high or when serious natural disaster occurs, for example. These are matters out of the hands of ordinary people that must be responded to rather than influenced. Is the journey towards an information society any different?

The paradoxes soon surface when the social implications of change are considered, particularly the power of individuals and groups to have impact on future trends. For example, is the opening scenario, with a global media environment linked to an apparently neutral world wide web, a real possibility? Does the average user of the web realize that they are part of a trend that represents a radically different set of connections, relationships and freedoms than anything previously experienced? Probably not. I have already raised the topic of the delicate balance that will be needed between the public good value of an open network that fosters exchange and innovation and the powerful effects of large organizations that wish to manage and direct the use of the services that they provide. 'Walled gardens' may be a concern to those for whom free access to unbiased information is a matter of philosophical concern, but to the avid home shopper it may not be. Could the future turn from friendly free-for-all into a world of 'information prisons' that control and restrict what people can obtain from where?

The answers to such questions will depend on an assessment of the value that ordinary people place on the information they locate in cyberspace. Is it relevant, easy to find and reliable? Is it useful to their everyday lives? That places great emphasis on public policy not simply to provide people with access to the technology at reasonable cost, but more importantly to provide them with the skills and competencies to use and exploit networked resources and to make judgements about the information that they find. In this sense the best chance for sustaining in the future the diversity that is the web now will be those interventions that the government and public service institutions are currently making.

We can expect, then, that over the coming five years there will be more people making more discerning judgements about the quality of content they require to lead their lives. It is already normal for students to use web resources to support their learning and the trends that are observable in places such as libraries and community learning centres in the UK suggest that there is a growing demand from all social groups, all age groups and cultural groups for access to networked resources. Some of that arises from general interest about what the web can offer, much of it concerned with using simple tools such as e-mail to keep in touch with families and friends in distant countries. The trends that drive progress will not necessarily be those at the cutting edge of the technology. Public investment in quality content such as cultural heritage and learning resources will be essential to boosting demand and testing ideas.

On the other hand, it is absolutely clear that there are more people in the UK with more money and more time to explore new technological opportunity. The consumer electronics market appears to be booming as DVD with widescreen TV and 'cinema surround sound' are taken up with enthusiasm, and more people expect to be able to travel with libraries of music on portable juke boxes or minidisk systems. Homes fill up with televisions, and spare mobile phones become the norm. Those who can afford to spend money on non-essential items (and according to recent research by the Henley Centre for the Arts Council of England (2000), that is now a majority of the population) expect to have high-quality experiences; hence the move towards cinema-like presentation in the home and top quality sound when travelling. Expectations have risen and will continue to rise as technology improves and so long as prices are competitive. There is the risk in all of this that the temptation for integrated solutions (the entertainment command centre) that will deliver all the media and information to the home and be able to interface to a local network of interfaces will overwhelm any recognition of the value of open and free access to networked resources. Buying such hardware brings with it a discrete and controlled set of service options. Here we have again the concerns that were expressed at the end of the last section: going for the no-choice soup-to-nuts solution restricts the opportunity to eat at another restaurant.

We should not get too hung up on such issues. In a society where there are reasonable policies to maintain a balance between regulation and market forces it is likely that most of the time most people will be satisfied with what they are able to do. Those who are aware of the potential for growth and innovation that could arise in a population that is skilled to use information and has access to limitless information resources will argue that to fail to achieve that potential is to fail society. Others might suggest that to force that information freedom on to people who do not see the need for it is just as oppressive as the domination by one or more large organizations. People will do what they want to do and are able to do. It may be quite reasonable to expect the current move to provide access to ICT resources and offer the skills to use those resources in productive ways, but that does not mean all those people will suddenly adopt completely new lifestyles. There will be a transformation, but slowly over time as the information and those resources become invisible, a normal part of the average life. Lifelong learning will become no more conscious an act than breathing.

Nevertheless, the social impact of the broader balance of free-for-all networking and managed media remains to be played out and will depend on the aggregation of individual decisions across countries across the globe. There will be social transformation as the technology integrates more with our lives, but we cannot be sure how far it will support the thrust of the information society described in the earlier part of this chapter.

Conclusion

Any attempt to write about the potential and likelihood of an information society (in whatever form it might take) always ends up talking about an Easter Island landscape where the stone figures are replaced by question marks. We can begin to see where the questions need to be asked, but there are few easy answers to be found. The title of this chapter was predicated on the question, what will be (or should be) the balance between public policy and the traditional supply and demand market? Will public policy push us in the 'right' direction sufficiently or will the personal pull of individual choice in a free market get us to a more robust and long-lasting society where information can be traded and exploited within traditional economic models? Although the consequent title seemed a good idea at the time it was probably a bad question to begin with. If the subsequent exploration has shown anything at all, it is that we are not at a junction where we are able to make a choice between one or the other, and we are never likely to be. Any future reality will see the playing out of various policies and forces in a rollercoaster journey that will lead to addictive exhilaration for some, but for others a feeling of uncertainty and nausea.

I like to think that there is still the chance to create the sort of information society where the act of taking learning journeys is as joyous as watching a good film or TV programme and where entertainment and learning can be intertwined; that reading a paper or indeed reading a book can be the key to unlock other interests and ideas. That more than anything we can use the technological opportunities to make people's lives better and in doing so create better, more stable and more tolerant communities. That through greater understanding of different lifestyles, individuals and communities we can become confident to live in harmony with those from different traditions. It is within this development framework that our great public institutions must see their future evolving: access to cultural assets, to new learning opportunities and to the services of government are both the means to unlock the information society and essential building blocks for that new order. Museums, libraries, advice services, archives, schools, universities, colleges, broadcasters must all have places in the jigsaw of a society where there is a balance between the right to know and the right to supply. Where people have the skills to know what is available and where it can be found. Where the strengths of what we already have are sustained into the future.

Should those goals be achieved we would have an informed society that is a learning society, and that would be a noble achievement. If I am asked to predict what might be the most significant of the drivers at this juvenile stage, then I am sure that it will be effective public policy together with joined-up investment. Those two things could make a difference to individual opportunity and create the universal access that will generate increased demand for information and information support services.

By way of final comment I wish to return to the question asked previously about the nature of the post-information society. The concept of an information society has always been and always will be impossible to define in an objective way; rather it reflects a series of trends that might dominate social change. However, beyond an informed learning society we need to see other landmarks, the knowledge society and the wisdom society. Information is only useful if it is put to good use, and a knowledge society will be one where people are competent to combine information with their own experience of the world to create new knowledge and ideas. The wisdom society I envisage as a place where everyone is capable of taking their knowledge and ideas and sharing them in useful ways with others – the recycling of their wisdom back into the information resource. Were we to aim for the latter landmark it would certainly require a very liberal and open web of communication freely available for use by everyone without hindrance. To end, I cannot resist offering a new slogan for my vision of the future. The most powerful driver of success with end-users will be the scope, quality, accessibility and relevance of what the various channels will offer and the networks can deliver. On that basis I can think of no better title for our goal than the Content Society.

References

Bell, D. (1974) *The coming of a post-industrial society. A venture in social forecasting*, London, Heinemann.

Henley Centre for the Arts Council of England (2000) *Towards 2010: new times, new challenges for the arts*, London, Arts Council.

Lessig, L. (2001) *The future of ideas. The fate of the commons in a connected world*, London, Random House.

5
Information literacy and the information society

J. Stephen Town

Introduction

Information literacy is 'a theoretical and practical response to the cultural, social and economic developments associated with the Information Society' (Webber and Johnston, 2000). In other words information literacy and the information society are not only inextricably linked, but the very concept of the former flows from the demands of the latter. In simple terms the impact of the information society on individuals is to create a requirement for functioning effectively within it, and that some of the associated capabilities might be encapsulated in a concept called 'information literacy'. The concept, if valid, should help define the practical steps required to develop those capabilities in individuals. This chapter links the growth of understanding in societies with a theoretical model developed to define and inform practical efforts to achieve information literacy.

This chapter considers how the sequence of events in national contexts might be seen as one of rising national concern about information society and knowledge economy issues, leading to some analysis of the processes associated with building such a society (including both infrastructure and individual processes), and this analysis leading to products which assist the growth of the desired society, including a recognition of the need for individual information literacy and the associated educational programmes required to attain this.

The chapter considers briefly how the concept of information literacy has developed and been used, and contrasts other national approaches with UK analyses and approaches. In particular it focuses on the work of the SCONUL Information Skills Task Force in elaborating and linking a theoretical model to practical programmes to develop information literacy. It contends that clarification of what is important about these programmes, and definition and measurement of the outcomes in individuals, might be key to helping create the information society.

Information literacy: definitions and distinctions

A recent useful survey covers the range of work on definitions and differences in the developing concept of information literacy (Bawden, 2001). The first usage occurred a quarter of a century ago (Zurkowski, 1974), referring to the workplace, and since then there have been attempts to link the concept with the information society and stress its importance in this context (for example Oxbrow, 1998), and also to track the development of information society technologies by coining fresh terms (for example 'digital literacy', Lanham, 1995). The fundamental concept or name of information literacy has however changed little. Bawden lists information literacy, computer literacy and synonyms (IT literacy, electronic literacy), library literacy, electronic information literacy, media literacy, network literacy, internet literacy, hyper-literacy, digital literacy and digital information literacy. While full justice cannot be done here to the terminological debate, this chapter assumes that while there have been radical changes in information technologies, sources and services, the challenge for the individual remains to master format, content and variety to function effectively in the information society. The most critical distinction, and the most damaging elision for the understanding of information society issues, is that between information literacy and IT/computer literacy. Societies which fail to understand the distinction are unlikely to create the full range of programmes necessary for their citizens.

Is there a disease?

If information literacy is a valid concept and is either the outcome in the individual of a functioning information society or a prerequisite for effective individual functioning within it, then one would expect some recognition of this by governments, policy makers and other stakeholders. The next section will address to what extent this is the case. It is however important to test the alternative position. Is information literacy a real and necessary concept demonstrating a critical issue for the information society? Or to put it another way, is there a 'disease' of information illiteracy which in some might need to be cured, and which must be prevented by appropriate education within the normal system? 'Information illiteracy' has been used as a term in this context (for example Mensching and Mensching, 1989)

It has been argued that information literacy is 'an exercise in public relations' for librarians and may not be a real problem (Foster, 1993). It might also be assumed by some that information skills and information literacy are developing apace with information and communication innovation (for example see The Pulse, 2002), and that therefore both societally and professionally we need put no more effort into information skills education than we have hitherto.

The validity of the concept can be shown if the absence of information literacy is a serious problem both for individuals and for aspiring information societies. If there is a disease of 'information illiteracy' with recognizable symptoms, diagnosis, treatment and cure, then it will be worth elaborating the concept and addressing the problem in national policies relating to the information age.

Two examples of information illiteracy are put forward in confirmation. One relates to a workplace environment, in which information management was considered to be an important enough issue to generate a national research project. The AIM-UK study (Hanley, Harrington and Blagden, 1998) drew on senior managers and around 400 aerospace engineers and scientists engaged in research and development. Of this highly educated workforce, 90% believed that access to information is either important or very important. However 'an almost total lack of awareness of major electronic sources was revealed and a significant amount of information seeking activities were ineffective . . . around 50% of . . . critical information incidents surveyed were unsuccessful in meeting the information need that prompted the search'. Among the specific proposals generated was 'the development of a research skills training course to enhance the information and searching capabilities of aerospace scientists and engineers'.

The second example is that of UK higher education, where one might have assumed information literacy levels would be high. The JUSTEIS project (reported in Armstrong et al., 2001) indicated that students are relying uniformly on the web and show a lack of understanding about the resources available to them 'because all the information is in the same place'. The web may have 'changed everything' but in doing so it has created a new problem of information illiteracy; that of false confidence in the internet as a complete information resource. The higher education experience also suggests very strongly that the growth of new information technologies has been accompanied by a growth of both demand for and delivery of information skills education. This might in turn suggest that national infrastructure developments and increased content access to create information societies will be accompanied by both need and demand for accompanying information literacy or skills programmes.

The driving forces and national analyses

National aims and perspectives

It is not the purpose of this chapter to cover in detail the driving forces arising from individual national contexts towards developing the information society. There appears to be common ground in three main connected issues, which leads to a national recognition of the need for progress. Firstly, a nation perceives a need for competitive reasons to be a player in the global knowledge economy. Secondly, this suggests a need for the upskilling of its population to work effectively in this sort of economy, resulting in a national 'learning agenda'. The 'learning agenda' also tends to become explicitly associated with the skills of citizens, the development of these skills within educational programmes, and their subsequent application in the workplace. Thirdly the growth of digital media and communications results in widespread information overload, leading to the need for both individuals and corporations to have effective information and knowledge management. The sequence tends to run from national concern to process analysis to products for developing information literacy. We shall consider this sequence in various specific national contexts below. The following very brief pictures are presented from English-speaking contexts, where 'information literacy' appears to be a commonly understood concept.

The USA

Information literacy had been recognized sufficiently as both a concept and a challenge related to the information age for a National Forum to be created in 1989, bringing together a coalition of interested parties, from librarians through educators to politicians (www.infolit.org/). Subsequently an Institute for Information Literacy (www.ala.org/acrl/nili/), and a set of competency standards for higher education (www.ala.org/acrl/ilstndardlo.html) followed. When the national skills debate was in progress information literacy and its component skills were therefore recognized, with a clear distinction made between information and technology and systems. The Secretary's Commission on Achieving Necessary Skills (SCANS, 1991) produced the following analysis:

Foundation skills	*Competencies*
Basic	Resources
Thinking	Interpersonal
Personal	Information
	Systems
	Technology.

Since then this early recognition of need has led to information literacy programmes at all levels of education in the USA. There has been no real issue of definition, and apparently little divergence of opinion about what practically is sought. A US model was provided at an early stage with outcome measures (Doyle, 1992); and more recently the Big6 model and programmes for schools (see www.big6.com/) has been created as a commercial venture.

Australia and New Zealand

The national analysis in Australia was not far behind. The relevant government body (Mayer Committee, 1992) suggested the following 'Competency strands':

- collecting, analysing and organizing information
- communicating ideas and information
- planning and organizing activities
- working with others in teams
- using mathematical ideas and techniques

- solving problems
- using technology.

Once again technology skills are clearly separated from information-related skills. There has been much subsequent activity in Australia, particularly in higher education, to which full justice can hardly be done here, but including task forces, conferences, standards and a joint Australia and New Zealand Institute for Information Literacy (see Bundy, 1998). A distinctive model for information literacy has been developed to reflect personal 'conceptions' (Bruce, 1997).

More recently in New Zealand the government became keen to see all citizens in possession of the opportunity to access and effectively use ICT. This led to proposals for a 'digital opportunity' strategy and action plan. Stakeholder respondents raised the need for an overall 'information society' strategy, and alongside the now expected access and infrastructure issues was the recognition that the government could encourage more people to acquire 'information literacy', seen as a key set of skills that people will need in the 'information age' (again based on Doyle, 1992). The fact that these skills were not explicitly taught was recognized, and many felt that 'children should be taught how to manage information from a young age'. LIANZA called for a national information literacy strategy to be strongly championed by 'one strong central agency' (New Zealand, 2001).

The UK

In the UK the information age was recognized as a key issue by the new Labour Government in 1997. The Government published two papers which combined the citizen's right to an information infrastructure (UK. DfEE, 1997) with the necessary learning agenda for a successful society in a knowledge-based future global economy (UK. DfEE, 1998). The main contextual driver in the UK was the desire for improved national performance and competitiveness in the global economy, which led to the wish to provide coherent packages for lifelong learning for UK citizens. A defined national set of 'key skills' for learning, for careers, and for personal life, were identified (at www.qca.org.uk/nq/ks/). The six skill areas were:

- number application
- communication
- information technology
- working with others
- improving own learning and performance
- problem solving.

When this approach was applied to UK higher education, the Dearing Report (NCIHE, 1997) identified a concept of 'graduateness' defined by the following skills:

- communication
- numeracy
- use of information technology
- learning how to learn
- subject-specific skills.

Both these analyses failed to explicitly identify information literacy as a requirement or to separate information skills from technology skills.

Welfare versus wisdom

In the UK, in contrast to the USA and Australia, the concept of information skills is consequently not recognized as a separate domain. This gap in the UK analysis leads to a failure to identify a requirement for information literacy in the information age, in spite of the recognition of a requirement for skills that relate to information technology. This lack of a well-defined and accepted concept of information literacy in national policy and planning appears to be a key difference between the UK and other English-speaking countries. This failure is remarkable given that information skills needs were recognized in both higher education and schools more than 20 years ago in various reports (for example Marland, 1981; CIRUE, 1975) as collected and reiterated more recently (Corrall, 2000).

There are three possible reasons why this has occurred. The first may be the inability in the UK to look beyond the immediate problems associated with the technology and the infrastructure. The solution to the information society problem often appears to be presented as simply one of dispensing IT infra-structure and services, and this in turn results in an elision of IT skills with information skills, with the consequence that the latter disappears as an issue. This even occurs in strategies produced by professional library bodies (see, for example, Library Association, 2001). It is almost impossible to find a UK policy statement with the term 'information literacy' specifically identified (the exception was the superseded Library and Information Commission's *Keystones for the information age: a national information policy for the UK* at www.lic.gov.uk/publications/policyreports/keystone.html, which listed 'developing universal information literacy' as one of its 'Competencies' issues). At present there seems to be little concern about planning for the information skills of the end-users, in contrast to the standardized approach to IT skills through, for example, the European Computer Driving Licence (ECDL). Training and skills issues seem currently focused on the staff of libraries and on their IT skills (for example through the People's Network initiative) rather than on the broader information skills of the citizenry. In a recent summary of national information policy it was recognized that while 'IT classes have been taught for many years' the issue of 'selecting and evaluating information' will only start to be addressed through the new Citizenship strand of the National Curriculum (Johnson, R., 2001).

The second reason, suggested before elsewhere (Town, 2000b), is that the UK policy mindset in preparing for the information society is one of dispensing welfare to its citizens rather than one of creating wisdom within individuals. The information skills needed for modern societies and economies are much closer to being a 'wisdom' rather than a 'welfare' problem. Wisdom may be defined as possession of expert knowledge together with the power of applying it practically. This would seem to be a suitable statement for defining the outcome of information literacy programmes. It recognizes that information literacy is a practical capability, but more importantly that it is 'knowledge' rather than simply 'skills' that are required. Consequently the solution requires 'education' rather than 'training', and an agreed theoretical framework on which to build sound information literacy education programmes. The recent change of terminology in libraries from 'user education' to 'information skills training' was therefore in some ways unfortunate.

The third reason is also bound up with the 'welfare' mindset. Concepts of 'information rich and poor', the need to combat the power of global media, and the need to ensure equality of information access in a healthy democracy all combine to suggest that information literacy is an issue of 'welfare'. Welfare may be defined (Oxford English Dictionary) as 'a satisfactory state of health and prosperity received by those in need' and 'organised efforts to improve conditions for the poor [or] disabled'. In addition the word 'literacy' itself has a dual meaning in the UK; for one class of citizens it suggests removal of the stigma of illiteracy, for another it suggests being cultured and 'well read'. There is certainly anecdotal evidence that 'information literacy' attracts a stigma from the former meaning which in some organizations makes it an unacceptable term.

There is recognition of the need for information literacy and information skills programmes from information professionals within national, education and workplace libraries in the UK (see for example Dale and O'Flynn, 2001), but this has not resulted in the explicit recognition of information literacy in national policies.

Conclusion

At the UK national level the need for information skills in the information society and the concept of information literacy are not explicitly recognized. The desired consequences of the investment in IT access and information and learning content are therefore less likely to be achieved, because the individual citizen will not have the ability to work with them in a fully effective way. The UK HE experience is predictive; students have access to a wide range of resources but fail to use them effectively, giving rise to increases in information skills or information literacy programmes. If this is happening to the most educated and motivated, then success is unlikely to be achieved with the rest of society. The UK is also likely to be less competitive in the global knowledge and information economies than nations who have planned and executed effective information literacy strategies. In the next section the work being undertaken in this area in HE is described, with a view to using it as a possible framework for application to the national situation.

Seeking meaning

Meaning, models, and measurement

'What is needed to accelerate interest in information literacy . . . is tangibility, and proof that it makes a difference to . . . learning outcomes' (Bundy, 1998). This challenge was addressed to teachers at all levels, but it applies generally. In other words the critical issues for acceptance and progress are practical definition and measurement. This section attempts to provide a practical meaning of information literacy through a UK model, and the following section provides an introduction to ongoing work to use the model (and other research and analysis) to create practical solutions for the achievement of information literacy as a useful element within broader learning. The work described started with an HE focus. In other national contexts it is not unusual for significant work to be done in higher education which is then diffused more widely. Higher education tends to have a complexity of information technology, content and access issues already and can therefore be an effective laboratory for information literacy experiments. HE students have the most significant access to information resources, both traditional and electronic, and their need for deeper subject-related information skills is usually recognized in academic programmes. In addition HE libraries have long been involved in 'user education' and its successor information skills programmes.

The SCONUL Information Skills Task Force

In the UK, there is significant activity in the field of information skills education (ISE) and in encouraging information literacy within the higher education sector. The involvement of HE librarians in this work led to the formation of the SCONUL Information Skills Task Force (ISTF) (Johnson, H., 2001). The drivers and antecedents for the creation of this body were:

- the development of the web and related electronic information resources, and the consequent need to re-engineer 'library induction' and 'user education' programmes to incorporate the changes
- SCONUL recognizing that in periods of rapid change a task force approach to some issues was needed, and that information skills were not addressed

by any of its existing committees

- the substantial growth in ISE activity undertaken by library staff, demonstrated by the LISU database of SCONUL statistics
- partnership issues between library and academic staff engaged in this activity
- different forms and methods of approach in ISE, identified through the SCONUL benchmarking pilots (Town, 2000a)
- issues that arose from overlap with IT skills training and education, especially in 'converged' library and computing services.

Some of the objectives of the ISTF were to:

- define and demonstrate the importance of ISE
- clarify the distinction to IT skills
- clarify the scope of activity and of contributions to it
- identify good practice
- relate ISE to institutional and national strategies, including information literacy.

Among the action lines and deliverables of the ISTF are:

- a briefing paper and the Seven Pillars model (SCONUL, 1999)
- a UK conference and published proceedings (Corrall and Hathaway, 2000)
- relating the model to UK Quality Assurance Agency subject benchmarks
- designing a generic skills course module, in association with the Open University
- co-operation with the JISC 'Big Blue' ISE research project
- developing performance measures for ISE
- exploring differences in approach in different academic subjects and disciplines.

Model definition

The model was originally constructed from a 'thought experiment' about using information services. As such it resulted from reflection on the professional practice of those involved in developing information skills within academic communities. It was also conceived deliberately to enable application to both traditional and digital information sources, and to relate to any level from that of the most naive seeker to that of the most expert producer of knowledge. It seems immaterial whether the user is approaching a virtual library through a desktop or approaching an existing physical system mediated by real people, or whether the user is a child doing homework or an academic undertaking leading edge research: the model should be able to encompass all contexts. It was, however, important to be able to link the model to the knowledge production role of universities. Another main influence on its development was the need for linkage to concepts of the 'graduateness' requirements of employers and other stakeholders, and to the skills lists arising from the relevant reports (for example NCIHE, 1997). The experience of users in libraries and their growing engagement with libraries and academic literature, and the understanding of these processes among members of the Task Force was profoundly influential.

Subsequent to its genesis the SCONUL model was mapped against some existing models (Bruce, 1997; Doyle, 1992; and the DEDICATE model from Fjallbrant, 1996). It combines almost everything inherent in the other models, but it was designed for use rather than being based on research findings. One intention was to come up with a comprehensive listing of information-related skills, irrespective of the source of the development of these skills. This placed those library-provided elements within a framework encompassing elements which might be provided by other parties, particularly teachers or IT staff. Thus the model would help point up the partnerships involved in developing these skills.

The diagramatic form of the SCONUL model is shown in Figure 5.1.

Here are the seven headline skills:

1 The ability to recognize a need for information.
2 The ability to distinguish ways in which the information 'gap' may be addressed by:
   — knowledge of appropriate kinds of resources, both print and non-print
   — selection of resources with 'best fit' for the task at hand
   — the ability to understand the issues affecting accessibility of sources.
3 The ability to construct strategies for locating information to:
   — articulate information need to match against resources
   — develop a systematic method appropriate for the need
   — understand the principles of construction and generation of databases.

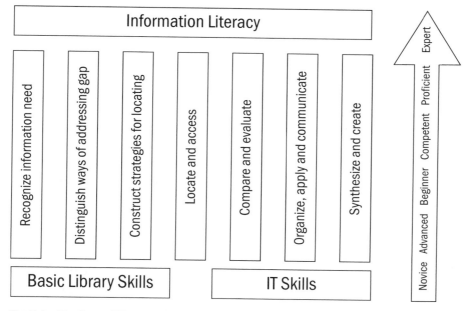

Fig. 5.1 *The Seven Pillars model*

4 The ability to locate and access information to:
   — develop appropriate searching techniques (e.g. use of Booleans)
   — use communication and information technologies, including terms for international academic networks
   — use appropriate indexing and abstracting services, citation indexes and databases
   — use current awareness methods to keep up to date.
5 The ability to compare and evaluate information obtained from different sources for:
   — awareness of bias and authority issues
   — awareness of the peer review process of scholarly publishing
   — appropriate extraction of information matching the information need.
6 The ability to organize, apply and communicate information to others in ways appropriate to the situation by:
   — citing bibliographic references in project reports and theses
   — constructing a personal bibliographic system
   — applying information to the problem at hand

- communicating effectively using appropriate medium
- understanding issues of copyright and plagiarism.
7 The ability to synthesize and build upon existing information, contributing to the creation of new knowledge.

The model was published in the Task Force briefing paper (SCONUL, 1999) and elaborated at the conference mentioned above (Town, 2000b).

The model separates the basic skills required for accessing IT systems, and the basic skills required for engaging with libraries as organizations, from the skills and understanding necessary to engage and work with information content, hence the distinction between the sub-boxes and the pillars proper. The model thus incorporates, and may reflect, the differences between computer literacy, information literacy and library literacy suggested elsewhere (see Bawden, 2001).

It is now recognized that the model does not represent a simple progression with each stage necessarily following another, although there is an underlying logical sense of development of skills within the model. The model will require different interpretation when applied to different subject fields, and to differing levels of user. This means that it does not provide absolute definitions, levels or standards for skills achievements. One of the proposed applications is, however, as a diagnostic tool for assessment of individual need, and some examples of this from the higher education context are provided in Town (2000b). Further work is required to develop an instrument for this form of measurement for a variety of individual contexts.

Seeking solutions

Accreditation through a generic programme

An early idea within the Task Force was the creation of an ECDL-equivalent accredited qualification for information skills. Given the parallel subject work described below this direct equivalence ceased to be seen as either possible or desirable. However the idea of a generic transferable skills course suitable for first-year undergraduate level, which might have wide applicability across different institutions, was taken up. Curriculum developers at the Open University (OU), working with Task Force members, used the SCONUL model to create a ten-credit module in information skills. This is now known as MOSAIC, and although based on the OU library and information resources, it is capable of customization to the services of other institutions. A pilot took place in May 2002. Discussions are in progress between the OU and SCONUL with a view to marketing this module throughout the HE sector.

Integration with educational programmes and subject relationship

The degree to which information literacy programmes are, or should be, integrated with formal academic programmes is a question that the Task Force set out to address, and evidence from the sector suggests that practice is varied, even within single institutions. This issue crosses professional boundaries between library and teaching staff, and is therefore likely to generate debates about demarcation and the skills and knowledge of those delivering programmes (see for example Noon and Heseltine, 2000).

Information literacy may be inseparable from context, and in higher education this may mean subject discipline. This is not a new suggestion: one model of 'learning information literacy' explicitly recognizes 'learning the intellectual norms of the subject domain associated with the production of knowledge' as one of its four areas of required learning (Hepworth, 2000). The way in which information skills and information literacy are being developed in different subject disciplines is under investigation by a sub-group of the SCONUL Task Force. Three subjects were chosen from across the spectrum – theology, chemistry and education – and librarians involved in information skills education in these disciplines were surveyed to ascertain methods, tools, curricular aspects and intended learning outcomes. The Quality Assurance Agency (QAA) subject benchmark statements for each subject were examined, and academic staff consulted through a web-based questionnaire. Results of this work will be presented soon.

In all of the above it seems that an ideological model built on 'specific practices embedded in particular social contexts' (Street, 1993), as opposed to a single autonomous model in which skills or competences can be viewed separately from the situations in which they are used, is more likely to be successful. The SCONUL model seems to be applicable in all of these contexts, but its application may be very different in each, and the definition of what each pillar might mean in different subject areas requires considerable further work. It is already clear that a simple generalized 'skills standard' approach is not adequate for either understanding or measuring information literacy.

Measurement

Measurement will be key to the future of information literacy as a useful concept. There is a need to recognize what is important about information literacy, information skills and associated programmes, and from that analysis specific measures may be identified. SCONUL's Advisory Committee on Performance Improvement has been collaborating with the Information Skills Task Force to elaborate what is important about information skills programmes in HE, in pursuit of a measurement framework. This is not limited to quantitative measures, and includes the collection of contextual data. The protocol for investigating this has been to use a Critical Success Factors (CSFs) methodology (from Oakland, 1993) and to apply it in small group settings across a range of staff involved in information skills programme delivery, organization or strategy. Findings have been collected so far from ten separate workshops involving more than 30 groups. Full analysis has not yet taken place, but it is already clear that there is considerable consensus on a number of significant elements which need to be right if successful programmes are to be created and managed. Interim results suggest the critical issues are:

- integration with institutional strategies, particularly those covering learning and teaching
- measuring student entry-level skills and subsequent outcomes
- student motivation
- staff training and qualifications for designing and delivering programmes
- resourcing programmes, including equipment
- pedagogic quality, methods and integration with subject disciplines
- partnerships between academic staff, librarians, national bodies and qualifications agencies.

Conclusion

Implications for the information society

How might these sectoral developments assist in developing the 'information society'? The preceding analysis and the work of the SCONUL ISTF suggests that the achievement of information literacy cannot be seen solely as 'skill' development or training, but needs to be recognized as a contextual and educational challenge. This is expressed through the idea of information literacy development as 'seeking wisdom' rather than resulting from 'dispensing welfare', and also demarcates information literacy from the issues of providing IT access and IT skills. The UK approach to developing national competitiveness through an educated and informed populace differs from approaches in other countries in its lack of recognition of the importance of information literacy, and the absence of provision for programmes to encourage it among the broader population. Applying the experience of higher education to the broader national context suggests the following actions.

Proposals for recognition

If the UK wants to have an information society then it must have information-literate citizens. If it wishes to avoid a gap between information rich and information poor (and the ignorant are clearly likely to be the poorest in this society), then appropriate levels of information literacy must be achieved throughout the population. This will involve both national recognition of the problem, and commitment and subsequent allocation of resources to address it. It was recently suggested that 'there is not enough investment . . . to help promote the acquisition of new media literacies that are needed by all citizens' and 'extending and deepening all citizen's capabilities for critical discourse about the origins and validity of information provided on the internet should become an urgent policy priority' (Mansell, 2002). A rewrite of the national skills list to explicitly recognize information literacy, and inclusion in the National Curriculum would be helpful steps. This requires policy makers and others to move on from the admittedly important issues of technology and access to those of the individual citizen's engagement with content and learning.

Proposals for action

One challenge to be met and a change required for the 21st-century information society in the UK is that of achieving universal information literacy. This will only be achieved if the actions suggested above result in the embedding of information literacy programmes within all national educational contexts. This will not be attained without a broadly shared understanding of what information literacy means, how it is defined from a practical point of view, and what programmes flow from this knowledge. This understanding must extend to the detail of programme content in all contexts, and to identifying who will resource and deliver them, and to measurement systems to demonstrate success.

In the UK, higher education has been leading the way in the recognition of these issues, in the practical experience of developing information skills and information literacy, and in using this experience to produce a meaningful model for further application. This work needs now to be applied to the broader national context if the UK is to be successful in the global information economy, and in creating a 21st-century information society.

References

Armstrong, C. et al. (2001) The JISC usage surveys: trends in electronic information services (JUSTEIS) project — supply and demand in higher education, *Library and Information Briefings*, **106/107**, (July).

Bawden, D. (2001) Information and digital literacies: a review of concepts, *Journal of Documentation*, **57** (2), (March), 218–59.

Bruce, C. (1997) *The seven faces of information literacy*, Adelaide, Auslib Press.

Bundy, A. (1998) *Information literacy: the key competency for the 21st century*, University of South Australia, available at www.library.unisa.edu.au/papers/inlit21.htm.

CIRUE (1975) *A language for life: report of the Committee of Inquiry into Reading and the Use of English*, London, HMSO (The Bullock Report).

Corrall, S. (2000) Skills for the future. In Corrall, S. and Hathaway, H. (eds) (2000), *Seven pillars of wisdom? Good practice in information skills development. Proceedings of a conference held at the University of Warwick, 6–7 July 2000*, London, SCONUL, 5–10.

Corrall, S. and Hathaway, H. (eds) (2000) *Seven pillars of wisdom? Good practice in information skills development. Proceedings of a conference held at the University of Warwick, 6–7 July 2000*, London, SCONUL.

Dale, A. and O'Flynn, S. (2001) Desperation: information literacy levels falling in Corporania, *Journal of Information Science*, **2 7**(1), 51–3.

Doyle, C. S. (1992) *Outcome measures for information literacy: final report to the National Forum on Information Literacy*, Syracuse, NY, ERIC Clearinghouse.

Fjallbrant, N. (1996) EDUCATE: networked user education project in Europe, *IFLA Journal*, **22** (1), 31–4.

Foster, S. (1993) Information literacy: some misgivings, *American Libraries*, **24**, (April), 344.

Hanley, K., Harrington, J. and Blagden, J. (1998) *Aerospace Information Management (AIM-UK): Executive Report*, Cranfield University, (October).

Hepworth, M. (2000) Approaches to providing information literacy training in higher education: challenges for librarians, *New Review of Academic Librarianship*, **6**, 21–34.

Johnson, H. (2001) Information skills, information literacy, *Library Association Record*, **103** (12), (December), 752–3.

Johnson, R. (2001) National information policy, *Library and Information Briefings*, **104**, (July).

Lanham, R. A. (1995) Digital literacy, *Scientific American*, (September), 160–1.

Laurillard, D. (2001) *Supporting the development of scholarship skills through the online digital library*, presented to the SCONUL Autumn Conference: *Supporting off-campus learning and ensuring service quality*, November, available at www.sconul.ac.uk/Conference/presegm01/index.htm.

Library Association (2001) *Libraries and lifelong learning: a strategy 2002–4*, London, Library Association.

McClure, C. (1994) Network literacy: a role for libraries, *Information Technology and Libraries*, **13** (2), 115–25.

Marland, M. (ed.) (1981) *Information skills in the secondary curriculum: the recommendations of a working group sponsored by the British Library and the Schools Council*, Schools Council Curriculum Bulletin 9, London, Methuen Educational.

Mansell, R. (2002) Where all citizens should be free to meet, *Times Higher Education Supplement*, (1526), (22 February), 16–17.

Mayer Committee (1992) *Employment related key competencies for post compulsory education and training: a discussion paper*, Canberra, ACT, Australian

Education Council.

Mensching, G. E. and Mensching, T. B. (1989) *Coping with information illiteracy: bibliographic instruction for the information age*, Ann Arbor, MI, Pierian Press.

NCIHE: National Committee of Inquiry into Higher Education (1997) *Higher education in the learning society: report*, London, HMSO (the Dearing Report).

New Zealand. Department of Labour, Labour Market Policy Group (2001) *Closing the digital divide: summary of stakeholder discussions*, Wellington.

Noon, P. and Heseltine, R. (2000) Developing information skills for students: whose responsibility? In Corrall, S. and Hathaway, H. (eds), *Seven pillars of wisdom? Good practice in information skills development. Proceedings of a conference held at the University of Warwick, 6–7 July 2000*, London, SCONUL, 66–77.

Oakland, J. S. (1993) *Total quality management: the route to improving performance*, 2nd edn, Oxford, Butterworth Heinemann.

Oxbrow, N. (1998) Information literacy — the final key to an information society, *Electronic Library*, **16** (6), (December), 359–60.

The Pulse (2002) *Information World Review*, (January), 3.

SCANS (1991) *What work requires of schools: a SCANS report for America 2000*, Washington, DC, US Secretary's Commission on Achieving Necessary Skills.

SCONUL (1999) *Information skills in higher education: a SCONUL position paper prepared by the Task Force on Information Skills convened by Hilary Johnson*, London, SCONUL.

Street, B. D. (1993) *Cross-cultural approaches to literacy*, Cambridge, Cambridge University Press.

Town, J. S. (ed.) (2000a) *SCONUL benchmarking manual*, London, SCONUL.

Town, J. S. (2000b) Wisdom or welfare? The Seven Pillars model. In Corrall, S. and Hathaway, H. (eds), *Seven pillars of wisdom? Good practice in information skills development. Proceedings of a conference held at the University of Warwick, 6–7 July 2000*, London, SCONUL, 11–21.

Town, J. S. (2001) Performance measurement of information skills education: what's important? Report and findings of a workshop held at the SCONUL conference, Glasgow, April, 2001, *SCONUL Newsletter*, **22**, (Spring), 21–4.

Town, J. S. (2002) Welfare or wisdom? Performance measurement for information skills education, *Proceedings of the 4th Northumbria International*

Conference on Performance Measurement in Library and Information Services, Pittsburgh, Pa, August 2001, Washington, DC, Association of Research Libraries.

UK. Department for Education and Employment (1997) *Connecting the learning society. National Grid for Learning: the government's consultation paper,* London, DfEE.

UK. Department for Education and Employment (1998) *The learning age: a renaissance for a new Britain,* Cm 3790, London, Stationery Office.

Webber, S. and Johnston, B. (2000) Conceptions of information literacy: new perspectives and implications, *Journal of Information Science,* **26** (6), 381–97.

Zurkowski, P. (1974) *The information services environment: relationships and priorities,* Report ED 100391, Washington, DC, NCLIS.

6
Imaginative communities: turning information technology to expressive use in community groups

Ian Beeson

Introduction

In this chapter the suggestion is made that communities must develop their imaginative capacity if they are to resist submersion in a global information culture. Electronic communities cannot be adequate substitutes for traditional locally based communities. An approach is developed towards using information technology not to transfer communities on to the networks, but rather to preserve and strengthen existing community groups (loosely defined) through harnessing and focusing their imaginative power. The *story* of a community group, as understood and told by its members, is taken as the basis for building a computer system which reflects and projects the life of the community. The True Stories project and a case study conducted under it with one community group in Bristol (UK), are described. The group used hypermedia technology to make a story of the community on the computer. Aspects of process and form in story making on a computer, in this project and more generally, are discussed, and prospects for future work with imaginative communities briefly explored.

Community

The demise of community

According to David Harvey (1989, 306), the intensity of 'time-space compression' in Western capitalism in the current era produces an experiential context not previously known, marked by excessive ephemerality and fragmentation in political, private and social realms. Anthony Giddens' (1990, 53) analysis of the 'extreme dynamism' of modernity makes the separation and standardization of space and time a precursor of the disembedding of social relations and their restructuring across space and time. Disembedding and re-embedding are in turn made possible by the reflexive appropriation of knowledge, in which abstractions and expertise replace tradition as the foundation of social life. Through these mechanisms, and through the relentless dynamism of capital, social life is not only fragmented, but also speeded up (Harvey, 1989, 343).

In these circumstances, what remains of *community*? Communal solidarities appear to be seriously – if not terminally – undermined by processes of dislocation, reconstruction and acceleration, experienced in communities as irresistible external pressures. There appears to be no possibility of a return to community based on locality, since communities can no longer be truly local in a mass culture, and are liable to be destabilized or derailed by currents from the surrounding society. In modern society, communities are bound to be more permeable, more interpenetrative, more voluntaristic and less stable than their predecessors.

These developments are not beyond analysis, and are not universally deplored. Giddens' (1990, 150) position of 'radicalized modernity' recognizes processes of fragmentation, dispersal and globalization, but proceeds to analyse them, and sees possibilities for self-identity, systematic knowledge, empowerment, appropriation and political engagement in the transformation of modern institutions. The question is, who can take up these possibilities?

Attempts to invoke something like a traditional notion of community based on locality as an antidote to (post)modernity's dislocations are met with suspicion as romanticizing or retrogressive. Thus Harvey (1989, 351), recognizes that one response to the travails of time–space compression has been 'to find an intermediate niche for political and intellectual life which spurns grand narrative but which does cultivate the possibility of limited action. This is the progressive angle to postmodernism which emphasizes community and locality, place and regional resistances, social movements, respect for otherness, and the like.' He is not sanguine about the prospects as 'at its best it produces trenchant images of possible other worlds, and even begins to shape the actual world. But it is hard to stop the slide into parochialism, myopia, and self-referentiality in the face of the universalizing force of capital accumulation. At worst, it brings us back to narrow and sectarian politics in which respect for others gets mutilated in the fires of competition between the fragments.'

Zygmunt Bauman (1993, 44–6) has reservations about the invocation of community by the communitarian writers. Although the retreat from universal moral values to a 'community first' position appears attractive, it seems unlikely that, in modern times, communities bound by local moral consensus can exist long in reality, or can avoid curtailing individuals' moral discretion. For Bauman, the 'situatedness' of members in such communities, far from being given or natural, is socially produced, controversial and fragile.

And yet, the life of a human being is still a life with others. In our growing up and in our everyday lives as adults, we are formed in our relation to others. If these relations diminish in intensity or reliability, our development and capacity as persons (for ourselves and others) will falter. In so far as we are involved, all the time, in living and working with others against a background of common understandings, expectations and purposes, we are part of a community. This is a looser sense of community than the traditional one, no doubt, but it recognizes that our life is lived in a social and cultural setting, and that our biographies remain rooted in time and place. A community is thus an ongoing accomplishment of people acting, interacting, making joint cause, disagreeing, misunderstanding, compromising and improvising. When Bauman (1993, 44) comments, against the idea of community, that 'whenever one descends from the relatively secure realm of concepts to the description of any concrete objects the concepts are supposed to stand for – one finds merely a fluid collection of men and women acting at cross-purposes, fraught with inner controversy and conspicuously short of the means to arbitrate between conflicting ethical propositions', we can accept his stricture and still recognize a description of a community of people practically and fallibly engaged.

Scott Lash (1999, 5–10) criticizes both sociology and cultural theory for failing to pay sufficient attention to 'the ground', by which he means the substance of our lives as lived, and which variously takes the form of 'community, history, tradition, the symbolic, place, the material, language, life-world, the gift, Sittlichkeit, the political, the religious, forms of life, memory, nature, the monument, the path, fecundity, the tale, habitus, the body'. Sociology, embodying a rationality of 'the same' has overlooked the ground by concentrating too much on how subjects construct the world; while cultural theory, embodying a rationality of 'the other', has overlooked it by concentrating too much on deconstructing the world into signifiers and events. Lash develops a theory of a 'second modernity' which has the ground at its centre. No sooner has he done so, however, than he introduces the idea that, in the era of the global information culture, this second modernity is itself exploded as 'both symbolic and imaginary are exploded into fragments and disseminated outside of the subject into the space of indifference in which they attach to a set of humans and non-humans, to objects of consumer culture, to images, to thinking machines, to machines that design'.

Lash (1999, 14) believes the shift to the global information culture to be irreversible, but warns that:

> we ignore, . . . we forget, the legacy of the second modernity, and especially the ground, the broken middle of the second modernity, at our peril. The second modernity, as index, as haptic space, as the tactile culture, as community, as memory, is in many respects in the midst of the global information culture still with us. It is with us, and will be with us for a long time, in the interstices, the sometimes vast and sometimes intimate spaces left more or less untouched by the new millennium's information and communication flows.

Whether communities can survive in some form, and can live with the processes of radical change characteristic of contemporary society – whether some of them are capable of 'riding the juggernaut' (to use Giddens' phrase) – remains to be seen. If they can, they will need to be able to deal creatively and imaginatively with a rapidly changing reality. Perhaps part of the way of doing that will be to use some of the very tools and networks which have been instrumental in the production of globalization and dispersal – and so threatened the stability of communities – to make communities stronger. Can information technologies be used to strengthen existing communities or community groups, instead of breaking them up? Much has been said and written about new communities or virtual communities emerging on the internet, but perhaps this is not the only way community and technology can interact. IT does give us powerful new tools for creating imaginary or imagined communities with no real analogue on the ground; perhaps it can also be appropriated by actual communities to support their own imaginative work. I should like in this chapter to hold on to Lash's notion of 'the ground' and explore ways of keeping his 'second modernity' alive – and even consolidating and expanding it – in the nooks and crannies of the global information culture.

The idea of an imaginative community

Stanley Fish (1980, 318–22) has ascribed to community an indispensable role in supplying *meaning* to texts. Fish, addressing the question of where the meaning of a text resides, locates it neither in the text, nor in the writer, nor in the readers, but in an *interpretive community* where 'meanings are the properties neither of fixed and stable texts nor of free and independent readers but of interpretive communities that are responsible both for the shape of a reader's activities and for the texts those activities produce'. Texts can never have determinate meaning, according to Fish, because communication and understanding are never context-free as 'communication occurs within situations and . . . to be in a situation is already to be in possession of (or to be possessed by) a structure of assumptions, of practices understood to be relevant in relation to purposes and goals that are already in place; and it is within the assumption of these purposes and goals that any utterance is *immediately* heard'. The force of the 'immediately' here is to deny the possibility of any 'pure' receipt of a text prior to interpretation, and simultaneously to avoid a fall into relativism: the reader's attention is always enabled by a set of norms of values, selected from and shaped by background and experience, which may change over time but are for the present unexamined, undoubted, and deployed with confidence.

Meaning, then, is not given to texts (nor, by extension of this argument, to the world) by individuals subsisting in isolation, but by communities of individuals who share common backgrounds and understandings. Fish's analysis takes us from a basic understanding of community as rooted in the vital processes of living and working together into the area where practices are developed and deployed by which communities make the world meaningful. We can take the opening from joint interpretation towards co-creation further by examining Paul Ricoeur's analysis of the foundations of social action in the imagination (Ricoeur, 1991 and 1994; Kearney, 1991). This will give us a framework for understanding how a community can be *imaginative* (and then active) – rather than simply interpretive.

Ricoeur suggests a path leading from a theory of the imagination through to practical action in society. His starting point is a theory of metaphor which draws on Gaston Bachelard's analysis of the poetic image and the notion of reverberation. For Bachelard (1964, xix), the poetic image is an original process in consciousness, not a thing in consciousness, and particularly not a trace or side-effect or by-product of perception or of a subconscious movement in the psyche. Bachelard offers a *dialogical* account of the imagination: the poetic image comes from the rising of a poetic power which surpasses the consciousness intending it and reaches out from self to other. He enjoins the reader of a poem not (first) to analyse an image but to seize its specific reality. For the reader, the multiple resonances of the image coalesce into a *reverberation* which unites reader to writer as 'the image has touched the depths before it stirs the surface. . . . The image offered us by reading the poem now becomes really our own. It takes root in us. It has been given us by another, but we begin to have the impression that we could have created it, that we should have created it.'

Bachelard sees the imagination as surpassing or transcending reality (and self and other), but only in order to return renewed. Ricoeur (1994, 124), in a like (but less poetic) manner, sees metaphor as involving semantic innovation through the unexpected or deviant use of predicates: new meaning emerges as the logical distance between remote semantic fields temporarily falls away. By engaging in a free play of possibilities away from the world of perception or action (for the time being), the imagination works with metaphor – developing, extending, linking, consolidating – so schematizing metaphorical attribution and thereby providing the basis for a redescription of the world. Such redescriptions are essentially *fictions*, but fictions which have and unfold new dimensions of reality, taking us beyond earlier descriptions into new understandings and new possibilities.

Poems, stories and other kinds of fiction go beyond factual descriptions because they get to the essence of action and because, through the use of techniques (established and appreciated in a community of hearers) of abbreviation, articulation and condensation, they can achieve 'iconic increase' – remaking reality in a richer vein. In their telling and retelling, stories have the capacity to reflect, unite, and mobilize a community 'between what could be a logic of narrative possibilities and the empirical diversity of action, narrative fiction interposes its schematism of human action' (Ricoeur, 1994, 125).

From the originating power of the imagination, the notion of fiction as redescription, and the concentrating power of story, Ricoeur further develops his analysis towards action, examining first the grounds of action (individual and intersubjective), and then the general imaginative practices by which a society remakes itself (the realm of the 'social imaginary').

We move from narrative play to pragmatic play, from description to projection, whenever an actor borrows a story's structuring capacity to form a *project*. Ricoeur sketches a progression from schematization of projects to the articulation of possible actions. To move beyond individuals' plans of action to intersubjective action, he uses Schutz's analysis of relations with contemporaries, predecessors and successors, simultaneously to embed the individual in the field of historical experience and to achieve the imaginative transfers (I to you, us to them, here to there) characteristic of *empathy* (Schutz and Luckmann, 1974).

In his examination of the more general imaginative practices that constitute the social imagination, Ricoeur singles out two opposed but interlocking practices for further analysis: *ideology* and *utopia*. The prime function of ideology is to integrate, recollect and reaffirm a society, and to legitimate a social order, though in its pathological form it can bring distortion, dissimulation and social stagnation. Utopia, on the other hand, has a subversive, challenging function, which can bring about social renewal but might raise impossible hopes or create schism. Ideology confirms the past, and utopia opens towards the future; the two are bound together in an irreducible tension and become pathological if separated.

Bauman's analysis of social space (1993, 146) will give us further help in filling out the possibilities and characteristics of imaginative communities. He regards socially produced space as combining *cognitive, aesthetic* and *moral* elements. 'If the cognitive space is constructed intellectually, by acquisition and distribution of knowledge, aesthetic space is plotted affectively, by the attention guided by curiosity and the search for experiential intensity, while moral space is "constructed" through an uneven distribution of felt/assumed responsibility.'

The construction and maintenance of cognitive space involves planning, design, allocation, regulation and the categorization and typification of others. By contrast, moral space is not calculated nor regulated, but involves us in direct relations with specific others – non-typified others whom we live *for* rather than merely *with*. The moral space is populated by those we care for. The aesthetic space is a space of spectacle in which amusement value overrides other considerations. The other here is an object of curiosity or a source of entertainment.

These three kinds of space overlap, but may have different relative saliences in different communities. So long as people are born and live and die with people who care for them, they continue to inhabit a moral space charged with specific mutual responsibilities, even if this becomes residual or attenuated for them. To the extent that they work, fulfil roles, exchange knowledge and move about within orderly cities and institutions, they are in a cognitive space, rationally laid out and organized. As consumers and spectators, they inhabit an aesthetic space filled with shows and commodities. One may see the shift from small traditional communities to an urban industrial culture in terms of an expansion of cognitive space at the expense of moral space. In the movement to post-industrial society, cognitive space comes to be eclipsed by aesthetic space.

How do these kinds of social space relate to our analysis so far of imaginative communities? Empathy belongs most clearly in moral space, and is threatened by over-expansion of cognitive and especially of aesthetic space. Aesthetic space, filled with new ideas and possibilities, supports the free play of the imagination and opens up the utopian horizon; if aesthetic space is kept too cramped, censure and stifling orthodoxy may be the result. Cognitive space provides the rationality and stability around which narratives and projects can form; confining it too far will limit the schematizing, projective and testimonial potentials of the imagination. It seems plausible that these three kinds of social space need to be kept in reasonable balance in an adequately functioning community: unchecked reduction or expansion of one kind of social space may lead to degeneration from imaginative deficits such as sectarianism (loss of empathy), simulation (loss of reference) or stultification (loss of play).

Electronic communities

Since any general return to traditional locally based communities seems blocked, do the electronic communities emerging across the internet provide a better model for community under post- or radicalized modernity? On the face of it, they seem to be more in the spirit of an age of mass media and global information networks.

Most commentators regard electronic communities as pseudocommunities at best, in which personal communication is simulated by impersonal connections without genuine commitment or the possibility of authentic relationship, and without most of the ingredients of face-to-face communication (taken to be the prototypical form of human communication). Bauman (1993, 178), referring primarily to mass media or electronic games rather than to electronic communication, speaks disparagingly of the 'telecity', in which strangers are reduced to pure surface on a glass screen, and so sanitized as 'telecity is the ultimate *aesthetic space*. In the telecity, the others appear solely as the objects of enjoyment, no strings attached (they can be zapped out of the screen – and so out of the world – when they cease to amuse). Offering amusement is their only right to exist – and a right which it is up to them to confirm ever anew, with each successive "switching on".'

Vivian Sobchack's attack is equally strong (1994, 100–2). Describing electronic space as 'all surface' and so uninhabitable, she traces the disembodiment and dispersal of the user:

> Television, video cassettes, video tape recorder/players, video games and personal computers all form an encompassing electronic representational system whose various forms 'interface' to constitute an alternative and absolute world that uniquely incorporates the spectator/user in a spatially decentred, weakly temporalized, and quasi-disembodied state. . . . Living in a schematized and intertextual metaworld far removed from reference to a real world liberates the spectator/user from what might be termed the latter's moral and physical gravity. The materiality of the electronic digitizes *durée* and the situation so that narrative, history and a centred (and central) investment in the human lived-body become atomized and dispersed across a system that constitutes temporality not as a flow of conscious experience but as a transmission of random information.

Bauman and Sobchack both identify the electronic community with aesthetic space; the moral space created by the caring encounter of human beings is absent, but so are many of the orderly structures of cognitive space. A community of this kind is seriously defective, and in fact no community at all.

Other commentators adopt a more positive attitude to computer-mediated communication. Lyotard (1984, 67), for instance, comes to the following conclusion regarding 'the computerization of society':

It could become the 'dream' instrument for controlling and regulating the market system, extended to include knowledge itself and governed exclusively by the performativity principle. In that case, it would inevitably involve the use of terror. But it could also aid groups discussing metaprescriptives by supplying them with the information they usually lack for making knowledgeable decisions. The line to follow for computerization to take the second of these two paths is, in principle, quite simple: give the public free access to the memory and data banks.

Nancy Baym (1995, 160–1), also in positive mood, asserts that, contrary to the usual analysis, computer-mediated communication 'not only lends itself to social uses, but is, in fact, a site for an unusual amount of social creativity'. She sees community as emergent in computer-mediated communication since 'social realities are created through interaction as participants draw on language and the resources available to make messages that serve their purposes'.

Among the resources that shape the development of computer-mediated community, she identifies temporal structure, external contexts, system infrastructure, group purposes, and participant and group characteristics. Although relations are constrained in some ways compared to face-to-face encounters, system features can be exploited in computer-mediated communication 'to play with new forms of expressive communication, to explore possible public identities, to create otherwise unlikely relationships, and to create behavioural norms. In so doing, [group members] invent new communities' (Baym, 1995, 151).

It may well be that views similar to Baym's reflect more clearly not only how history is running, but the plasticity of the human organism. We must acknowledge that new forms of communication, interaction, and access to information are emerging on the networks, and that the structure and spread of the networks reflects and contributes to patterns of dispersal and globalization characteristic of postmodernity. But these electronic communities, in which human presence and material structure are inevitably attenuated, must remain truncated in their moral and cognitive dimensions, and so cut off from historical social development. Although it is possible we may be left marooned in electronic communities by default, these cannot – lacking ground and substance – themselves adequately replace local communities, nor become imaginative communities able to play a full part in shaping modern society.

Technology and the imaginative community

But we do not just have to wait and see what happens. We could instead explore the possibility of using new information and communication technologies to support the imaginative potential of whatever communities already exist. At least some of these, we can presume, will be better grounded, morally and cognitively, than any virtual substitutes. Instead of moving from discrete local communities in the real world to self-contained electronic communities in a virtual world, we can stop halfway and use the electronic technologies to help groups and movements of diverse kinds strengthen both their self-awareness and their hold on the real world.

Let us now ask whether new information technology can be used effectively to support imaginative work of the kind described in Ricoeur's analysis. Although information technology has been commonly associated with systematizing, rationalizing and controlling human activities in work contexts in formal organizations, new formations of the technology more suited to support creative or expressive uses are increasingly available. With the arrival of multimedia systems, images, sound and animation can be included in documents. Furthermore, it is possible to create 'hypertexts' with multiple threads running through them, so that texts can be produced which do not have to be linear, nor even finite, and can include many voices and styles. By integrating different media and supporting multiple voices, these technologies appear to open up new avenues of self-expression and collaborative creativity. The suggestions made long ago by pioneers such as Engelbart (1963) and Kay and Goldberg (1977) that computer systems could be built which would enhance or augment the intelligence or creativity of the users, instead of limiting or controlling them, are now realizable.

Can these recent software arrivals be used by community groups to schematize invention in the direction of action, or to make narratives which can concentrate and focus a community's understanding of itself? Current hypermedia technology certainly can be used to support the construction and sharing of rich 'little narratives' and even the maintenance of multiple perspectives within a narrative. Such narratives might give a community a resource from which to project future actions. To move in the direction of action, the tools need to be deployed within the context of a community project. The formation of projects will require deliberation among community members, perhaps assisted by further schematization and speculative story-telling.

But if a community group can form a project to tell its own story, it may be able to make itself a narrative which parallels and scripts the community's action in the world. In this way imagination and reality transform one another. And because the story is made and stored on the computer, the community gains a cumulative repository which it can use to develop larger imaginative practices and track and project its own history.

The True Stories project

The True Stories project at the University of the West of England (UK) is one attempt to explore the potential use of hypermedia technology by community groups for telling their own stories. The purpose is to see how, in practical cases, hypermedia technology can be used by community groups to express and reflect their experiences, and their imaginative power, and to focus their collaborative action through a story they make together on the computer. The project has been described in more detail and at various stages in other publications (Beeson and Miskelly, 1998a, 1998b, 1998c, 2000; Beeson, 2000, 2002). It takes its theoretical starting point from Ricoeur's analysis of the condensing and mobilizing potential of narrative for communities. The title of the project reflects the tension between story as a work of the imagination and truth as the ground for action. Although in ordinary usage, the word 'story' often has a connotation of untruth, in the sense of story we want to pursue a story ought rather to be *true*, or at least true enough to gain sufficient assent in the community to be credible and to provide a basis for realistic action. This fits with Ricoeur's observation (1991, 199) that 'the domain of action is from an ontological perspective that of changing things and from an epistemological perspective that of verisimilitude, in the sense of what is plausible and probable'.

It was clear that established methods of systems analysis and design would not be very useful for working on this kind of project, since those methods were predicated on finding the users' requirements and then designing a solution to meet them. Not only was it important in this project for the 'users' themselves to construct their 'solution', but the theoretical position assumes that imaginative work will always transcend existing realities, so that any approach which assumes that a requirement can be captured from a factual description or analysis cannot be sufficient. The task is not to introduce a technical support system for existing community activity, but rather to see what kind of stories are told by community members with the technology. Stories not previously told or considered may emerge in the course of the project. New kinds of story might be tellable with this technology, or in the particular context of this project. Such a project is essentially a voyage of discovery, expression, and learning. There may be no end product, or even no definable end to the project itself. The story will not be designed first and realized later, but will emerge in the telling and making.

Another difficulty was that the emerging forms of IT which were identified as of great potential use in community groups had been invented primarily for the use of media design professionals, and only subsequently marketed to home PC users. They were in consequence complex and unfamiliar for most users and would need some adaptation or facilitation to get them working in community groups. If the introduction of this new technology is a new departure for the community in question, both the technology and an analyst or researcher that comes with it are likely to be experienced as intrusions into the community's life (and story). The technology must not be allowed to dominate the life of the community but must as far as possible be absorbed into it. If a human agent accompanies the technology, that person must strive to facilitate the process of absorption, not direct it. To deal with this aspect of the work ahead the project team had recourse to Certeau's analysis of users' practices.

Tactical confabulation

In his account of the practice of everyday life, Certeau (1984, 35–7) uses the terms 'strategy' and 'tactics' to distinguish between the respective situations and possibilities of system owners and users. A group in control of a territory, or of a technical system, can produce a strategy for maintaining its boundary, rationalizing its operations, and reproducing its power. Users, on the other hand, operating in a space which is not their own, can only produce tactics – isolated and opportunistic actions conducted ad hoc against the background of a dominant strategy, to take whatever advantage might momentarily present itself. Certeau (1984, xii) sees the actions of users or consumers of television, urban spaces, newspapers, supermarkets, and so on, not as being merely forms of consumption, but as being hidden *productions*, in which they to some extent appropriate, modify and subvert, more or less invisibly, the products increasingly imposed upon them.

Applied in our area of interest, Certeau's analysis supports the idea that the use of a new technology (by people who did not invent it) should be studied as a 'production', an emergent process of making and doing. Users who feel themselves to be in someone else's world when working with technology, will operate 'tactically'. Their mode of operation will not in general be particularly concerted or coherent, but rather a patchwork of attempts, experiments and withdrawals. At the beginning of an engagement with a daunting new technology, confronted by 'unreadable writings' on the screens, in the tutorial files, help systems and manuals, and in the spoken advice of other people trying to help, community members will be in no position to take part in the *design* of a system. If they persevere, they will by tactical operations begin to 'colonize' the system and make something of their own in it. What we might hope and look for is that the members of a community group, through the making of their own story, could evince a sense of ownership of their work and their situation, and so eventually proceed to 'strategic' engagement with the technology. This analysis also sheds light on the problematic nature of participation in the system development process: users' involvement in a rationalized project plan and a methodology may be tentative, reluctant and obscure.

One of the alienating aspects of living tactically may be that truth is seen to belong to others – to the dominant party. The more we move from consuming stories to making them, the more we move from a tactical towards a strategic position. As we move in that direction, we should also be moving in the direction of truth, since the need to dissemble diminishes. We should furthermore resist, Certeau advises (1984, 160), the notion that the true meaning of a story is unknown to the tellers and only available to certain skilled others (he calls this 'folklorization'); if stories become objects for collectors, archivists, analysts and producers, the vital link in the community between imagination and action may be cut.

Introducing technology

Supposing then that hypermedia technology can be a useful vehicle on which to put together a story, because it will support diverse forms of expression and multiple perspectives, how should it be introduced into a community group? This technology is complex, so to introduce it into a community may trigger tactical responses and counter-moves. Such counter-moves could include not only resistance to the technology, but falling under its spell to the extent that the story was forgotten or made subordinate to the programs. In general, the approach should be to encourage the emergence of the community's story, so that the community can establish a strategic space for itself, and then bring in the technology as non-invasively as possible, in the hope that the community may be able to absorb it rather than react to it. There also needs to be awareness at the outset that when constructing this kind of work as a project (with some end point, and some end product, probably), it can only ever be a finite episode within the wider current of community life.

The general line adopted was that the computer equipment should be taken into the territory of the community group, and that the equipment should be relatively cheap and simple to operate, so that there would be a good chance of its continued use. The project team wanted to act as advisers rather than directors in their relations with the user group, and thought they should start off the process by providing examples of – or making suggestions about – stories, rather than definitions or rules which would constrain users in their story making.

These various considerations gave the researchers a basis for a cautious and modest intervention. They looked for partners among community organizations who would be interested in trying to tell their story with a hypermedia system. The project team would provide the initial system, and a facilitator, but the community organizations would have to commit themselves to learning the technology and trying to tell their story with it.

The story of St Paul's Carnival: a case study

The main piece of fieldwork within the *True Stories* project so far has been with a community organization in Bristol (UK) called the St Paul's Carnival Association. This is a group which has for several years put on an annual carnival in the St Paul's area of Bristol. The Carnival reflects and celebrates Afro-Caribbean culture in Bristol, but is of wide general appeal in the city. The Association employs a paid full-time co-ordinator and has some funding for educational activities. It relies on student placements and volunteers to plan and run the carnival day and events leading up to it. It is managed by a committee made up of local people. The focus is the annual carnival: two months of school-based *mas* (masquerade) camps preparing the elaborate costumes and dance routines for the Carnival procession, and two weeks of cultural and sports events, leading up to carnival day in July, which attracts about 35,000 visitors. Because the Association wanted to have more year-round activities and were interested in exploring new media as one aspect of carnival events and workshops, it seemed appropriate to them to work with us in using hypermedia to tell the story of the St Paul's Carnival. In the course of our project with the Association, its members put together their story of the Carnival, on a PC installed at their office, and eventually wrote it on to a CD-ROM which was then shown at the Carnival itself.

Working with the technology

Installed at the Association's office were an ordinary PC with a printer, a photo drive (for scanning in photographs), and Photoshop and Director software. At the time of the fieldwork, the Association already had a PC it used for ordinary office applications, but it was not connected to the internet. The majority of participants had little or no experience of computers, and none had experience of the packages we were using. Only a few had a concept of what hypermedia was and in those cases it came from viewing CD-ROMs or using the world wide web.

Photoshop (from Adobe) is a powerful tool for manipulating pixel data in photographic images. Director (from Macromedia) combines an authoring system capable of handling animation with a scripting language (Lingo), and so provides a full multimedia programming environment. Director works with a theatrical or film metaphor: the user creates interactive 'movies' which consist of a sequence of frames, where each frame contains elements called 'cast members', which are rendered and composed frame by frame as the movie is played back. These packages together certainly gave us a system with sufficient power and versatility to support hypermedia work and a rich notion of story. But both are complicated to use and they are not designed specifically to fit together. Probably the system was over complex and made making a story more difficult than it might have been. Perhaps we should have opted for simpler, more restricted packages and pushed them to the limit before moving on to heavier software. In this case, we hoped that the powerful packages could be introduced gradually from the beginning, with the help of a few modest examples and at a pace governed by the users' learning. This approach, as it turned out, worked reasonably well.

A great deal of one-to-one work between facilitator and individual participant was required to get people on to the system. Participants had to be ready and able to invest significant amounts of time into learning how to negotiate the Windows platform and the new software, and then into managing the file space and manipulating images in (and between) Photoshop and Director. Some participants persevered sufficiently to be able to make creative use of the software packages without assistance. The significant learning requirement impeded participation. Not everyone who might want to contribute to the story, or had something to offer, had the time or inclination to engage fully in making it on the machine. Having to learn and follow exact procedures for creating story elements and manipulating images was seen by everyone as a block to creative engagement. The PC platform itself impeded collaboration between learners and story makers – simply because only a couple of people could work at the machine at one time. PCs are by no means an ideal tool for collective working, either in the set-up of the hardware or in the orientation of the software interface. In this project, much of the working together was done first off the machine and then transferred to it.

Nevertheless, participants found ways round their difficulties. They developed small repertoires of procedures which worked for them and which they could use repeatedly. People who had not learned the software themselves could give photos or pieces of writing to someone else to add to the story, or could offer themselves for interview. People who persevered established a modus vivendi with the system – routines and tricks that worked, that they sometimes picked up from one another, and from which, when feeling adventurous, they could extend into new areas. Their use, in short, was tactical in Certeau's sense: they made forays into the system and withdrew, building their skill sporadically and opportunistically. This process is only partly visible to an observer. Given the fluidity and complexity of the technology, we are of the opinion that the general mode of use will remain tactical for most users, without ever becoming truly strategic. This has significant implications for (future) project set-up and the conduct of participative work.

Making the story

What model of participation is appropriate for this kind of project? The clear intention is for the 'users' to develop their story. The researcher's role is not to direct the project but to facilitate it and provide some assistance and continuity. It would be detrimental to a project of this kind for the researcher/facilitator to act as an expert, either at the technical or the aesthetic level, since the work is essentially the community's, and external direction would either distort the story or provoke a tactical withdrawal by the group members. The role needed here, it seemed to us, was one which combined participant observation with technical guidance when requested. The kind of relationship between researcher and community members we were looking for is akin to that proposed by Paulo Freire, in his dialogical model of adult literacy education in Brazil. Freire's concept implies joint responsibility and ownership for the educational process. Knowledge is developed *through* the process, in 'a constant unveiling of reality' (Freire, 1993, 62). In an echo of Certeau, there are no 'consumers' here, who may read a story and pass on, but only a community of co-producers. All the participants (including the teachers) have to become 'partners in naming the world' (Freire, 1993, 69–71).

The story of the St Paul's Carnival began to emerge as the core group supplied a collaborative lead and as other contributors were drawn into the work. Contributors with more clearly defined roles in the Association – such as the co-ordinator and the emergency planner – thought through what they wanted to say from what was already a clear position in the Association. They did some pre-planning of their parts of the story, and gained an initial understanding of the technology, before they tried to build the story on the machine. This put them in a position to use the software with some confidence. Contributors with less defined roles took a more improvisational or tactical approach, experimenting with the technology and trying things out while they looked around for what it was they wanted to tell. Some of them became involved with the technology by helping others make elements of their story on the computer, or became drawn into the story by seeing what others were doing or by coming across materials that interested them in the office, or in the archives. Marginal contributors moved towards the centre of the process as their own sense of purpose and of a personal connection to the emerging story developed.

An early sense of an overview of the Carnival story came from the co-ordinator, who came up with the idea of representing the whole of Carnival as an *island* which would serve as an organizing principle for the whole story.

He wanted to think of carnival as a place through which you could travel. The idea appealed to other participants, partly because of the reference to Caribbean islands and also to the St Paul's area itself, an African-Caribbean 'island' within Bristol. The co-ordinator drew a rough map of the island (on paper), writing on it text abbreviations for different aspects of Carnival. He referred to this as a dictionary or encyclopedia of the Carnival. Other people fed into and developed this initial idea. Another participant translated his map into a drawing of an island on the computer, with animated waves surrounding it, and with icons created from photos of carnival replacing the original text annotations.

The island map became a central focus for the developing story. An early indication of this was when printouts of the island map (from the computer) began to be stuck on the wall beside the earlier maps, and to be referred to instead of the originals. It also became (at the facilitator's suggestion) the centrepiece for the evolving Director application. Subsequent development of the story revolved around the island map, which was added to and altered as discussions around it and about individual work took the story forward. The annotated map on the office wall became the basis for subsequent work on the computer, and for explaining the project to enquiring visitors. So, what had started as an organizing metaphor for a community event had become a framework both for the process of telling the story and for the structure of the associated application (and its interface).

The story that came out was to some extent historical, tracing the history of the Carnival partly through its successive programmes, but was more importantly thematic, covering music, food, stalls, processions and other typical carnival subjects. The various parts of the story were by and large created by different individuals working mainly separately (whenever they had time to sit at the computer and make something). The parts of the story were not subjected to editing or stylistic control except by the individual authors. A story with multiple authors and with many ways to navigate through the material was in fact thus made, as had been hoped. It made use of pictures and sound as well as text, and was extensible, although in the event no significant use was made of video or internet material.

A CD-ROM of the story, made at the request of the participants, was produced in time for use at the 1998 Carnival, immediately following the fieldwork. No contribution was edited out of the story yet it still exhibited sufficient coherence to be producible and readable by others as a single story, though clearly a story with a range of voices in it. It had the kind of coherence you might get in an edited collection of articles, but, in this case, instead of an editor providing shape after the event, the participants agreed on the core metaphor, the top level interface and other matters, during the course of making the story.

The CD-ROM holds an ambivalent position in the project. On the one hand, it shows that a community group, largely by its own efforts, can make a version of its story on the computer which gives expression to different voices. The story is thus in a sense realized and can be disseminated within and beyond the community. On the other hand, the CD-ROM, as an uneditable product, marks a finishing point, an end to the project. The story of the community of course moves on, but this artefact of the story recedes in the rear-view mirror.

It is also important to note that the story of St Paul's Carnival, as inscribed on the CD, is the story from the vantage point of 1998 rather than the story of the Carnival in general. The difficulty in handling time in a cumulative multilinear work may have been at the root of the reticence of participants to build comprehensive links across the story elements (below the top level interface). It could be that this reticence was due to difficulties in conceptualizing and building such links within the constraints of the software package. But it may also be that the endlessness and multilinearity of this form of story works against pulling ideas and materials together. The island glues the elements together at the top level, but below that, it may be easier just to keep on adding in new pieces than to try to make a coherent structure.

Conclusion

As George Landow (2000, 166) has noted, the kinds of stories that are produced with hypermedia technology have characteristics similar to *collage* (or *montage*). The story elements (nodes) are mixed media creations which can be arbitrarily linked and juxtaposed. Describing hypertext as digital collage, Landow notes the defining characteristics of digital words and images as

- virtuality
- fluidity
- adaptability

- openness (or existing without borders)
- processability
- infinite duplicability
- capacity for being moved about rapidly
- networkability.

Landow (2000, 157–9) argues that, with hypertext, we are able to make connections between texts and between texts and images so easily that we are encouraged to *think* in terms of connections. He points out that hypertext shares certain characteristics with Cubist collage – juxtaposition, appropriation, assemblage, concatenation, blurring of limits, edges and borders, and blurring of the distinction between border and ground. A hypertext consists of elements which are linked together to bring out common qualities, meanings or relationships, but which at the same time remain as different nodes, and so retain a sense of separation.

Likewise, in a community story produced in hypermedia, the possibility is presented of sharing concepts or aspects of a story, while at the same time expressing differences. The ability to add links into a hypertext arbitrarily and without explanation also tends to produce a collage-like quality in a story. Links can be inserted without the author giving a reason: the connection may be metaphorical or obscure, and different readers may interpret it differently. The whole hypertext may not have a worked-out coherence in the mind of the author(s). It may be a loose and inconclusive accumulation of fragments out of which readers may nevertheless be able to achieve a reading that is coherent enough for them. In a community story, where there are several authors, it may be that the reader, charting a path through the hypertext, moves between contributions from different people without knowing it. Such a blurring of authorship emphasizes the looseness of the form. While this can undermine the consistency or integrity of the work, it also opens up the possibility of stories which contain different, even opposing, voices and which can therefore be said to be stories of the community itself.

Seen positively in this light, as a collage, a community story made in hypermedia – despite (or because of) its loose structure and lack of finish – does look like an appropriate vehicle for bringing together little stories and a plurality of voices, in a way which allows a sharing of experience and imagination without undue pressure to conform in content, style or structure.

Nevertheless, it remains an open question whether a story of fragments can bring a community together and catalyse community action in the way Ricoeur says a (coherent) story can. Perhaps stories that mobilize and unite communities cannot be as loose as these. Perhaps a multiplicity of Lyotardian little stories cannot serve as a good base for community.

This chapter has sketched an approach to using hypermedia technology to tell the stories of community groups. The approach was built on the basis of Ricoeur's theory of imagination and action, Bauman's analysis of social space, and Certeau's account of users' practices. In tracing in outline the True Stories work with the St Paul's Carnival Association, we have seen a story-making project developing in a balanced fashion within the social space of a community. We can see all three aspects of social space opening up in parallel: moral space in the interaction of the participants, cognitive space in the planning of the Carnival and the computer application, and aesthetic space in the invention of the story's components, representations and interface. There is some cause for optimism from the work described here that the use of IT in communities might indeed be turned towards strengthening their expressive potential and thereby reinvigorating them, within and against the erosive flow of the global information culture.

Important questions that deserve further consideration and research are whether the production of a story as an artefact interrupts the story as an ongoing production of the life of the community, and whether the loose and open-ended texture of a hypermedia story reduces its suitability as a mobilizing focus for the life of a community.

To return briefly to the moral dimension of imaginative practices discussed in the earlier part of this chapter, there is a question of with what kinds of community this work could or should be done. Hypermedia technology, as we have seen, offers a possible platform on which members of a community can tell all or many of their stories in an accessible and extensible manner. The same story can be told in different ways, and many stories can be told at the same time, and connected to one another. Complementary stories can be linked together, but so can oppositional or contradictory stories. Because there is no need for a finished version, and because it is possible to make many voices heard, there is no need to cede control to an editor, and no need to silence any of the voices, nor to impose a harmonization not already achieved by the speakers. It could therefore be that the approach we are developing in the True

Stories project might be useful in communities which are in conflict, or which have in some way been silenced. In view of the difficult territory this may take us into, and in view of the other questions raised that still have to be answered, this final question can only be raised tentatively: if stories made on the computer can help reflect and mobilize the life of a community, can they also be useful in processes of reconciliation, or even liberation?

Acknowledgements

The ideas and work represented here have arisen in significant part from collaboration with colleagues. Clodagh Miskelly carried out the fieldwork with the St Paul's Carnival Association discussed above. The positions and approaches presented have been developed over some time in discussion with her and Marcus Lynch.

References

Bachelard, G. (1964) *The poetics of space,* Boston, Beacon Press.

Bauman, Z. (1993) *Postmodern ethics,* Oxford, Blackwell.

Baym, N. K. (1995) The emergence of community in computer-mediated communication. In Jones, S. G. (ed.), *CyberSociety: computer-mediated communication and community*, Thousand Oaks, CA, Sage.

Beeson, I. A. (2000) Holding on to the ground, *Proceedings of DIAC 2000 – Shaping the network society: the future of the public sphere in cyberspace*, Palo Alto, CA, CPSR (Computer Professionals for Social Responsibility).

Beeson, I. A. (2002) Exquisite variety: computer as mirror to community, *Interacting with Computers* (special issue on Intelligence and Interaction in Community-Based Systems, forthcoming).

Beeson, I. A. and Miskelly, C. (1998a) Software for sustaining community: metaphors in collision. In Allen, J. K. and Wilby, J (eds), *Proceedings of the 42nd annual conference of the International Society for the Systems Sciences, Atlanta, GA*, ISSS (International Society for the Systems Sciences) (on CD).

Beeson, I. A. and Miskelly, C. (1998b) Tactical confabulation, *Systemist,* **20** (special edition).

Beeson, I. A. and Miskelly, C. (1998c) Discovery and design in a community story. In Chatfield, R. H., Kuhn, S. and Muller, M. (eds), *Proceedings of the*

5th biennial participatory design conference, Palo Alto, CA, CPSR (Computer Professionals for Social Responsibility), 147–56.

Beeson, I. A. and Miskelly, C. (2000) Dialogue and dissent in stories of community. In Cherkasky, T. et al., *Proceedings of the 6th biennial participatory design conference*, Palo Alto, CA, CPSR (Computer Professionals for Social Responsibility), 1–10.

Certeau, M. de (1984) *The practice of everyday life*, Berkeley, University of California Press.

Engelbart, D. (1988; original publication 1963) A conceptual framework for the augmentation of man's intellect. In Greif, I. (ed.), *Computer-supported cooperative work: a book of readings*, San Mateo, CA, Morgan Kaufmann.

Fish, S. (1980) *Is there a text in this class*, Cambridge MA, Harvard University Press.

Freire, P. (1993) *Pedagogy of the oppressed*, London, Penguin Books.

Giddens, A. (1990) *The consequences of modernity*, Cambridge, Polity Press.

Harvey, D. (1989) *The condition of postmodernity*, Oxford, Basil Blackwell.

Kay, A. and Goldberg, A. (1977) Personal dynamic media, *IEEE Computer,* **10** (3), 31–41.

Kearney, R. (1991) *Poetics of imagining: from Husserl to Lyotard*, London, Routledge.

Landow, G. P. (2000) Hypertext as collage-writing. In Lunenfeld, P. (ed.), *The digital dialectic: new essays on new media*, Cambridge, MA, MIT Press.

Lash, S. (1999) *Another modernity, a different rationality*, Oxford, Blackwell.

Lyotard, J.-F. (1984) *The postmodern condition: a report on knowledge*, Manchester, Manchester University Press.

Ricoeur, P. (1991) *From text to action – essays in hermeneutics II,* London: Athlone Press.

Ricoeur, P. (1994) Imagination in discourse and action. In Robinson, G. and Rundell, J. (eds), *Rethinking imagination: culture and creativity*, London, Routledge.

Schutz, A. and Luckmann, T. (1974) *The structures of the life-world*, London, Heinemann.

Sobchack, V. (1994) The scene of the screen: envisioning cinematic and electronic 'Presence'. In Gumbrecht, H. U. and Pfeiffer, K. L. (eds), *Materialities of communication*, Stanford, Stanford University Press.

Part 3

The information society and policy

7

Information policy: complexity, scope and normative structure

Ian Rowlands

Introduction

This chapter offers some theoretical frameworks for getting to grips with the scope and definition of information policy and the values that underpin it in practice. In doing so, it draws on concepts from information science, information law and political economy.

Information policy is an important component in the deliberations of national governments and international public bodies, yet it is much less immediately visible than other areas of public policy. In the UK when we think of health, education or housing policy, for instance, we can readily identify laws, regulations, responsible cabinet ministers, royal commissions, think tanks and other trappings and apparatus of government. To a more limited extent, the same is true of information policy. For example, we have laws and regulations that exist to regulate the processing of personal information (e.g. data protection), or to create the market conditions within which information products and services can be traded (e.g. copyright), or to protect national security (e.g. official secrecy). At the same time, there are broader policy aims that deal with information, not framed in purely legal terms. We have measures that are concerned with creating information infrastructures – from public libraries, to the training of information professionals, to the provision of broadband networks in higher education, as well as measures to help achieve an information society. Within the pages of our newspapers, we find fierce debates on the big political issues of the moment, many of which have a strong informational component, such as the introduction of compulsory identity cards or video surveillance in our high streets and shopping centres. These highlight some interesting questions for information policy, such as: Who owns personal information? Should citizens sacrifice some privacy in the fight against crime? How should digital broadcasting be financed?

These questions form a backdrop to the emergence of information policy as an academic speciality. There is now a reasonably extensive body of literature on information policy matters at national and international levels but, while progress is being made, it is widely agreed that the subject is at an early stage of intellectual maturity, with little consensus or agreement on what precisely the field comprises. This chapter argues that we can only understand something as complex, slippery and *political* as information policy by reference to models from the policy sciences. Despite the obvious relevance of its subject matter to library and information professionals, little coherent disciplinary mapping of the information policy construct is evident in its own literature. In fact, there are many reasonable people for whom the term 'information policy' smacks of intellectual inflation:

> As a stranger to the discourse of information policy, I have found some difficulty in identifying a unified set of topics which might be the subject of something called 'information policy'. Indeed if one considers the nine categories referred to by Rowlands, the stranger might readily conclude that the only element unifying information technology policy, intellectual property, information disclosure, confidentiality and privacy, and others is that they are all of concern to librarians and information scientists. (Aldhouse, 1997)

To which one might perhaps add that these issues are also of direct concern to their suppliers (i.e. the information industries) and their user communities, a not insignificant coalition of interests. Aldhouse does however indirectly raise some important questions: Where does information policy sit in relation to library and information science? Is the natural home for information policy within the library and information science tradition or does it share more features in common with broader public policy? Or are there unique characteristics of information policy which legitimate treating it as a field of studies in its own right?

Many commentators on information policy have noted that it seems very different from other, more established, areas of public policy. The differences are not difficult to identify. Information policy differs from say, education, housing or health policy in that:

- it is a relatively new area of policy concern
- it involves an unusually large and diverse number of interest groups
- decisions about information can have an enormous impact on events and policies in other areas – the reverse is true to a much lesser extent
- information, in contrast with, say, labour or capital, does not fit into the traditional categories employed by policy analysts
- information policies are made at very different levels of the political and social structure, from the local to the global, and are remarkably inter-dependent.

These differences are all, of course, relative. They may not be unique (i.e. exclusive) characteristics, but they certainly seem to be atypical of other areas of public and organizational policy, where the issues tend to be relatively more clear cut. There are other issues around the notion of information that make information policies unusually complex. We are dealing here with an area of human activity that is characterized by unusually rapid change, both in terms of the emergence of newer, more powerful technologies for capturing, storing, processing and sharing information, and the continuing efforts of regulators to keep pace with that change. The problem is that the sheer complexity of information policy results in a reduction of the capability of the state to make policy coherently and effectively. Much of our public information policy is latent rather than explicit: it exists in the form of attitudes, values and ways of doing things that, while not written down, are just as important as formal policies. The problem here of course is that unstated policy is capable of infinite shades of interpretation and realization.

Information access and disclosure are critical elements in the working of participative democracies and measures concerning these aspects can be found in most areas of public policy. The UK 1993 White Paper on open government, for example, lists some 40 Acts of Parliament and 380 Statutes, enacted since the war, which place various restrictions on the use of information, often tucked away within the small print of how the consumer credit market, for example, should be regulated. To be fair, there are many examples of both legislation and government practice which conversely guarantee the availability of information to the public in areas as diverse as pollution registers, food labelling and agricultural statistics. However, if we decide to take a view, at least for the sake of argument, that we can treat 'access to information' as an independent variable in society, is it not possible to conceive of the whole apparatus of information law and regulation, including public libraries, education, broadcasting, universal service, cryptography, freedom of expression and other related concepts, as forming a kind of gigantic 'information ecosystem'? And, just as in natural ecosystems, is it not the case that each element is interdependent and that even relatively small changes to one component can lead to unpredictable large-scale changes in the rest of the system? It is this kind of thinking that led to a great deal of interest in the notion of 'national information policies' in the early 1970s, and to a recent, post-internet, revival of interest.

The scope of information policy

At its highest level, information policy thus comprises all the laws, regulations and public policies that encourage, discourage or regulate the creation, use, storage and communication of information. It follows that information policy is a broad concept, and the topics that may be taken as generally indicative of its scope are:

- government information resource management policy and practice
- telecommunications and broadcasting policy
- international communications policy
- information disclosure policy
- information, confidentiality and privacy
- computer regulation and computer crime
- intellectual property
- library and archives policy
- government information dissemination.

In many ways, information policy is a problematic concept intellectually. What binds together such an apparently disparate and combustible mix of issues such as privacy, electronic government, access to official information, internet provision in libraries, SuperJANET and identity cards? Information policy is an example of what a political scientist might recognize as an 'issue area', one that draws together a bundle of apparently unrelated concerns around a single (if highly ambiguous) integrating concept – in this case, the power of information to 'make a difference' in the social, cultural and economic life of the nation.

Of course, a wide range of forces other than public policy are relevant to a consideration of the issues affecting the creation, use, storage and communication of information. These include, among many others, the commercial strategies adopted by publishers and database providers, consumer behaviour, the influence of pressure groups, and the proliferation of new information media and platforms. One of the characteristics of information policy that makes it a challenging area to study is that it simultaneously *shapes* and *responds* to the outside world. As an *independent* variable, information policy can be thought of in terms of its impact and outcomes, both on the wider environment and on the political process itself. When it is viewed as a *dependent* variable, our attention is drawn to the environmental, cultural, economic and other factors that shape and guide policy and its implementation. This insight leads us to the view that we should define information policy as broadly and as inclusively as possible. Information policy is about much more than laws and white papers; it is better to think of it as referring to all those societal mechanisms used to control information, and the societal effects of applying those mechanisms.

In theory, many different future information societies must be possible. The big questions for policy makers are therefore: What kind of information society do we want? What kind of informational organization best serves that kind of society? What kind of regulatory structures best build and sustain that kind of informational organization? These are clearly highly political issues, with a capital P.

The emergence of information policies

Historically, information policies have evolved in direct response to the emergence of specific technologies, such as print, telephony, radio or value-added and data services. Not surprisingly, the responsibility for these policies has tended to fall within the domain of whichever professional information community was most directly concerned with the particular technology involved (as librarians, computer scientists, broadcasters or information scientists). In other words, while information policy has been *technology driven*, policy analysis and research has typically been *discipline bounded*. The fragmentation of information policy research is mirrored by a fragmentation of policy-making institutions. In the UK, for example, the Department of Trade and Industry is the lead agency for developing policy in relation to tradeable information, standards and intellectual property, while data protection is under the jurisdiction of the Home Office, legal deposit under the Department of National Heritage, and public records under the Lord Chancellor's Department.

Prince Metternich once described early 19th-century Italy, then composed of a collection of regional entities, as little more than a 'geographical expression'. Such a viewpoint has some relevance to information policy and finds reflection in the long-standing debate about whether we should more properly speak of an all-embracing 'National Information Policy' or 'national information policies'. Other public policy areas, like social exclusion, are arguably just as fragmented as information policy and a coherent programme to tackle poverty might well include such diverse elements as innovations in education and training, tax reform, the restructuring of welfare benefits and action on housing.

The question of whether we speak of information policy or information policies is not merely a source of vexation for academics. Singular and plural forms represent differing worldviews. Consensual approaches to thinking about a particular issue area in ways that provide a basis for decision making are called 'regimes'. A regime may be thought of as a framework of shared values and assumptions that sets the context within which specific laws and policies are developed. In education, for instance, there is almost universal consensus on the need to provide compulsory schooling up to age 16 and to encourage participation in higher education, and there is a clear understanding of the benefits of high-quality education in relation to continuing economic prosperity. These values transcend party political divides and frame the debate on education policy in terms of the relative merits of the means at our disposal, rather than fundamentally questioning the ends themselves.

Towards an information policy regime?

The legal and regulatory environment within which we capture, store, use and process information is complex and multifaceted. Indeed, taken at face value, many of our information laws and public policies appear to be rather uneasy bedfellows. Thus, we create information markets by treating information as intellectual property, while at the same time offering subsidized public library services that 'distort' the workings of the marketplace. We endeavour to make government more transparent and accountable through freedom of information legislation, while contracting out many formerly public services to the private sector, thus placing information that was once protected by the cloak of official secrecy into the realm of the 'commercially sensitive'. Similarly, when we think of some of the stories in today's newspapers, we find tensions between the rights of editors to free expression, the rights of certain politicians to safeguard their personal privacy, and the balancing wider public interest. As the list of specific information laws and regulations necessarily expands to cope with the need to respond to new technologies and applications, inter alia, digital signatures, consumer protection on the internet, data encryption, 'voluntary' smart cards, and so on, we can anticipate many more such dilemmas in the future (with considerable earnings potential for suitably qualified lawyers!).

What is missing, it seems in the actuality of public policy in the UK, is a clear sense of an integrating overview or 'information policy regime'. Just how do we make sense of the complex ecology of information laws, regulations, information management practices and institutional cultures that shape information transfer activities at the national level? Information professionals are key stakeholders in this debate and have an unique opportunity to play a role in the development of a coherent information policy regime.

Information policy is a verb, not a noun

Our understanding of this complex and fascinating topic will be very limited if we limit our study just to the formal expressions of information policy: acts of Parliament, green papers or discussion documents. The analysis of policy documents can be a dull and sterile activity. We would do much better to think of information policy as a dynamic process, as an interplay between various stakeholder groups, vested interests and power structures.

There are many frameworks in the academic literature to help us to better understand the dynamics of policy making. Some writers view policy making as the reaction of a political system to external stimuli, representing politics as a kind of black box that regulates change in the outside world, a little like the thermostat that tells your central heating system when to come on or off. Others view policy making as the result of a series of choices or bargains negotiated between stakeholders and represent it as an essentially chaotic, non-linear, process determined by shifting networks of power and influence. A review of all the frameworks potentially available for use in the context of information policy studies is beyond the scope of this chapter, but one immediately useful and productive way of trying to understand information policy is to employ a systems approach. This recognizes that policy making comprises a series of inputs (people, ideology, expediency, information, research, investment) and outputs (wealth creation, better healthcare, access to democracy). By conceiving of information policy making as a set of INPUT–PROCESS–OUTPUT (I–P–O) activities for organizing our thinking, we shift to the view that information policy governs a *process* (such as the storage and transmission of information) rather than a *thing* (such as technology). 'Information policy' might therefore be better thought of as a verb than a noun. Just as the I–P–O model can be used to describe how data are transformed into information and then knowledge, so it can also offer insights into policy making. So, rather than addressing policy issues relating to a specific advance in software or data communications (technology-driven) we can switch our attention to the underlying functional aims and objectives of policy.

Conceptualizing policy as a *process*, rather than a specific outcome or event, is very useful. It helps us to understand how policy develops over time and how policy is shaped by (and, in turn, shapes) economic, cultural, organizational and social factors. Policy is not an abstract ideal, it takes place in an imperfect and sometimes confusing world. A typical representation of the policy-making process is to break it down into a series of stages, and a relatively simple example of this approach is illustrated in Figure 7.1.

As we move from left to right, a problem is first recognized and defined and then finds itself on a decision-maker's agenda. Alternative 'solutions' are developed, presented and rejected in favour of the option that offers the maximum net benefit (or is the most convenient, expedient or cheapest). This is then officially adopted. Implementation begins and some kind of evaluation

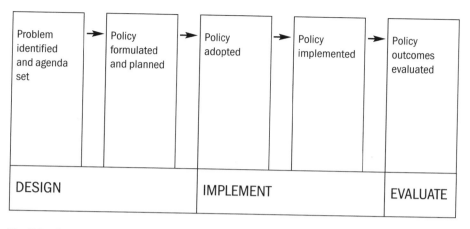

Fig. 7.1 *Staged model of the policy-making process model*

or monitoring procedures are usually invoked so that any undesirable outcomes can be identified and mitigated against. In many cases, the results of that evaluation will require adjustments to be made earlier in the chain, perhaps resulting in a complete re-design of the policy. This is a rational and idealized model of policy making. It conceptualizes policy as a planning activity. To a large extent, once a policy-making process gets underway, it tends to be continuous. It has been said that policy making has no beginning and no end. This overstates the case: it is possible to define reasonable starting and termination points in a pragmatic way. Within those bounds, however, the process can be regarded as continuous.

The power of the staged model is that it offers us a way of grouping a wide range of apparently disconnected decisions, phenomena, observations and data into meaningful units. It has a certain intuitive appeal that is not easily to be discounted. It also has its limitations. Many critics would immediately point out that real life, with its rough-and-tumble of politics and horse trading, is not nearly as tidy as the model suggests. Nonetheless this is how policy making is most often presented in the media and many policy makers would still justify and defend their own actions, however apparently irrational at the time, in terms of this ideal framework.

Despite their apparent abstraction, theoretical models can be very powerful and shape the course of events in the real world.

Information policy is highly political

Information policy, like public policy in general, derives its values and goals from the dominant political, economic and cultural contexts within which it is forged and developed. As observers of a phenomenon as complex as national information law and policy, we would do well to employ some of the intellectual tools that underpin critical theory. We might usefully start from the proposition that although reality exists, it can neither be fully understood or explained, and that objectivity in our enquiry into the political realm can never be value free. However, it may be possible to unlock and share knowledge through joint reference to an appropriate value system. Ideological diehards aside, there can be no objective 'truths' in information policy. Instead we need to focus our attention on the values – rather than the specific laws and regulations – that underpin our conceptions of information. Political and professional ideologies are fundamental to the way that information policy problems and dilemmas are perceived – and, more urgently, how problems are screened and represented by different stakeholders.

Scholars use the term 'frame' to describe the sets of values and concepts that people use in making sense of the world around them. Frames offer a powerful tool for understanding, for example, how different people may read and understand the same text quite differently. The historian Jonathan Rose (2001) has shown that some early readers of John Bunyan's *The pilgrim's progress*, wholly unacquainted with works of fiction, let alone allegorical tracts, 'read' the work quite literally, as factual reportage of Christian's journey and its travails. For many other readers, right up to the Victorian era, the book was simply an exciting story, to be enjoyed in the same way as an adventure yarn, or even as a horror comic with its lurid colour illustrations. Later critical interpretations have positioned *The pilgrim's progress* as a Chartist political fable, a conservative tool for the suppression of the working classes, even as an early exploration of feminism. Rose's contention is that working-class readers gradually learnt how to construct appropriate frames that enabled them to differentiate between literary genres, whether those be 'travelogue', 'novel', 'religious allegory' or 'political tract'. As well as being immensely useful in their own right, Rose argues that shared frames of reference were instrumental in enabling the British working classes to become increasingly politically aware. He notes in passing how many pioneers of the Labour Party openly acknowledged their political debt to the radical subtext of Bunyan's great work.

Frames are equally crucial in understanding policy processes, especially the early stages of problem identification and agenda formation. This point may at first seem rather obvious and unremarkable, until we reflect further on some of the implications of the staged model. Why is it, for example, that some issues capture the interest of policy makers, while others are neglected? Is it just because of circumstances, or is it because powerful lobby groups are able to get themselves noticed above the general din? Even when an issue bubbles up on to the political agenda, the ways in which it may be dealt with can vary enormously. Consider the following sequence of events:

Issue identification and problem definition – 1

Issue – People sleeping on the streets

Problem definition – Vagrancy

Policy response – Tougher forms of policing

What counts as a problem and how that problem is defined depends very much on the way that we perceive it. If we see people sleeping on the streets as a problem of vagrancy, then the policy response is more than likely to be framed in terms of law enforcement and policing. However, the following sequence gives a different perspective:

Issue identification and problem definition – 2

Issue – People sleeping on the streets

Problem definition – Homelessness

Policy response – Provision of low-cost housing

We might just as easily view the same issue as an indicator of social deprivation or a sign of failure in other policy areas such as community care – in which case the policy response will obviously be very different (we might provide low-cost housing, for example, or appropriate mental healthcare).

Information policy issues are equally ambiguous. In the UK the recent trend towards the electronic delivery of public services provides a good example. Local government has been quick to embrace electronic communications, using e-mail, the internet and the world wide web. Official borough websites contain a wide range of information, including 'What's on' guides of borough activities, council reports and plans, tourist information, and links to local community and voluntary groups. Many authorities use innovative forms of electronic communication to provide information about local services – examples include public libraries with computers hooked up to the internet, electronic kiosks displaying pages of local information in public places like supermarkets, and videotelephony for hearing-impaired people. Simultaneously, it is possible to see these developments as informing and empowering local communities, extending democracy, as instruments to reduce administration costs and head count by re-engineering local government services, providing a stimulus to the information industry, a new weapon in the councils' public relations armoury, or merely as gesture politics, pandering to the technology fetishists. The truth probably lies somewhere (everywhere?) on this list, but it is not immediately evident where.

Frames politicize the discussion of information policy problems by relating policy outcomes to value systems. By making the frames that structure our views of information policy and regulation more explicit, we could enter into a more transparent debate about what kind of information policy environment we want and how to achieve it. In other words, issue identification and problem definition in information policy are hardly value free. The same is true at all points in the policy cycle, even the evaluation of policy outcomes. Economic arguments over whether information should be treated as a tradeable commodity or cherished from a public good perspective abound in the library and information science literature, perhaps in their most crystalline form in relation to intellectual property rights. The continuing creation and development of information content requires that investors be properly rewarded for their efforts. This means conferring property rights and enabling a marketplace to develop. On the down side, these property rights may erect a barrier to the world of ideas for those who are unable to pay. This in turn necessitates a further set of public policies, such as universal service, investment in libraries, civil research and development, and education, which seek deliberately to distort the information marketplace in favour of the wider public interest. Questions of this kind, which hinge on the respective roles and responsibilities of the state and the market, of the rights of creators and users, are ubiquitous in the professional literature.

Aside from monetary considerations, access to information and knowledge is also a function of power structures. In many situations, the widest possible access to information is seen as a 'good thing' – health promotion, information about school performance, consumer information, access to local government records being classic examples. In other circumstances unfettered access to information is more problematic – the policy advice given to ministers, personal information, information that might be prejudicial to national security or a firm's commercial position. Restrictions on the free flow of information are sometimes essential, but there is always a danger that powerful forces in society will constrict these flows to their own advantage.

Progress in our understanding of information policies depends on finding ways to make our assumptions, prejudices and values more transparent – information policy, like all aspects of public policy, is after all deeply embedded in a political and social context. Information policy makers constantly find themselves between a rock and a hard place. Just consider the following intractable dilemmas of:

- market-led versus state-led visions of the information society
- rights of freedom of expression versus rights of personal privacy
- the monopoly functions of patents and copyrights versus their informational aspects and the needs of users in the UK science base
- the philosophy of open government versus the retention of crown copyright and continuing restrictive licensing practices in the UK.

The tensions between the main stakeholders (information industry, government, journalists, celebrities, inventors, library users) in each case are painfully evident. Without recourse to a broader framework that makes the underlying value systems clear, how can we find a way to resolve these tensions openly and fairly?

A normative model of information policy

The model (Figure 7.2) was generated automatically using a data-mining technique. It relates a number of information policy concepts to one another in a two-dimensional space, depending upon how frequently pairs of concepts co-occurred in a large bibliographic database.

It is not unreasonable to suppose that closely related concepts (e.g. fish AND chips) will tend to occur together more frequently in bibliographic records than concepts which are less mutually connected (e.g. fish AND oranges). If the intensity of these relationships is represented by distance, we could construct a map which would show 'fish' and 'chips' quite close to one another, while 'fish' and 'oranges' would be much further apart.

The concepts in the information policy map appear to be reasonably coherent and probably will not come as any great surprise to anyone with more than a passing interest in the subject. Five clusters of concepts are evident and are summarized in Table 7.1.

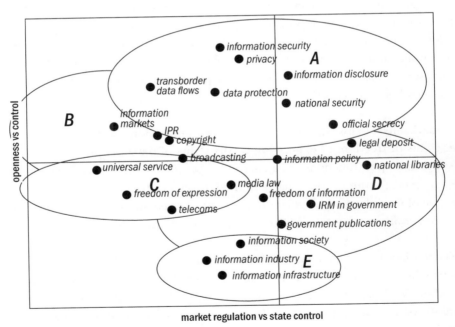

Fig. 7.2   *Information policy concepts*

Table 7.1 *Information policy sub-domains*

Cluster	Label	Interpretation
A	Information protectionism	Regulations and mechanisms controlling information access and disclosure in the public sphere (e.g. official secrecy) and in information markets (e.g. data protection).
B	Information markets	Laws and regulations that protect investment in the creation of information content (e.g. copyright) and enable market exchange to take place.
C	Broadcasting and telecommunications	Public policies that regulate the mass media and communications, balancing commercial and citizen interests (e.g. universal access).
D	Public access to official information	Policies and regulations that frame citizens' access to information held within government (e.g. freedom of information).
E	Information society and infrastructure	Public policy measures to invest (or encourage private sector investment) in the information infrastructure, broadly defined.

The axes on the map have been set (arbitrarily) to originate from the term 'information policy'. Broadly speaking, concepts lying to the right of the origin seem to relate primarily to the direct management by the state of its own internal information resources. From the top down, these responsibilities extend from the control of sensitive official information ('Information protectionism' cluster), through the effective storage and management of official information ('Public access' cluster) to the provision of infrastructures for its wider dissemination ('Information society and infrastructure' cluster). In contrast, concepts on the left-hand side of the map seem to more closely match the state's *indirect* role as a regulator of private sector information activities. Again, scanning from the top down, we see the state first acting to constrict information flows where these are held, for instance, to be invasive of personal privacy ('Information protectionism' cluster), then creating the conditions within which market exchange can take place ('Information markets' cluster), and finally mitigating the worst excesses of the marketplace by guaranteeing fundamental rights of freedom of expression and universal service ('Broadcasting and communications' cluster). For the sake of convenience, the *y* dimension can be summarized as expressing a spectrum between unrestricted, open (bottom) and restricted or controlled (top) information flows. The x dimension seems to indicate two distinct information policy roles for the state – as a regulator of information markets (left) and as a major gatherer and disseminator of information itself (right).

Conclusion

This model offers a new framework for helping us to think first and foremost about the system of values – rather than the specific laws and regulations – that underpin information policy. It may well be illustrative of aspects of the information policy 'regime' that were discussed earlier. Without a better understanding of the nature of that regime, and the shared meaning that it implies, the policy debate around information issues will remain fragmented, partial and lacking in intellectual coherence.

References

Aldhouse, F. (1997) Implementing information policies: some data protection experience. In Rowlands, I. (ed.) *Understanding information policy*, London, Bowker-Saur, 114–27.

Browne, M. (1997a) The field of information policy: (1) fundamental concepts, *Journal of Information Science*, **23** (4), 261–75.

Browne, M. (1997b) The field of information policy: (2) re-defining the boundaries and methodologies, *Journal of Information Science*, **23** (5) 339–51.

Rose, J. (2001) *The intellectual life of the British working classes*, London, Yale University Press.

Weingarten, F. W. (1989) Federal information policy development: the Congressional perspective. In McClure, C., Hernon, P. and Relyea, H. (eds), *United States government information policies: views and perspectives*, Norwood, NJ, Ablex, 112–36.

Further reading

Hogwood, B. W. and Gunn, L. A. (1984) *Policy analysis for the real world*, Oxford, Oxford University Press.

Rowlands, I. (1997) *Understanding information policy*, London, Bowker-Saur.

8

Knowledge management in government

Margaret Haines and Paul Dunn

Introduction

This chapter takes a broad look at the influences and expectations of public sector organizations evolving in an information age. It provides a general look at knowledge from the perspective of the public sector organization, explores the KM activities occurring in one area and reflects upon the theory versus the reality. It also includes a public sector example of knowledge management through a case study of the UK National Health Service.

What is government knowledge?

Most papers written on knowledge management (KM) begin with a dictionary definition of knowledge supported by a quote from a leader in the KM field. Not wanting to disappoint readers the following is offered:

> Knowledge: the facts, feelings and experiences known by a person or group of people.
>   (Collins English Dictionary)

The oft-quoted definition developed by Tom Davenport and Larry Prusak (1997) is:

> Knowledge is a fluid mix of framed experiences, values, contextual information and expert insight that provide a framework for evaluating and incorporating new experiences and information. It originates and is applied in the mind of knowers.

This doesn't take the topic of KM in government too far or resolve an underlying question: What are we trying to manage? Prusak argues that one cannot manage knowledge, only the knowledge-supporting environment. Peter Senge (1997) believes the West has a weak definition of knowledge and all too easily allows it to be interchanged with information. He draws a distinction between information and knowledge, saying information can be acquired and passed on much like a purchased item, whereas knowledge is the *capacity for effective action*.

The capacity for effective action probably better describes the public expectations of government and public services. It provides a suitable definition for KM in government and provides a focus for our final conclusions. Effective actions will be the result of different types of interactions and communications. Simply put, government services are responsive to internal public sector communications, to those with the public, and the naturally occurring societal forces. The KM landscape is therefore both broad and variable.

The criminal justice system alone highlights the range of relationships that can be linked to KM including in this case victim support, the police, the court services, prison services, prisoner health, the family of the prisoner, local authority and probation, policy authors and many more, a seemingly endless list. How does one share an experience and introduce one policy driven activity with that of another for the benefit of all concerned? How can all those involved be better prepared to act?

The changing public sector service

The service is about managing relationships and, like all areas of life, public service relationships are constantly changing. The assumptions of 19th-century ideology that either through Marxism or laissez faire the state would have a less significant role have not been realized. Indeed the protection of states through strong economic or social structures (the welfare and warfare states) has seen some powerful examples recently. The 2001 UK foot and mouth outbreak required integrated public service action (army, DEFRA, medical), and through knowledge sharing these actions had to determine the level of intervention that best served public interests. The collapse of Enron in 2002 is just one of the stories that has provoked calls for more regulation and audit powers in the financial sector. The first example highlights the scope for KM in the public services, where different organizations work together to resolve issues. Similar work patterns occur as a matter of course in other areas, e.g. defence, health, education, revenue, civil registrations. Furthermore these organizations create a significant customer relationship to the private sector.

Overall each part of the public sector will, however, create quite different interaction experiences. For example, a person concerned by poor health creates a very different experience of KM to that of a business selling to government. It may be argued that one of the strengths of the public service is having many departments that can deal exclusively with one category of public service or be part of a knowledge structure when required.

The regular changes to departmental scope and structures reflect changing priorities and the desire to improve efficiency and the capacity for effective action. If KM can be delivered across the public sector it may provide different options for achieving this goal and for delivering joined-up services. Of course the powerful new information and communication technologies, epitomized by the internet, provide a new incentive for exploiting information and knowledge systems. The public sector is seeking changes with technology – unsurprisingly, because governments are known historically to embrace developments of science and technology to help achieve success (Carter, 1965).

In 1998 *Our information age* (HMSO, 1998), the de facto UK national information policy stated:

> In this policy statement, we set out our ideas on how the Government will act to enable people to take advantage of the new information age – a co-ordinated strategy which will focus on transforming education, widening access, promoting competition and competitiveness, fostering quality and modernising government. The prize of this new age is to engage our country fully in the ambition and opportunity which the digital revolution offers. That prize is there for the taking. We must stretch out our hands and grasp it.

Our information age provided an umbrella for many of the modernizing public sector policies that emerged in 1997 and 1998 including:

- *Open for learning, open for business* (National Grid for Learning, 1998) – challenged learners, the education & lifelong learning services, industry and government to commit to a national grid for learning

- *Modernising government* (HMSO,1999) – committed government to modernizing public services, all capable of being delivered by computer by 2005
- *E-government* (UK. Cabinet Office, 2000) – a strategic framework for public services in the information age.

Most of these policies were designed to equip the public sector for functioning in an information society. Developments have addressed exploiting the tacit knowledge within, and improving knowledge transfer across the public sector. In December 2001, the *Second UK online annual report* stated:

> OeE [Office of the e-Envoy] successfully delivered the Knowledge Network as a unified cross-Government communications infrastructure to enable officials in all Government departments and associated bodies connected . . . to communicate electronically with each other and share common, secure access to databases, discussion forums, web-based community sites and 'knowledge pools'. The Knowledge Network will now provide the underlying technical infrastructure for a new programme of modernisation led by the OeE, known as Knowledge Enhanced Government. The embedding of knowledge management practices and processes will support and utilise the KN infrastructure to underpin this programme.   (Office of the e-Envoy, 2001)

Crucially, these strategies place government and the public services in more than one role and specifically those of adopter, leader and regulator of change. If a private sector organization found itself in this position it might introduce restructuring to remove possible tensions. It may be that a restructuring is occurring in the public sector as Lester Thurrow (1997) has observed there are signs of a changing state relationship. He sees regionalism occurring fast in the USA, former USSR and the UK with stronger roles for the new devolved authorities. It might be assumed that in this model of governance the central powers would be reduced. However, the role of the centre is underlined by the paradox that, while there is fragmentation, these authorities often then seek membership of a broader agreement, the new centre, which manages the then shared macro environment. The EU is an example of a country-based model, and multinational corporations provide another example where the individual operations serve the locality or specialization yet benefit from a central brand and communal overarching strategy.

The public service implementation could be compared to the multinational corporation model. An emerging example is the devolved financial and performance management of the UK health sector, local National Health Service organizations and networks, which focuses on the development of national standards, securing resources and setting direction, maintaining relationships with other government departments, helping services integrate and modernizing and ensuring delivery (UK. Department of Health, 2001b).

A restructuring of public services is likely to introduce issues concerning legal reform, information ownership, stewardship and ownership of the intellectual capital that is generated through access to the information or by the privileges of public services. While these matters will not be tackled by this chapter they are raised here to underline the issues that will occur in any transition, and therefore the importance of sound information management policy to deliver KM in government.

The impact of technology

The modernization predicted in the 1960s may now occur, as science and technology are more able to cope with the decentralized nature of public services and provide an infrastructure to enable engagement with society at large. There will need to be changes so that the building blocks of knowledge – data, information, people and experiences – are accessible. A knowledge-centric environment is about responding to unstructured questions and not assuming the enquirer has an intimate understanding of the subject in question. The current examples of knowledge services (the Knowledge Network, Knowledge Enhanced Government, portal search tools, education/libraries) build upon this viewpoint.

Assuming the decentralized model outlined earlier, the centres will no longer be the primary sources of information. To be effective the new centres will need to establish knowledge networks through close co-operation with the devolved administrations. The approach taken by the UK government recognizes that enabling a co-operative environment requires a central technological infrastructure independent of, but available to, the public sector organizational silos. This evolution is beginning to show itself through the work of the government portal site UK Online. Behind the scenes lies an investment underpinning common service solutions such as electronic authentication, information access and retrieval. The focus of public service reform is expressed in the *Modernising government* White Paper (HMSO, 1999). Government plans have been to harmonize operations to enable seamless interaction across both central and local government. This seamless interface would reflect the 'hypertext organization' model of Nonaka (1995). This development is designed to provide more than just service reform as it acts as an incentive and opportunity for closer procedural reforms across each existing relationship (public/government, etc.) so all unite uniformly behind a knowledge-centric solution – the focus thus being content rather than department.

Change involving IT can lead to horror stories. Heeks (1998) explores the reasons for transformation failure and observes that the emphasis on IT solutions has led to a widening gap between informal and formal information. Perhaps the headline stories could have been avoided had the new IT systems addressed the 'full' knowledge process chain. While the rigidity of departmental IT has assured accountability and privacy protection, it may have been to the exclusion of the informal networks, thereby losing the all important opportunity for organizational learning (Nonaka, 1995). These discussion points suggest new public services must be based upon knowledge transfer and have the IT capacity for system integration throughout the transactional chain.

Business management strategy for KM

Government public sector services are not generally geared for generating demand or funded on a performance-profit basis. However, commercial practice is permeating public sector ways of performance monitoring and assessment. It is not possible to shoe-horn the public services as a whole into any one of the four organizational models underlying business strategy (Whittington, 2000). However, in the past couple of decades the *classical* approach, considered the bookkeeper's approach, may have been targeted over a *systemic* and more holistically purposed strategy. (See Figure 8.1). If so this is unfortunate as the latter may be more favourable for an integrated public service where there is a need to be flexible and adaptive to multiple interactions.

	Deliberate	**Emergent**
Profit-maximizing	Classical (Profit/Strict Plans)	Evolutionary (Profit/Fittest Survives)
Pluralistic	Systemic (Pluralistic/Direction)	Processual (Pluralistic/Adopting)

Fig. 8.1   *Generic perspectives on strategy*
(Source: Whittington, R. (2000) *What strategy and does it matter?*, Thomson Business Press.)

The choice and identification of business strategy is relevant to KM thinking, for the implication of a *classical* approach is one of segmented business units with independent delivery targets. This segmentation was a symptom in all sectors of the 1980/90s explosion of IT solutions resulting in localized independent approaches. It led to a great variance in people skills and technology solutions, and to narrowly focused processes, and this direction would seem to be in direct opposition to the core KM principles of integrated people, processes and technology.

Re-engineering the public sector services from this background will be difficult. In addition the public service transformation will need to address differing stakeholder interests, among them a minister's vision, the accountability of departments and a shifting and volatile public demand. Resolving the interests of the first two stakeholders is likely to need compromise on implementation. The third is relating to public expectation. To achieve joined-up services and closer engagement with the public, the public sector service must be capable of addressing new and variable demands or a 'mass customization' at a national level. Perhaps the greatest challenge awaiting public services is the management of an ever larger number of 'experiences' from a larger and more vocal group. In meeting the challenge it must ensure that all participants in the services are suitably engaged and informed.

The present government KM environment

In the UK the Office of the e-Envoy (OeE) has recently considered the development of a knowledge management policy framework, to provide a holistic view of knowledge management in its varied facets and associated recommendations for activity. (www.e-envoy.gov.uk). Early proposals have suggested that such a knowledge management policy framework could be based around ten key areas of activity:

- *knowledge capture* – policies and processes for the initial identification and capture of knowledge in its explicit and tacit forms
- *knowledge transfer* – policies and processes for the effective transfer of knowledge among its various sources and between its various forms
- *knowledge retention* – policies and processes for the retention of corporate knowledge, particularly in times of personnel or organizational change
- *content management* – policies and processes for the efficient management and maintenance of the corporate knowledge base
- *knowledge capital* – policies and processes for measuring and developing the government's human and social capital foundations
- *enabling communities* – policies and processes for identifying, promoting and supporting knowledge-based community working across and between departments
- *supporting a knowledge culture* – policies and processes to develop and embed the necessary cultural change and business environment to embed knowledge management activity and ethos
- *knowledge partnerships* – policies and processes for identifying, promoting and supporting knowledge partnerships between central government and key partners, including local government and the regions, the NHS and agencies/non-departmental public bodies (NDPBs) and the voluntary and community sector
- *supporting key business activities* – policies and processes for supporting key business activities within government, including project management, the legislative process, delivery monitoring and committee support
- *knowledge benchmarking* – policies and processes for benchmarking current knowledge capacity and practice against domestic and international best practice and for raising relative performance.

The Knowledge Enhanced Government (KEG) team has recognized the need to capture and use knowledge about the public's experience with government. Knowledge capture methods such as 'story-telling' and discovery interviews will facilitate thematic analysis of a wide range of public sector experiences captured in narrative databases.

The KEG team is working with the major central government departments in ensuring that there are departmental teams and processes to support participation in the KEG and in developing the KM policy framework, and the Department of Health is already a key player in these processes. The next section will describe the approach to KM within the Department of Health and touch upon the wider NHS.

A public sector example of KM: a case study of the National Health Service

In one chapter it would be difficult to adequately describe the approaches to knowledge management across the entire public sector in the UK. This section will describe the policy context and the implementation approach to KM in the National Health Service and in the Department of Health as a backdrop for the conclusions presented.

The National Health Service is the highest-profile public service in the UK. Modernizing the NHS is a key pledge of the current government and modernizing the way in which the Department of Health does business is part of its overall commitment to modernizing government.

In *Our information age* (HMSO, 1998), a promise was made that information technology would be fully exploited by the NHS, with electronic communications supporting seamless care. The White Paper *The new NHS – modern, dependable* (UK. Department of Health, 1997) further promised a flexible and adaptive interface which would allow:

- easier and faster information through NHS Direct, a new 24-hour telephone advice line staffed by nurses
- use of the NHS information superhighway NHSnet and the internet to deliver quicker test results, online booking of appointments and up-to-date specialist advice to patients
- use of the internet and emerging public access media (e.g. digital TV) to provide knowledge about health, illness and best treatment practice to the public.

Other health policy documents promote reform towards a more client-centred service based on better value for money, clinical quality improvement processes, increased efficiency and effectiveness in delivery of services, and partnerships with other sectors. Examples include:

- *Our healthier nation* (UK. Department of Health, 1998c), which put tackling health inequalities at the top of the agenda and encouraged partnerships with other sectors
- *A first class service: quality in the New NHS* (UK. Department of Health, 1998a), promoting a clinical governance framework addressing quality through effective underpinning knowledge systems
- *A health service of all the talents* (UK. Department of Health, 2000a), proposing a comprehensive review of information requirements to support workforce planning and all education- and training-provider partnerships
- *R&D for a first class service* (UK. Department of Health, 2000d), proposing new knowledge systems relating to research findings and scientific development that assist clinical management and policy decisions
- *An organisation with a memory* (UK. Department of Health, 2000c), making the case for knowledge management systems to capture and disseminate the learning through work and tacit knowledge generated.

The information strategy for the NHS, *Information for health* (UK. Department of Health, 1998b) outlined a programme of modernization based on information systems and technology. Its purpose was 'to put in place . . . the people, the resources, the culture and the processes necessary to ensure that NHS clinicians and managers have the information needed to support the core purpose of the NHS in caring for individuals and improving public health'.

The strategy explicitly states that it will address the need for better access and management of information resources by patients, healthcare professionals and policy makers and managers. Initiatives that have developed as a result include:

- *NHS Direct Online* – providing accredited, independent multimedia information and advice on health, lifestyle and participation in the NHS policy development
- *The National Electronic Library for Health* – providing NHS professionals with online access to national information, guidance and supporting evidence.

The *Information for health* strategy has been revised and updated to reflect the goals of the NHS plan 2000 (UK. Department of Health, 2000b) and the revised strategy appeared in 2001 under the title *Building the information core: implementing the NHS plan* (UK. Department of Health, 2001a). The NHS plan is driving change in the health service through ten core principles, including a commitment to continuous quality improvement, to valuing staff and to providing open access to information about services, treatment and performance. It further requires the NHS to introduce major initiatives to support greater sharing of information by the various organizations and improved patient access to services and knowledge resources – including their own electronic patient records.

The government's response, *Learning from Bristol* (UK. Department of Health, 2002), to the enquiry into the management of care of children receiving complex cardiac care at the Bristol Royal Infirmary (UK. Department of Health, 2001b) reaffirms the government's commitment to the principles of the NHS plan. It specifically promises to deliver a common core of evidence-based health knowledge delivered by a single integrated National Knowledge Service (NKS) by 2003. The NKS will meet the needs of professionals, patients and the public for up-to-date, cross-referenced, evidence-based information by fully integrating the development of NHS knowledge systems. Funded by the Department of Health it will cover:

- the analysis of knowledge needs of providers and consumers of health services
- the creation of high-quality knowledge resources using providers funded by the Department *or* the selection and procurement of externally produced resources that meet agreed selection criteria
- the delivery of the knowledge resources via traditional and new technology systems to agreed technical and service standards
- the development of individual and organizational knowledge skills to use the resources effectively
- the active promotion of the NKS to support the spread of good practice and further the development of local knowledge mobilization strategies.

Work to co-ordinate the online delivery of NHS-focused information is already underway as is national procurement of national licences to evidence-based resources. The challenge for the NKS leadership is to integrate local delivery systems in a way which allows local variation and ownership but avoids a post-code lottery in relation to health information provision and knowledge transfer.

This new focus on knowledge resources rather than just information systems continues in the recent framework for lifelong learning in the NHS – *Working together, learning together* (UK. Department of Health, 2001d) which states that the health service and its partner organizations need effective learning strategies to use the knowledge assets available to them. A university for the NHS is proposed which will embrace e-learning, knowledge management and network technology in order to deliver education and training appropriate for a modern health service.

The direction of a knowledge-based NHS is taking place while the NHS is undergoing a major reorganization. The government announced in *Shifting the balance of power* (UK. Department of Health, 2001c) its plans for devolving power and decision making to local NHS organizations, allowing local choice consistent with a nationally integrated service. In the context of information and knowledge management this means that the Department of Health will provide the national leadership, setting national frameworks and some centralized procurement, but implementation of knowledge and learning-focused policies will devolve to new health authorities and trusts. To assist local NHS organizations with this challenge, the Department's Modernisation Agency is introducing knowledge 'mobilization' projects to spread best practice throughout the NHS in order to radically improve the delivery of services to patients.

While the policy focus described above is primarily NHS related, recent papers produced as part of a departmental review of the Department of Health suggest that better internal knowledge systems are critical to improve the ways of working and in particular to improve the policy management process. Emphasis was placed on the need to base all departmental activities on sound evidence provided by internal knowledge sources and drawn from other departments, the NHS and the public.

For the Department of Health, KM as 'capacity for effective action' will depend on having the appropriate content, systems, processes, leadership, culture and skills development in place. Various initiatives have been introduced that will address all of these areas and will inform the development of a department-wide KM strategy. These initiatives, which have attracted considerable interest from other public sector bodies, include:

- the ministerial briefing system CHIP, which provided a benchmark for the development of the Knowledge Network
- the KLIMT Project (Knowledge Learning and Information Management Toolkit), which explored workgroup knowledge management requirements
- the South East Regional Office knowledge harvesting project, which is evaluating a system for capturing tacit knowledge
- the piloting of the European Computer Driving Licence, which is developing information literacy and IT skills for departmental employees, etc.

As an active member of the Knowledge Network, the Department should be well placed to improve its capacity for sharing knowledge with other government departments, while its work to co-ordinate the online provision of knowledge resources should lead to effective information dissemination to NHS staff, patients and the public. The challenges for the Department remain how to improve access to the knowledge of these clients of its services and how to facilitate knowledge transfer between and among clients and providers within the wider NHS.

Conclusion

In the first section of this chapter the subject of KM in government has been approached from various theoretical positions to provide an overview of the role of government and the public sector, technology and the service types. There are some repeating and crucial aspects that stand out as significant for a broad assessment of the subject. They are as follows:

- There is a high public expectation that public services will be flexible to meet a specific requirement and adaptive for specific needs.
- Devolution and a decentralized model of governance will create legal and technological complexities that may obstruct knowledge transfer and limit the opportunity for interoperability.
- Commercial strategies and target management may lead to a service strategy moving away from that which is conducive to knowledge sharing or creative service delivery.
- A successful knowledge environment in the public sector will require a sound information management strategy to underpin integrated and co-operative working.

To complement the theoretical view, the chapter has also looked at the actions and activities of a cross-Whitehall initiative where the main focus is knowledge management to improve the public sector operations and the services. References are made to the work supporting a UK knowledge economy and electronic service delivery by the Office of the e-Envoy and also to work undertaken by the Department of Health. The examples show:

- the OeE leadership through the knowledge team delivering to a Knowledge Enhanced Government agenda
- the value of closer working across the health sector and of the public sector practitioner examples that provide a frame of reference for others wishing to make changes.

The evidence is there to suggest that considerable activity is taking place across the UK government to prepare the public sector services and the public at large for the new information society. The theoretical study argued that a multinational corporation model would need central initiatives to provide both a technical and working level infrastructure. The NHS model examined and the work of the public sector generally guided by the Office of the e-Envoy is evidence that central and local government is involved in developing good practice communities, know-how transfers and learning directives. Further examples can be found in the DTI Knowledge Unit, Local Government IDeA and in other areas. UK government policy is seeking to improve its *capacity for effective action* through KM principles.

What can we conclude about this?

The UK is no different from many G8 countries in its attempts to reform and modernize its delivery of public services. The authors are active in inter-government debates and open forums regarding public sector changes and KM. From this perspective it is suggested that measuring who is leading within the G8 is difficult because of underlying differences and specific agendas. However, the UK policy would seem commensurate with that of others and is visibly moving to a knowledge-centric form. The UK Online portal is providing a symbol of this direction.

In the first section of the chapter the government and public service position was simplified as needing to be responsive to internal public sector communications, to those with the public, and the naturally occurring societal forces. It would be valuable to consider some of the arguments and evidence under these three headings to determine the gaps and opportunities for positive KM intervention and the future outlook for KM in government.

Public sector communications

The modernization of government and the harmonization work underpinning electronic delivery is leading to a strong IM programme. The KEG framework provides a direction and goal for joined-up government and policy making. Change in processes and operations will also need changes in the culture with incentives for knowledge sharing. The discussed business strategy that is focused upon performance targets may prevent inter-services joint working or the likelihood of informal knowledge exchanges. A strong feature of the civil service was its career civil servant who moved across departments and thereby physically transferred good practice and know-how. Somehow this needs to be reinforced and so it is important that public services invest in the people side as well as the technology and process transformation. This may come through secondment, mentoring or shared projects but importantly the investment must be retained and reused to ensure continuous improvement.

The technology and vision is one that is shared across governments and the learning of what works and product value is something that should be quickly ingested as it is a worldwide change concept. It is recognized by writers and analysts of change management that what works in one country or region may not work in another. Often it is as a result of cultural values being at odds with the working of the business system. To move forward and benefit from the experiences of others, the changing structure of government must be readily acknowledged and each authority prepared by first understanding its cultural dynamics and then its contribution overall.

Public sector communicating with the public

The introduction of IT systems combined with the record management rigour applied within the public sector is probably the reason why it has been relatively easy to deliver information to the public. There have been websites for most departments for many years, some providing guidance and forms. More recently there have been transactional services allowing for the two-way exchange of information (see www.ukonline.gov.uk).

It is not enough to present electronic versions of what may have been paper documentation. As discussed above, there is a need to make information available in the form that best suits the enquirer. There is a need to understand how information is required and when joined-up services are appropriate, and to be sure a client response is being dealt with appropriately. As Trish Williams (2002) comments, 'some countries and governments actually set deadlines for launching a host of online initiatives only for schedules to slip as agency officials grappled with complex information sharing and collaboration issues'. While there is work to build services around key life episodes (see www.ukonline.gov.uk) it will not be possible to foresee every interaction and so meet each specific need. To overcome this gap there will need to be a greater investment in codification of rules, regulations and complementary information (tacit and explicit) accessible with tools that enable natural language inter-rogation and retrieval. This will be a defining area in that it will present a seamless environment – at least within broad clusters of public sector services.

Crucially, then, any investment in providing a knowledge-supporting environment within the public sector must reflect the client capability. The potential gap, if not carefully managed, would otherwise greatly reduce the knowledge transfer between the public sector and public client.

In preparation for a UK electronic infrastructure there must be development of public skills and accessibility through preferred technology. The skill of the use of technology is important but more so is the ability to interpret the knowledge content when discovered. The services will need to be embedded with instructional knowledge and be capable of presenting results in alternative formats, for example story-telling and narrative databases. It is one thing to have a do-it-yourself manual and another to make use of it.

Having the preferred technology is critical in meeting greater demands and providing service flexibility. Knowledge transfer must be consistent in content (i.e. it should be possible to infer the same conclusion regardless of technical interface) if the services are to be universally inclusive. The most recent UK Online annual report (Office of the e-Envoy, 2001), confirms that investment will continue in broadband and universal service delivery but there is a fast-moving growth in technology diversity that will see games consoles to organizational systems wishing to interact with the government services.

The public influence and e-democracy

A change is predicted in how people will generally learn, join forces and communicate in the future, and the emerging digital channels are largely responsible for this belief. E-democracy is beginning to take form and e-voting for leisure or political purposes is closer to being a reality. Governments of the day will need to attune to a range of communities of interest operating at local, national and international level. The new knowledge-rich information society will have a new and possibly more direct relationship with government and the public services. Earlier the new structure and regionalism of government was identified. So one can expect that at a local level e-democracy will be active. It was also suggested that with the changing structures one should anticipate changing relationships between ministers and the public sector service providers.

Presently governments are actively encouraging public interest in the opportunities of the new technology and encouraging online interaction. KEG has stated that it is concerned to improve public interest in the process of governance and thereby improve election turnouts. However, in an interview carried by the *Big Issue* magazine Tony Benn, former Labour MP for Chesterfield, states 'They say that the public are apathetic about the government but most people think it's the government that is apathetic about them. It's a matter of getting people at the top to listen to everybody else, not the other way round' (Daly, 2002).

Benn continues 'People are meeting each other, exchanging information'. Clearly he anticipates an active e-democratic environment and recognizes the need for the government sector to be more active in talking and listening. Ultimately we would suggest connecting the formal information networks to these developing information-sharing communities if the knowledge networks are to be effective. If Benn is right about the disengagement then KM principles present the opportunity for re-establishing the political relationship.

The government sectors worldwide will also experience another culture change. The open access to public sector information (e.g. freedom of information), surely a key facility for e-democracy, will create a new breed of knowledge worker. These will be monitoring services, regulations and future programmes, and be capable of providing new perspectives on public affairs, not only within national borders but also at an international level. The emerging communities of action will have the democratic power to create a very different experience that will present new challenges to all governments and the basis of governance. As reasoned by R. A. W. Rhodes (1997), 'governance is a broader term than government – with services provided by any permutation of government and the private and voluntary sectors'.

To be effective in this environment governments of the day will need to be a part of the new communities, providing leadership and creating a constructive knowledge-sharing partnership to facilitate creative change and reform.

The outlook for KM in government

Governance and the shape of government would appear to be changing and this will create transitional relationships that need to be managed. The three roles of government as leader, user and regulator will all figure actively during the transition and as such the communication structures and ultimately the knowledge networks need to be highly receptive. In government's role as 'leader', the work of public services, exemplified by the NHS study, will act as a benchmark for changes in the private sector and for citizen communities.

The capacity for effective action (our definition of KM in government) will depend upon continual cultural changes and the capability to capture the voice of community relationships. There would seem to be an interesting time ahead but the KM building blocks that will underpin a responsive government sector are being laid.

References

Carter, G. M. (1965) *Government and politics in the twentieth century*, London, Thames and Hudson.

Daly, M. (2002) *The Big Issue*, Reported comment by Tony Benn in article by Max Daly, (474).

Davenport, T. H. and Prusak, L. (1997) *Working knowledge*, Boston, MA, Harvard Business School Press.

Heeks, R. (1998) *Reinventing government in the information age*, London, Routledge.

HMSO (1998) *Our information age: the government's vision*, London, HMSO.

HMSO (1999) White Paper *Modernising Government*, Cm 4310, London, HMSO.

National Grid for Learning (1998), *Open for learning, open for business*, London,

Department for Education and Skills Learning

Nonaka, I. (1995) *The knowledge creating company*, Oxford, Oxford University Press.

Office of the e-Envoy www.e-envoy.gov.uk.

Office of the e-Envoy (2001) Second UK Online annual report, Cabinet Office.

Rhodes, R. A. W. (1997) *Understanding governance*, Buckingham, Open University Press.

Senge, P. (1997) Through the eye of the needle. In Gibson, R. (ed.) *Rethinking the future*, London, Nicholas Brealey.

Thurrow, L. (1997) *Changing the nature of capitalism – rethinking the future*, Nicholas Brealey.

UK.Cabinet Office (2000), *E-government, a Strategic Framework for the public service in the information age*, London, Cabinet Office IT Unit.

UK.Department of Health (1997) *The new NHS – modern, dependable*, Cm 3807, London, The Stationery Office.

UK.Department of Health (1998a) *A first class service: quality in the NHS, Consultation document*, London, DH Publications Unit.

UK.Department of Health (1998b) *Information for health*, London, DH Publications Unit.

UK.Department of Health (1998c) *Our healthier nation: a contract for health*, Cm 3852, London, The Stationery Office.

UK.Department of Health (2000a) *A health service of all the talents: developing the NHS workforce. A consultation document*, London, DH Publications Unit.

UK.Department of Health (2000b) *The NHS plan: a plan for investment – a plan for reform*, Cm 4818, London, The Stationery Office.

UK.Department of Health (2000c) *An organisation with a memory: report of an expert group on learning from adverse events in the NHS*, chaired by the Chief Medical Officer, London, The Stationery Office.

UK.Department of Health (2000d) *R&D for a first class service: R&D funding in the NHS*, London, DH Publications Unit.

UK.Department of Health (2001a) *Building the information core: implementing the NHS plan*, London, DH Publications Unit.

UK.Department of Health (2001b) *The report of the public inquiry into children's heart surgery at the Bristol Royal Infirmary 1984-1995. Learning from Bristol*, Cm 5207, London, The Stationery Office.

UK.Department of Health (2001c) *Shifting the balance of power within the NHS:*

securing delivery, London, DH Publication Unit.

UK. Department of Health (2001d) *Working together, learning together: a framework for lifelong learning in the NHS*, London, DH Publications Unit.

UK. Department of Health (2002) *Learning from Bristol: the government's response to the report of the public inquiry into children's heart surgery at the Bristol Royal Infirmary 1984–1995*, Cm 5363, London, The Stationery Office.

UK Online www.ukonline.gov.uk.

Whittington, R. (2000) *What strategy and does it matter?*, London, Thomson Business Press.

Williams, Trish (2002) Statement available at www.washingtontechnology.com/news/15_23/features/16111-1.html 2002.

Part 4

The information society and the information professional

9
Freedom versus protection: the same coin or different currencies?

Graham P. Cornish

Introduction

There are three basic concepts in the information world which appear, on occasions at least, to be at odds with each other: the right of freedom of expression, the right of freedom of access to information and the right to protect what we create (mostly copyright). All three concepts contain elements of both freedom and protection and the exercise of one seems to lead to inhibition of one at least of the others rather like the children's game of 'Stone–Paper–Scissors'. Are these three concepts really in conflict or is there a creative tension that will allow all of them to flourish? This chapter will not necessarily answer that question but it is hoped it will at least point a way through the maze of ethical, technical and professional questions that surround these issues.

Rights or privileges?

'Rights' is a very emotive word and it is often surrounded more by emotion than reason. There is no basic agreement on exactly what constitutes a 'right'. Some philosophers see it as primarily a legal matter – something granted to individuals by virtue of being a citizen of a particular state. Others prefer to see it as something rooted in 'natural law' or justice and therefore something that may be enshrined in law but, if it is not, then it ought to be. Whatever definition we use, it must be acknowledged that rights are never absolute in practice and often have to be moderated to accommodate other people's rights. Shavell (2000) quotes the trivial example of owning a garden over which you have total rights, but making a compost heap there that emits noxious fumes may cause other people offence or even become a health hazard, in which case steps must be taken to remove the compost and so limit your rights over your land.

In the context of the information society, we are trying to grapple with a property right (mostly copyright) and two less well-defined rights (freedom of expression and freedom of access), so perhaps the comment by H. L. A. Hart (1968) that 'a right constitutes a justification for interfering with another's freedom, the very existence of the practice presupposes a background right to liberty in general' gives us a clue to just what it is we are trying to disentangle. This general right is affirmed in Article 3 of the *Universal declaration of human rights* (United Nations, 1948): 'Everyone has the right to life, liberty and security of person.' To try to understand this issue in a modern information-based world it is necessary to examine each of the three elements in turn to see how and whether they conflict with, or complement, each other.

Protecting what we create

The concept

The idea behind intellectual property is rooted in the notion that anything we create is an extension of 'self' and should be protected from general use by anyone else. This gives rise to the idea that the person creating something has exclusive rights over the thing created, partly for economic reasons but also because we have a right to protect our 'self' of which our creativity is a part. This protectionism is expressed mostly through copyright, trademarks and patents with some less common additions as well. Copyright is by far the most commonly encountered in the information society and is important to ensure the continued growth of writing, performing and creating by giving the creator a certain amount of control. This right is enshrined in the *Universal declaration of human rights* at Article 27 (2) (United Nations, 1948) which states: 'Everyone has the right to the protection of the moral and material interests resulting from any scientific, literary or artistic production of which he is the author.'

Copyright law aims to protect this growth but, at the same time, tries to ensure that some access to copyright works is allowed as well. Without this access creators would be starved of ideas and information to create more copyright material. Copyright divides into two main areas: economic rights and moral rights. In the Anglo-Saxon tradition the emphasis has always been on economic rights, i.e. what economic benefit rights can bring in terms of royalties, sale of all or part of copyright, licences, and so on. Moral rights include the right to be named as the author, the right not to have another person named as the author instead, the right not to have works falsely attributed to oneself and the right to prevent the alteration of the work.

It is clear that copyright has the potential to be the basis for a serious conflict with the concept of freedom of access. If owners can control access then how can it be unfettered? On the other hand copyright might be seen as an ally for freedom of expression as any views expressed will be protected by copyright. However, there is a further conflict here in that some forms of freedom of expression may rely on using material that expresses the views of other people or claims to need to use material owned by others to enable a view to be expressed. This was a major consideration in the case concerning publication of a memo by Paddy Ashdown to the prime minister (*Ashdown and Telegraph Group Ltd* at www.lawreports.co.uk/civjul1.9.htm). Libraries are in a unique position as custodians of copyright material (Cornish, 2001). They have the duty to care for, and allow access to, other people's copyright works. This places special responsibilities on all those working in libraries, archives and the information world generally. Librarians and information intermediaries in the widest sense of the phrase, practise their profession by using this property, so they should take all possible steps to protect it, while, at the same time, ensuring that the rights and privileges of users are also safeguarded.

Because copyright is such an intangible thing, there is often a temptation to ignore it. Those who take this approach forget that they, too, own copyright in their own creations and would feel quite angry if this were abused by others. Some of the restrictions placed on use by the law may seem petty or trivial but they are designed to allow some use of copyright material without unduly harming the interests of the creator (author).

The impact of IT

The rapid growth in the dissemination of information by electronic means has had the dual effect of heightening awareness of their rights for owners and increasing disregard by users as copyright infringement is facilitated by the same technological developments. This has the potential for increased conflict between owners and users.

There are those who think that, in an electronic world, copyright has had its day. In an electronic world where anything can be copied and everything can be transmitted, downloaded, modified and repackaged, where, they ask, is the logic in maintaining a right that can no longer be enforced? Better to let everyone use whatever they want any way they care to and charge them for it. Licences, compulsory and voluntary, are often seen as replacing copyright law altogether. This rather cavalier approach ignores the fact that it is copyright law that defines what is owned in the first place and therefore determines what can and cannot be licensed and for which purposes. In a debate on the future of intellectual property, Chris Blake (2001) raises the question: is copyright really dead? Viewing the issue from the context of the music industry, one of the most vulnerable and valuable copyright industries in the world, he concludes it is not dead but that it will need to change to cope with the future and so will the attitudes of those who own it.

Weakest link or cornerstone?

Unlike trademarks and patents, copyright is automatic upon creation so there is no central record of ownership, novelty or uniqueness, neither is it the total monopoly given by the other two. As infringement of copyright becomes more and more simple to achieve, so this weakest but most prevalent member of the intellectual property family is likely to become more and more abused.

Yet it is also going to remain the cornerstone of creative activity in this dynamic and fluid time. Unless those who create can exercise some kind of control over what they have created the incentive to carry on creating will gradually disappear. Certainly many people do not create for money, as Fytton Rowland (1997) explains, but many others do, especially but not totally in the leisure-related industries. But even if authors do not themselves create to generate income their publishers certainly do publish for this very purpose in many instances. Even those so-called 'learned publishers' who do not generate profits as such still generate surplus revenue which they use for the purposes of enabling more publishing to take place. In UK legislation copyright is weak and its weakest element is the so-called moral rights referred to above. A weak link they may be, but they have already become a vital element in the electronic world because of their significance to authors of all kinds. Copyright will also remain essential because it defines what is owned and what the owner can do and allow, or prevent, others from doing. How those actions are managed will the crucial issue, not whether or not copyright continues to be a concept.

Neglect and abuse

Of course neglect is really a facet of abuse but the two terms are useful to distinguish between those who own something, but fail to exploit it properly, and those who do not own it but aim to exploit it without the right to do so. It would be wrong to make the assumption that creators and owners always understand what they can do with their own property or, indeed, that they own any property at all. Many owners are blissfully unaware of the extensive rights that they own or the market value of them. Copyright is both a moral right and a property right, which is acquired automatically upon creation of a work that qualifies for protection. The absence of formalities for registration (as exists for trademark and patent protection) will often mean that the owner is totally unaware of what is owned or the power it gives. Only when owners are aware of their rights can they decide whether or not to exercise them. Many rights owners do not wish to exercise some or all of their rights, but they do have them and they are often surprised when someone approaches them for permission to copy or put something on a website or even use it in an advertisement (Cornish, 2000b). But the user cannot know what the owner is or is not willing to allow and on what terms without consultation taking place, an often complex and unsatisfactory process which may lead to an equally unsatisfactory outcome for everyone involved. Some kind of coding system would help to alleviate this situation where users chase permissions that owners do not feel it necessary to give (Cornish, 2000a).

Users, on the other hand, can be equally cavalier in their attitudes to rights. Many users are only vaguely aware, if aware at all, of the rights that owners enjoy. On the other hand, they are often so badly informed that such concepts in Anglo-Saxon law as 'fair dealing/use' are often used as an excuse for doing what users want to do, regardless of the finer points of the law. While users of copyright material need to be aware of the rights that the owners enjoy (even if the owners themselves are not), they also need to remember that those rights may be limited by the users' own needs (Hart, 1968). It is this conflict that is at the heart of this chapter.

Stopping abuse: education

One of the best ways of stopping neglect and abuse of any kind is education. As many users are unaware of their rights and their potential economic value this needs to be a focal point for an education programme. The UK government has identified education of the general public on copyright as a major topic and is proposing some important initiatives in this area. For example the Report from the Creative Industries Task Force states (UK. Department of Trade and Industry: Creative Industries Intellectual Property Group, 2000): 'Awareness about intellectual property can be improved by campaigns targeted at people who are not conscious that they need any knowledge, or, even, feel that they have enough knowledge and do not need to know anything else.'

From a library and information point of view the cynic might say that the less owners know about their rights the better. This is not the case. Ignorance can take the form of over-protection as well as under-protection so it is better that each player does understand their rights and the limitations placed on them. Educating the owner is a long-term strategy that will require patience and investment. Penetrating the Small and Medium-sized Enterprise (SME) environment, for example, can be a slow business but this sector is a major creator and owner of copyright material. In the electronic information world the whole question of who owns what is becoming highly complex, with websites, for example, having many elements often owned by an equally confusing variety of owners.

However even the fiercest defenders of rights owners' interests, such as licensing agencies, will freely admit that the library and information community is one of the most diligent in respecting copyright law as they understand and interpret it. This puts the library community in the envious position of being seen as an 'honest broker', which can and should be a valuable asset in the immediate future. Considerable efforts have been made to educate library and information staff and lead them through the labyrinth of legal niceties that surround the profession in the UK. Various training initiatives exist for the library and information community (see websites at www.cilip.org.uk/; www.bl.uk; www.aslib.co.uk; www.copyrightcircle.co.uk) as well as those provided by publishers' organizations, the music industry and the legal profession.

Essentially the role of education should be to emphasize the balance that needs to exist between owners and users. The law in the UK and many other countries recognizes this balance and users need to be aware that copyright is not a monopoly and materials protected by it may, within strict limits, be used by others without reference to the original creator or owner (Norman, 1999).

Education is the best way of managing the balance between the three elements of control, freedom of access and freedom of expression. When the interaction between the three is understood, then there is some real hope of developing a balanced rights environment.

Stopping abuse: licences

An increasing amount of use of copyright material is being governed by licences rather than the law. Licences are already prevalent in many areas and the trend will continue as owners and users prefer to rely on mutually agreed terms rather than unclear elements in the law which give the user only very limited rights of access and use. Licences enable copyright owners to permit anything they wish in return for agreement to the terms by the user. At the same time licences can free users, especially those offering information services such as libraries and information centres, to develop all kinds of new and dynamic services in partnership with the owner. An obvious example is the Copyright Fee Paid Service (www.bl.uk/) offered by the British Library, which enables libraries to avoid much of the bureaucracy of the UK legislation, and offer a wider range of services.

The danger of licences is that the owner may see them as replacing rather than complementing existing statutory exceptions that benefit users. A licence which does not acknowledge that users have privileges under the law is an inhibiting rather than liberating instrument for information delivery. This is a major concern in a world where licences are becoming almost the norm to accompany access to information carriers. While printed materials continue to be made available under familiar conditions, increasingly CD-ROMs, videos, multimedia packs and, almost universally, online materials are accessible only under licence of some kind. Often these licences are not noticed by the user and the terms of the contract are not therefore readily known or understood but can still be binding. This can lead to unintentional breach of contract for which the copyright owner can often achieve greater damages than copyright infringement. Properly constructed licences can and should be a benefit to both parties, but the terms need to be examined carefully and owners need to know what they are entitled to license, and users equally to know what they need to be licensed to do and what they do not. Poor licences will eventually deter users from buying materials and do the owner no good; good licences can help to expand the market and enable the publisher to reach parts of the market that would not otherwise be attainable.

Stopping abuse: technical measures

One of the most controversial phenomena in the information world is the development of electronic rights management systems (ERMS). The theory behind these systems goes back to the 1980s with the research into the theoretical CITED (Copyright In Transmitted Electronic Documents) model for copyright management (www.newcastle.research.ec.org/esp-syn/text/5469.html). Any such system should provide for a range of controls including access (possibly variable within a single document depending on user status), payment, modification, use (copying, printing, networking, etc.) and use data. No one such system has yet been produced but CITED provided the model on which such systems subsequently are being designed. The benefit to owners of such systems is that they give them almost complete control over all aspects of the use of electronic documents. The economics of devising, installing and operating such systems are far from clear. The issue of control has become such a contentious one between owners and users that it significantly delayed the introduction of the latest European Directive on copyright (European Union, 2001). As a result the Directive contains clauses that require governments to give protection to ERMS but, at the same time, can override this protection if the owner does not implement a system that adequately reflects any national provisions to allow some exceptions for users. Many owners argue that exceptions to their exclusive right are unnecessary in modern times as they can be provided for by licences or through electronic mechanisms. Users see this as a real threat to access and have fought long and hard to retain the balance between ownership and use. Publishers, in particular, have pressed for the removal of such concepts as 'fair dealing/use' in a digital age but it is worth noting that the preamble to the 1996 WIPO Copyright Treaty (www.wipo.int/treaties/ip/copyright/copyright.html) does affirm the validity of the concept of exceptions in any context, as the preamble says: '*Recognising* the need to maintain a balance between the rights of authors and the larger public interest, particularly education, research and access to information, as reflected in the Berne Convention'.

Complete and unfettered control would give copyright owners a monopoly they have never enjoyed in modern times and would severely limit access to information. Many owners give assurances, sincerely meant, that they would not implement total control but these are given in a technological environment that is in a state of constant flux and an economic world that is in a similar state for publishing in general. Guarantees, sincerely meant now, may have to be overturned in two, five or ten years' time and the setting of precedents is more important than vague statements of good intent.

Expressing what we think

The right to protect what we create has occupied a large part of this chapter – but why? Essentially because it is this ownership of forms of expression that both underpins and undermines the other two element of this trinity of rights. As the *Universal declaration of human rights* famously states in Article 19 (United Nations, 1948), 'Everyone has the right to freedom of opinion and expression; this right includes freedom to hold opinions without interference and to seek, receive and impart information and ideas through any media and regardless of frontiers'.

However, holding opinions is one thing, expressing them is another. To quote an Eastern European politician who shall remain nameless: 'Freedom of thought, fine; freedom of expression, that's another matter altogether.' Once anyone expresses their opinions in any fixed format they immediately acquire copyright in them. As stated above, they may not wish to exercise it but, nonetheless, it is there to be exploited, neglected or abused just as for any other copyright material. In fact it is probably the case that the majority of material protected by copyright falls into the category of Article 19. So it would seem that the right to protect what we create and the right to express ourselves are complementary rather than contradictory.

Unfortunately the issue is not so clear. Very few ideas or opinions are totally the creation of an individual and each person feeds on the creativity of others to further build and expand nascent ideas or implant new ones. This then may require that the right to freedom of expression necessarily means using the creativity of others to express those ideas, thus causing a conflict of interest between these two fundamental principles.

Despite these conflicts the role of the librarian is clearly set out in the IFLA statement on libraries and intellectual freedom (International Federation of Library Associations, 1999):

> IFLA declares that human beings have a fundamental right to access to expressions of knowledge, creative thought and intellectual activity, and to express their views publicly.
>
> IFLA believes that the right to know and freedom of expression are two aspects of the same principle. The right to know is a requirement for freedom of thought and conscience.

This last sentence is crucial to the whole debate: intuitive thought is fine from a philosophical point of view but rarely exists in a total vacuum. Therefore the right to know (whether really defined as a 'right' or not) is fundamental to being able to develop forms of thought and expression. Professionally it is incumbent on librarians and information workers to acknowledge that 'It is the responsibility of libraries to guarantee the right of free expression by making available all the library's public facilities and services to all individuals and groups who need them' (Canadian Library Association, 1997).

Librarians have a duty to facilitate freedom of expression by making available whatever information users legitimately want to see. The subsequent legitimate use of that information is the responsibility of the user. Copyright owners, while recognizing the vital role of libraries in facilitating the exercise of human rights in the widest sense, still often become nervous about unlimited access to information. This is a problem which is becoming crucial in the world of the internet as libraries provide wider and wider access to information for all.

There will then appear the creeping paralysis of censorship unless great vigilance is exercised. As public and academic libraries offer a wider range of communications facilities, users may find themselves constrained as to the type of message they can compose, the persons to whom they can be sent and which websites can be accessed.

The other side of this coin is that those who create works and make them available usually want to provide wider access to their thoughts, ideas and creations. Making anything available to the public always carries risks with it. These may be economic (exploitation), personal (criticism) or intellectual (plagiarism). But it is only through this process that human thought and insight can continue to develop. Therefore it is clear that expressing what we think is as crucial as protecting what we create but there are areas in which they will come into conflict.

Gaining access

Creators have rights over what they create and the right to freedom of expression, but is there a right of access to what has been created and expressed? This concept is eloquently expressed by the Library and Information Association of New Zealand which asserts that (Library and Information Association of New Zealand Aotearoa, n.d.).

Free circulation of information safeguards our democratic society. The members of our society have a fundamental right to access to information. A basic right of citizens in a democratic society is access to information on matters which affect their lives. At times the interests of the individual have to be subordinated to the interests of the community . . . The right to be informed, to be consulted, and to intervene is essential and fundamental to the democratic process.

This is further reinforced by IFLA's own statement on libraries and intellectural freedom (International Federation of Library Associations, 1999).

IFLA declares that human beings have a fundamental right to access to expressions of knowledge, creative thought and intellectual activity, and to express their views publicly. . . . freedom of thought and freedom of expression are necessary conditions for freedom of access to information.

Gaining access is, therefore, not only the third side of the triangle but inextricably intertwined with the other two sides – protection and expression. But, as with the other two, there is an interplay between them that is both positive and negative. Clearly access can be gained only if there is something to access. Therefore the creative element in the triangle is essential, otherwise access becomes nothing but a theory. In the same way, unless there is freedom of expression, what point is there in allowing freedom of access? A system which allows the reader merely to consult and read what has been predetermined by some other authority is not freedom of access at all but merely censorship. But access raises the same problems as making information available from a different angle. Here it is important to distinguish between 'access' and 'availability'.

For many years IFLA has had a Universal Availability of Publications (UAP) programme (Cornish, 1996) and this has focused on making published material available, regardless of format or method of outlet. But availability is essentially a passive activity – here it is if you want it. So emphasis in the programme has changed to looking at the barriers to access such as legal issues, charging, linguistic issues and lack of knowledge of what actually is available.

Here the role of the library is essential. If libraries are not about providing access then it is difficult to see what they are about at all. Essentially the library is a neutral place providing access to any publicly available material or information regardless of its origin, content or form, and providing that access to any person legitimately entitled to use the library's services, again without any bias or favour. This neutrality is at the heart of gaining access to information and the pivotal role of the library is recognized in many codes of practice such as that from Australia (Australian Library and Information Association, 1997):

> Libraries [s]hould not exercise censorship in the selection, use or access to material by rejecting on moral, political, gender, sexual preference, racial or religious grounds alone material which is otherwise relevant to the purpose of the library and meets the standards which are appropriate to the library concerned. Material must not be rejected on the grounds that its content is controversial or likely to offend some sections of the library's community.

This accords with the UAP principle of 'Any published document to any person in any place at any time and in any format necessary to access it'.

Ironically the advent of the web should have swept away many barriers to access but others have taken the place of the traditional ones. For the barriers to freedom of access will be found mostly in the technology. Certainly there will be the technologically rich and the technologically poor but, from the perspective of rights, the basic issue will be payment for use. In the past, users of libraries have paid little, if anything, to use the library. The library bore the cost of acquiring and maintaining the collection and users were not expected to contribute to this. Any item in the library was freely available to any user (the ideal library philosophy). But in the world of the web, access may be denied to individual documents within a single website or whole websites unless and until the user can pay for it. And the crucial question will have to be faced: who is going to pay? Some will argue that providing access is simply another form of acquisition but, unlike conventional purchasing, demand to access websites is not finite like purchasing a book or subscribing to a journal. Yet, if the library fails to confront this issue then either limited budgets will soon be exhausted or users will be denied the access which all librarians believe they need to have.

Once more copyright is the key issue. How owners will allow access and under what terms they will issue licences will determine much of the shape of information provision and free flow in the next five years. We may need to shift from a 'free-for-all' attitude to a more discerning system based on social-security-type principles. Owners complain that their income is reduced by exceptions to copyright law such as 'fair dealing/use' but this concept is crucial if the idea of delivering information to anyone is to survive. In principle, owners are not averse to 'fair' use of their works but do not see why they should have to carry the cost of providing free information for society as a whole. Perhaps we are moving towards a system where those who can afford to pay for access to information do so and those who cannot are given assistance from public funds rather than everyone having the same access rights. If society decides to provide cheap housing to a sector of society, this is not done by making the builder subsidize the building but from the public purse. This change in financing access to information in the future will be a major one. But what must not be allowed is that access is denied to anyone. The economic models may change but the principles must not.

Conclusion

These three basic rights of protection, expression and access, however defined, are essential to the proper development of an information-based society. Their different functions and concerns are the cornerstone of society so that the perceived conflicts between them needs to be resolved in a creative manner for the benefit of all those concerned, whether creator, intermediary or user. Each is essential to the survival of the others but each can conflict with the others. However their interdependence makes it clear that their union is not dissoluble and they are indeed three expressions of two sides of a single coin.

References

Ashdown and Telegraph Group Ltd www.lawre ports.co.uk/civjul1.9.htm.

Australian Library and Information Association (1997) *Statement on professional ethics*, available at www.ifla.org/faife/ethics/aliacode.htm.

Blake, C. (2001) Is copyright really dead? In *Publishing after copyright: maintaining control. Proceedings of Keynote/EPS conference, March 2001*, 30–2, available at www.epsltd.com.

Canadian Library Association (1997) *Intellectual freedom position statement*, available at www.cla.ca.

CITED www.newcastle.research.ec.org/esp-syn/text/5469.html.

Cornish, G. P. (1996) Universal Availability of Publications (UAP), *Encyclopedia of Library and Information Science*, **58**, 325–46, available at www.ifla.org/ VI/2/uap.htm.

Cornish, G. P. (2000a) Copyright: black and white or just making you see red? In *New frontiers in grey literature: fourth international conference on grey literature, Washington, October 1999*, Amsterdam, Greynet Conference Bureau, 164–9.

Cornish, G. P. (2000b) *Understanding copyright in a week*, London, Hodder & Stoughton.

Cornish, G. P. (2001) *Copyright: interpreting the law for libraries, archives and information services*, 3rd rev. edn, London, Library Association Publishing.

European Union (2001) Directive 2001/29/EC of the European Parliament and of the Council of 22 May 2001 on the harmonisation of certain aspects of copyright and related rights in the information society, *Official Journal of the E.U. L167*, 22/06/2001, 10–19.

Hart, H. L. A. (1968) *Punishment and responsibility: essays in the philosophy of law*, Oxford, Clarendon.

International Federation of Library Associations (1999) *Statement on libraries and intellectual freedom*, available at www.faife.dk/policy/iflastat/iflastat.htm.

Library and Information Association of New Zealand Aotearoa (n.d.) *Access to information*, available at www.lianza.org.nz/index.htm.

Norman, S. (1999) *Copyright in public libraries*, 4th edn, London, Library Association Publishing.

Rowland, F. (1997) *Print journals: fit for the future?*, available at www.ariadne.ac.uk/issue7/fytton/intro.html.

Shavell, S. (2000) *Principles*, Chapter 7, available at http://econ.bu.edu/Weiss/Ec337/Shavell/bg7-1e.pdf.

UK. Department of Trade and Industry: Creative Industries Intellectual Property Group (2000) *The report from the Intellectual Property Group of the Government's Creative Industries Task Force*, London, Patent Office.

United Nations (1948) *Universal declaration of human rights*, New York, UN, available at www.udhr.org/.

WIPO Copyright Treaty and Agreed Statements concerning the WIPO Copyright Treaty (adopted in Geneva on December 20, 1996), available at www.wipo.int/clea/docs/en/wo/wo033en.htm.

10
Watching what happens to information about people: data protection

J. Eric Davies

I don't care what is written about me so long as it isn't true.

Dorothy Parker

Introduction

People and organizations have been noting down personal information for some time. Some of the earliest examples of recorded information survive on clay tablets in Sumeria. These 'abbreviated jottings', as Sampson (1985) calls them, of some 5000 years ago amount to administrative notes documenting things like tax payments and distribution of goods. Since they described somebody's payments and receipts they were/are personal information. Such incidental information about people – rich and famous, humble and poor – has given us much of our perspective on history. Culturally, we would be all the poorer without it. We could ponder, however, whether the people involved would have appreciated their personal affairs being paraded around during their lifetime, let alone being scrutinized for the next few millennia.

Formal gathering of information about people has also been important throughout the ages. The roll call for taxation at Bethlehem some 2000 years ago is but one example of data gathering that has become embedded in the cultural and historical canon. In the UK the Domesday Book is the manifestation of another, and the decennial censuses of the last century and a half or so have also added to the record. There is clearly no scarcity of personal information.

Nowadays, the exchanges of daily life, from where we live, how we learn and what we consume, to what we do at work, our financial standing and our state of health, all involve transactions that are recorded by a range of agencies; and it needs to be so if affairs are to proceed smoothly and efficiently. On the other hand, arguably, there do need to be limits on unfettered gathering and use of personal information if individuals are to enjoy a reasonable degree of freedom and privacy. One has only to take pause and consider just how many agencies typically hold data in some shape or form about one, to realize that the strands of information extend a great distance. What, why and how things are done with that information forms the basis of data protection.

The impetus for data protection

It is hard to imagine that compilers of the Domesday Book were particularly preoccupied with the fair obtaining of the information gathered though, for many reasons, they would have been keen to ensure its accuracy. King Herod does not appear to have been troubled with the niceties of respecting client confidentiality either when he quizzed the Three Wise Men. The idea that personal information deserves, and needs to be afforded protection is a relatively new one. Still more recent is the act of enshrining this concept in legislation. The earliest example of data protection law is credited to the Lander of Hesse in Germany in 1970.

Personal privacy has occupied people for some time. The United Nations *Universal declaration of human rights* (1948) asserts an entitlement to privacy as does the *European convention for the protection of human rights* (1950) from the Council of Europe. In the UK, privacy came under the scrutiny of the government-appointed Younger Committee (Committee on Privacy, 1972). It took a broad view of the topic and a more detailed review of data protection was later undertaken by another government-appointed committee under the chairmanship of Sir Norman Lindop (Committee on Data Protection, 1978).

Although current attention regarding data protection focuses on the activities of the European Union, that institution came relatively late to the field in terms of tangible output. Both the Council of Europe (1981) and the Organisation for Economic Co-operation and Development (1981) were in the van of initiatives to encourage the adoption of data protection measures by individual states, the former through a treaty opened for signature in 1981, and the latter with a set of guidelines published in the same year.

Concern about data protection has, to a large extent, been engendered by the advent of mass data processing and the power and potential that it has brought in its wake. It soon became apparent that the risks, some might even say threats, posed by inappropriate and unscrupulous use of machine and information could be damaging to a person's interests. The attitude prevailing, at least in the UK, is neatly summarized in a section of a government document, *Computers and privacy* (UK. Home Office, 1975):

> What is special about computers?
>
> None of the functions carried out by computers within information systems is different in kind from those which are, or could in principle be carried out by traditional methods. But there are important differences in the way, and the speed at which those functions can be performed by computer systems on the one hand, and by traditional systems on the other.
>
> The speed of computers, their capacity to store, combine, retrieve and transfer data, their flexibility and the low unit cost of the work which they can do have the following practical implications for privacy:
>
> (1) they facilitate the maintenance of extensive record systems and the retention of data in those systems;
>
> (2) they can make data easily and quickly accessible from many distant points;
>
> (3) they make it possible for data to be transferred quickly from one information system to another;
>
> (4) they make it possible for data to be combined in ways which might not otherwise be practicable;
>
> (5) because the data are stored, processed and often transmitted in a form which is not directly intelligible, few people may know what is in the records, or what is happening to them.

Lest the technology be pilloried too heavily, it is worth noting that it is what is done with the technology, for good or ill, that remains the fundamental issue. As Michael Gorman (2000) puts it, in a recent book that has a very balanced overview of privacy issues and libraries from a mainly US perspective, 'it is the human use and misuse of technology that arouses the emotions, and it is the human use and misuse of technology that we should observe, study, and seek to amend for the better'. He goes on to emphasize 'the point is that it is not technology that is the enemy of privacy but our joyful use of technology'.

The current thinking is that the need to safeguard the use of personal data is independent of the medium on which it is recorded, the mode of its processing and manipulation and the vehicle for its dissemination. This more generic approach accommodates manual paper records as well as digital data in its purview. Moreover, it includes other manifestations of personal information including electronic images and sound. It has been recognized that a person's interests can just as easily be compromised and damaged by inappropriate use of a piece of paper as they can through careless use of a mobile telephone, or misapplication of information gathered on a CCTV surveillance system.

It needs to be appreciated that legislation for data protection has several driving factors. There is, of course, the desire to safeguard personal data as a human right, but legislators have been equally concerned to facilitate the transborder flow of information engendered by commerce in a global 'knowledge economy'. Nations wishing to exchange data need to adopt a common approach to data protection that ensures easy movement of safeguarded information. Pan-national initiatives, discussed earlier, have followed this approach.

Current legislation in the UK derives from a Directive (1995) from the European Union and its objectives, as rehearsed in Article 1, are as concerned with the free flow of data between member states as they are with the fundamental rights and freedoms of natural persons:

Article 1 Object of the Directive:
1. In accordance with this Directive, Member States shall protect the fundamental rights and freedoms of natural persons, and in particular their right to privacy with respect to the processing of personal data.
2. Member States shall neither restrict nor prohibit the free flow of personal data between Member States for reasons connected with the protection afforded under paragraph 1.

Defining data protection

Arriving at a satisfactory definition of data protection is not easy since it is an amalgam of ethical, legal, technical, managerial and social factors that impinge on information management. According to the British Standard, BS-ISO 2382 (1986, Section 08.06.04), data protection is defined as:

> The implementation of appropriate administrative, technical or physical means to guard against the unauthorised interrogation and use of procedures and data.

A clearer focus on personal information is appropriate and this can be found in the definition of privacy protection which is in the same Standard (1986, Section 08.06.03):

> The implementation of appropriate administrative, technical, and physical safeguards to ensure the security and confidentiality of data records and to protect both security and confidentiality against any threat or hazard that could result in substantial harm, embarrassment, inconvenience, or unfairness to any individual about whom such information is maintained.

These do rather concentrate on the security and privacy aspects of the topic, and although these aspects are important, data protection, as has been discussed earlier, is made up of more.

The following is a definition that the author has developed and found workable over a number of years:

The creation of a legal, social and technical framework through which are achieved the objectives of ensuring that information pertaining to individuals is obtained, stored, used and transmitted in such a way that it cannot be consulted, applied, extracted, altered or destroyed by unauthorized persons, or to the detriment of an individual's interests.

Data protection is then a multi-faceted topic that goes beyond considerations of personal privacy and confidentiality of information although they remain vitally important aspects. Data protection also embraces such features as making fair use of whatever information is acquired as well as of ensuring its reliability and integrity. Thus, the expectation is that legitimately acquired personal information will not be used in such a way that it undermines a person's reputation, activities or interests and that whatever is used is reasonably accurate because misleading information would be damaging. It is this fusion of factors that gives the subject its complexity both in terms of fundamental theory and practical day-to-day management.

Legal underpinning for data protection in the UK

The current enactment regarding data protection in the UK is the Data Protection Act (1998). The full text is available on the web at www.legislation. hmso.gov.uk/acts/acts1998/19980029.htm. Its purpose is described in its preamble as 'an Act to make new provision for the regulation of the processing of information relating to individuals, including the obtaining, holding, use or disclosure of such information'.

The Act specifies in some detail what is acceptable activity with personal data and it creates mechanisms for monitoring and regulating the use of that data in order to protect the interest of the individual. A person's right of scrutiny of data and provision for redress in the event of its misuse are also included. In addition, the Act identifies special types of information and cases of use where different treatment, including exemption, is appropriate. The interpretation of data embraces manual records on paper as well as digital and other manifestations.

Definitions

As with many pieces of legislation, definitions are important because terms used in the Act have very specific meanings. A few important ones are summarized in brief below. The Act should be consulted for the complete wording of definitions noted here, and for additional ones.

Perhaps one of the most important things to define is *data*. At their simplest they are described as information which:

(a) is being processed by means of equipment operating automatically in response to instructions given for that purpose, or

(b) is recorded with the intention that it should be processed by means of such equipment, or

(c) is recorded as part of a relevant filing system or with the intention that it should form part of a relevant filing system.

Processing data is given a very wide meaning in the Act; it covers activity from beginning to end, from collection to disposal. In the Act, *processing* is described as: obtaining, recording or holding the information or data or carrying out any operation or set of operations on the information or data, including:

(a) organisation, adaptation or alteration of the information or data,

(b) retrieval, consultation or use of the information or data,

(c) disclosure of the information or data by transmission, dissemination or otherwise making available, or

(d) alignment, combination, blocking, erasure or destruction of the information or data.

People who have a role in the use of data are also given precise definitions. Thus, a *data controller* is a person who (either alone or jointly or in common with other persons) determines the purposes for which and the manner in which any personal data are, or are to be, processed. As such the data controller carries the responsibility for what is done.

A *data processor* is any person (other than an employee of the data controller) who processes the data on behalf of the data controller. It should be noted that since a data processor undertakes the processing on behalf of a data controller, consequent responsibility for data protection remains with the data controller. It is therefore very advisable that the data processor's obligations and operations are covered by appropriate contractual arrangements.

Personal data are data which relate to a living individual who can be identified:

(a) from those data, or

(b) from those data and other information which is in the possession of, or is likely to come into the possession of, the data controller. It includes any expression of opinion about the individual and any indication of the intentions of the data controller or any other person in respect of the individual.

An individual who is the subject of personal data such as that described above is defined as a *data subject*.

The Act identifies a range of information that is particularly important to the privacy interests of an individual. Such information is termed *sensitive personal data* and additional provisions regarding its processing are specified. *Sensitive personal data* means personal data consisting of information as to:

(a) the racial or ethnic origin of the data subject,

(b) their political opinions,

(c) their religious beliefs or other beliefs of a similar nature,

(d) whether they are a member of a trade union,

(e) their physical or mental health or condition,

(f) their sexual life,

(g) the commission or alleged commission by them of any offence, or

(h) any proceedings for any offence committed or alleged to have been committed by them, the disposal of such proceedings or the sentence of any court in such proceedings.

Acceptable activity

Generally, the Act tends not to discriminate between the purposes to which data are applied, but there are significant exceptions. There is a lengthy list of exemptions to the Act's provisions, and these are generally specified in relation to the purposes to which information is put. Exemptions are described later. In addition, the Act has specified a category of *special purposes* which include:

(a) the purposes of journalism

(b) artistic purposes

(c) literary purposes.

These *special purposes* are characterized by a more 'liberal' approach to regulation and to some extent this is understandable. For example, investigative journalism can hardly succeed if the informed consent of the subject of the investigation has to be acquired before any information is gathered. Perhaps this provision illustrates the European origin of the basic Directive from which the Act is derived and the characteristic freedom of expression that is embodied in law. There is a 'public interest' test that can be applied to the interpretation of special purposes. The Commissioner has made it clear, however, that artistic or literary purposes cannot be used as an omnibus description to avoid complying with the legislation.

Acceptable activity is specified through a series of eight general principles to be followed in activities involving personal data. Users must operate in accordance with the principles and other provision of the law and are liable to sanctions and prosecution for failing to do so. Briefly summarized, the eight principles require personal data to be:

1 processed fairly and lawfully [detailed conditions are specified]
2 obtained and processed only for specified and lawful purposes
3 adequate, relevant and not excessive
4 accurate and, where necessary, kept up to date
5 not kept for longer than is necessary
6 processed in accordance with the rights of data subjects
7 processed under appropriate technical and organizational security measures
8 not transferred to a country or territory outside the European Economic Area unless that country or territory ensures an adequate level of data protection.

The Information Commissioner

Monitoring and regulating activity involving personal data is the responsibility of the *Office of the Information Commissioner* which has powers to identify, record, approve and direct the activities of data users with reference to the principles and the law. Activities have to be formally notified to the Commissioner who maintains a *Register of Notifications from Data Controllers*. This is accessible through the Commissioner's website and is searchable by data controller name (www.dpr.gov.uk/search.html).

Except for examples of data use, or types of data controller covered by exemption, operating without notification is prohibited and a punishable offence, as is failing to update a notification if practice changes. Most data processing activity involving personal information has to be notified. A notification currently costs £35, lasts for one year and is renewable. It is a relatively straightforward process and can be undertaken by completing a form, or by telephone to a help-line when a draft notification form is compiled for later confirmation. Details that have to be notified include:

- the data controller's name and contact details
- purposes
- data subjects
- data classes
- disclosures
- overseas [non-European Economic Area] transfers
- security measures [which, for obvious reasons, do not get published in the *Register!*].

The Commissioner has important powers of regulation and scrutiny if circumstances warrant. These extend to serving notices on data controllers and to responding to requests from individuals to assess whether activity is being undertaken properly or not, if they have formally sought a 'Request for Assessment'. If the Commissioner is satisfied that a data controller has contravened or is contravening any of the data protection principles, the Commissioner may serve him with an 'enforcement notice' requiring compliance within a specified time. If the Commissioner needs to know more about a data controller's activity, say in acting on a Request for Assessment, before deciding on the merits of the situation then the Commissioner may serve an 'information notice' (or a 'special information notice' if processing for special purposes is being investigated). Such notices require the data controller to furnish the Commissioner with information needed within a specified time.

In practice the Commissioner has tended generally to develop a positive approach to regulation and enforcement that relies on encouraging good practice and compliance through information and discussion rather than seeking litigation at every and any opportunity. The result is that the Commission is held in respect by the mass of people and organizations that use personal data. Examples do occur, however, of cases being brought to court and these are noted in the Commissioner's annual report (Information Commissioner, 2001). There is a further mechanism that offers assurance to those who are wary of the power that the Commissioner wields, especially regarding the serving of notices. Appeals against the Commissioner's decisions and actions can be taken to the Data Protection Tribunal. There is further scope for appeal, on a point of law, against the Tribunal's decisions by recourse to the High Court.

Individuals' rights

The interests of the individual about whom data are being gathered are looked after by several mechanisms in the legislation. In most circumstances the individual has to give informed consent to processing, and in the case of 'sensitive data' acquiring consent is obligatory. Furthermore, the individual has, with some exceptions, the right to establish what data is held about them and to see a copy of any material so held. Normally, a request for access to personal data must be met within 40 days and a fee of up to £10 may be charged for this. Further provisions in the law allow for the correction, or even deletion, of inaccurate information. In addition, the sources and disclosures of inaccurate data have to be revealed and appropriate rectification made. Individuals may take complaints about data controllers' activities to the Commissioner and where they wish an activity to be investigated make a formal Request for Assessment.

Individuals may object to processing if they are likely to suffer substantial damage and distress. Moreover, they may seek compensation through the courts for damage and associated distress that they suffer as a result of any use of personal information about them. They also have a right to object to decisions being made about them that are entirely based on automated decision systems; these are being increasingly used to filter applications for credit cards, life assurance and other transactions, for example. In addition, they may also object to receiving unsolicited direct marketing material or 'junk mail'.

Exemptions

The Act specifies a great many exemptions to its provisions and many of them are rather specialized. Moreover, the degree of exemption varies from category to category. A brief summary of the types of purpose covered by exemptions is given here. The full text of the Act should be consulted for specific detail. Exemptions to the Act apply in the case of information being applied to:

- protecting national security
- prevention of crime and offences relating to taxation
- health, education and social work where there are conditions on data subject access
- regulatory activity such as that undertaken by agencies concerned with the

protection of members of the public, for example Ombudsmen and similar 'watchdogs'

- journalism, literature and art as they represent 'special purposes' that warrant a degree of protection of expression
- research, history and statistics
- information available to the public by, or under any enactment
- disclosures required by law or made in connection with legal proceedings
- domestic household purposes.

Exemptions also apply to information pertaining to:

- confidential job references
- the Armed Forces
- crown employment and ministerial appointments
- management forecasts
- corporate finance
- negotiations where a disclosure would change the balance of an advantage
- examination marks where a longer period is allowed to comply with data subject access
- examination scripts
- legal professional privilege
- information liable to result in self-incrimination.

Global issues, transborder data flow and safe harbours

The importance of data protection to global information exchange was noted earlier, and it is clear that this is an increasingly important aspect of transactions in the knowledge economy. It is now hard to imagine a world without extensive transborder data flow for a variety of purposes. The internet functions as a universal conduit for all kinds (and qualities) of information. Such traffic, where it involves personal information, raises the issues regarding privacy, reliability and integrity rehearsed earlier.

The UK legislation is very clear about the need for adequate measures to safeguard any data moved out of the European Economic Area. This has raised a particular set of problems with one key 'player' in the global arena – the USA – because its approach to data protection, characterized as it is by a considerable degree of voluntary self-regulation, differs vastly from that of the European model. (Indeed, it can be observed that there is a general aversion to overmuch Federal control and legislation in the USA.) A solution of sorts to this situation, which took some time to negotiate, has been found through the formation of a 'safe harbour' concept by the US Department of Commerce (*Export Portal – Safe Harbor* www.exports.gov/safeharbor). Through this arrangement organizations can affirm their compliance with prescribed controls that then enable them to operate globally. This 'self-certification' is overseen by the US Department of Commerce which publishes a list of participating organizations.

Priorities in managing personal data – policies and practices

Complying with UK data protection legislation and following good practice are formidable tasks which need to be taken seriously. Information managers have a great deal to contribute in this respect through their understanding of the fundamentals of gathering, assessing, organizing and exploiting information. Observing good data protection practice should be ingrained in an organization. A starting point should be the adoption of a formal policy that endorses the data protection principles and commits the organization to working to achieve the highest standards of performance involving personal data. The policy should cover data regarding those inside the organization, such as employees, as well as those persons with whom the organization deals externally. It should also be reviewed at intervals to ensure that it remains relevant.

It is important that someone take corporate responsibility for managing data protection; in larger organizations this may warrant a substantial portion of someone's time. Creating such a role ensures that there is a single identifiable point for queries and that someone is charged with seeing that policy is implemented and that operations are monitored.

A key feature of good data protection management is the need to ensure that the amount and nature of information that is being used is really required. This can be achieved through an information needs assessment exercise. Questioning what is done, why and how, and whether it can be done with less, can be advantageous. The more streamlined the use of personal data, the better for the organization – not only in terms of compliance, but also in terms of overall efficiency.

A policy will not be implemented successfully unless it is properly disseminated and understood throughout an organization. Therefore, appropriate awareness raising and training initiatives are needed, and these should be complemented with adequate process design and supervision covering all stages of the use of personal information – from acquisition to disposal – and relating to all types of personal information. Particular attention needs to be paid to the design of mechanisms to accommodate queries from data subjects, and in particular formal data access requests and complaints. In addition, a careful balance needs to be maintained between ensuring compliance through monitoring workplace activity, and behaving ethically and legally in managing staff.

Extensive detail on the practicalities of working within the data protection legislation is available in a British Standards Institution publication (1999) which the author has prepared in conjunction with others.

What recent research tells us

A project recently completed at Loughborough University (Sturges, Teng and Iliffe, 2001) looked at a whole range of privacy issues relating mainly to academic and workplace libraries. The findings revealed that there was a considerable degree of trust by the general user population in the way libraries and librarians used personal data and this was reassuring, particularly when set alongside people's attitudes to how other agencies were thought to handle their data. Whether this faith in the system was justified is another matter. The evidence suggested that the level of awareness, and depth of knowledge of data protection matters among managers was not overwhelming. Interviews with systems vendors, for example, suggested that when managers were assessing new systems, the systems vendors were rarely, if ever, quizzed about the privacy and data protection measures that their systems incorporated.

One of the most positive outcomes of the project was the creation of a set of guidelines for the development of a privacy policy. It should be stressed that this was not a draft or sample policy, but more usefully, a set of guidance notes that identified the stages of developing a local policy and the features that it should cover.

Conclusion

It is worth asking 'Is the UK Data Protection Act working?' The answer would seem to be a qualified – 'yes!' The whole system does allow data to be used sensibly and properly while at the same time there are reasonable safeguards for individuals against the data controllers who may be careless, or worse. Legitimate personal data processing in the UK appears by no means to have been hindered by the legislation.

The relatively few cases of data protection infringement that emerge (rightly) attract high visibility, but usually things are put right very quickly and individuals have access to recompense. Many are the result of flawed management and supervision, or technical breakdown, rather than some sinister design to undermine confidence in personal data processing. It would be naive to think that we live in a perfect world where people don't make mistakes and systems don't fail. That they don't do so that often is a tribute to the professionalism and commitment of those entrusted with all facets of managing information.

> Many the wonders but nothing walks stranger than man . . . .

> Clever beyond all dreams
>   the inventive craft that he has
>   which may drive him one time or another to well or ill.
> When he honors the laws of the land and the gods sworn right
>   high indeed is his city; but stateless the man
>   who dares to dwell with dishonor.
> > Chorus in *Antigone* by Sophocles.

References

British Standards Institution (1986) *BS ISO 2382/8 Information processing systems – Vocabulary – Part 08. Control, integrity and security*, London, BSI.

British Standards Institution (1999) *Data protection – guide to the practical implementation of the Data Protection Act 1998*, BSI-DISC PD 0012, London, BSI.

Committee on Privacy (1972) *Report of the committee on privacy*, Cmnd 5012, London, HMSO (the Younger Report).

Committee on Data Protection (1978) *Report of the committee on data protection*,

Cmnd 7341, London, HMSO (the Lindop Report).

Council of Europe (1950) *European convention for the protection of human rights and fundamental freedoms*, Article 8; Section 1, Strasbourg, Council of Europe.

Council of Europe (1981) *Convention for the protection of individuals with regard to automatic processing of personal data*, European Treaty Series 108), Strasbourg, Council of Europe.

Great Britain, *The Data Protection Act* (1998) (Public General Acts 1998 – Chapter 29), London, Stationery Office.

European Union (1995) Directive 95/46/EC of the European Parliament and of the Council of 24th Oct. 1995 on the protection of individuals with regard to the processing of personal data on the free movement of such data, *Official Journal of the E.U. Part (L)*, (23rd November), 31.

Gorman, M. (2000) *Our enduring values: librarianship in the 21st century*, Chicago, American Library Association, 144–57.

Information Commissioner (2001) *Annual report and accounts for the year ending 31st March 2001*, HC2 (2001/2002), London, Stationery Office.

Organisation for Economic Co-Operation and Development (1981) *Guidelines on the protection of privacy and transborder flows of personal data*, Paris, OECD.

Sampson, G. (1985) *Writing systems*, London, Hutchinson.

Sophocles (1960) Antigone. In Grene, D. and Lattimore, R. (trans), *Greek tragedies*, Chicago, University of Chicago Press.

Sturges, P., Teng V. and Iliffe, U. (2001) User privacy in the digital library environment: a matter of concern for information professionals, *Library Management*, **22** (8/9), 364–70.

UK. Home Office (1975) *Computers and privacy*, Cmnd. 6353, London, HMSO.

United Nations (1948) *Universal declaration of human rights*, New York, United Nations, Article 12.

11

Electronic publishing: what difference does it make?

Claire Warwick

Introduction

Technological change has always caused anxiety for those people whose task it is to negotiate the change between old and new media. Deprived of familiar points of reference, both publishers and users may feel disorientated when faced with new publication and distribution media. Although this chapter discusses the effects of electronic publication at the beginning of the 21st century, it is instructive to begin by looking at these kinds of anxieties from a much older perspective:

> To whom shall I give this handsome new book?
> Just polished up with dry pumice
> Cornelius, shall I give it to you?
> Since you thought something of my trifles
> Even when you alone in Italy had dared
> To set out the whole history of the world
> In three books.
> By Jupiter, that's a labour of learning
> Take this book then, for what it's worth
> And virgin patroness, may it last for a century or more.
>
> Catullus, *Carmina*, I.I

This is by the poet Catullus (1893), who lived in the first century BC. But the problems that worry him are those which still preoccupy those interested in the effect of novel publication media. It has become a truism to compare the revolution brought about by electronic publication to that caused by the invention of printing. Yet here we can see an author agonizing about the revolution caused by the beginning of publishing itself. Compared with this, printing itself was simply a technological refinement.

Who could blame an author then for asking questions. What is the future of this new publication? What control does the author have over the reception and readership of it? Where does it fit into the current market? Will it be preserved for posterity? How much information can the current technological medium cope with? Will other authors approve?

Catullus is expressing an anxiety in many ways caused by a changing medium. Whatever the format, his friend has clearly packed a huge amount of information into a small space of three scrolls. It is almost as if he is demanding a new 'delivery mechanism' for the information which is almost too copious for a conventional publication to cope with. He was also living in an age where two cultures of information provision were co-existent. Only those with appropriate information skills could use the new technology of reading and writing. Authors no longer declaimed their texts to audiences, they wrote them down, but they were still read out by a slave. The voice was still a faster and more reliable delivery mechanism that the laborious copying of a text. But the fact that it was copied showed that there was a demand for the dissemination of written information, and that this could be done for profit.

All of these considerations should suggest parallels with our current situation. Electronic publishing is becoming more widely accepted and available. It is reaching more users and making profits for its producers. But two publication cultures are still co-existent. Like a book being written, but read out, most journals, for example, are still printed and delivered electronically. It is still not clear what the effects of electronic publishing are, or what they are likely to be.

By no means all readers now use electronic text. Even well-educated users in information-intensive jobs still use print more extensively. Others are enthusiastic about the possibility of the new medium to hold unprecedented amounts of information, and are willing to admire the hard work of those who create such information resources, but they are worried about the ways in which their work, and organizational culture may be affected by this. Those who work in this new medium rather anxiously release the products of our effort into the world, unsure about how well it will be regarded, and indeed how long it may last.

The effect of the book on society has indeed been massive. So successful is it as a publication medium that although Catullus poems are now printed in codex form, they have lasted ten times the years that he hopefully asks for. Ironically enough, even 200 years would be a remarkable lifespan for a digital publication, since some early electronic text can now not be read, after only ten years (Lee, 2001). Nevertheless technology progresses at a much faster pace now than in ancient Rome. So is it indeed possible to assess the impact that electronic publishing has had? Is it too early to make predications about their future?

Electronic publishing – definition

It is important to pause here and consider what is meant by electronic publishing. Defined broadly this could include anything that is produced in a non-paper-based form. Since the internet is such a powerful and ubiquitous medium, there is a danger that it is assumed to be synonymous with publications. This is misleading, since the web is no more a publication as such than the paper that a book is printed on. But inevitably, any web page can be thought of as an electronic publication, if it contains text, even if the site is primarily commercial, such as a flight booking site, or one that compares utility prices. To adopt this definition would almost inevitably force a consideration of the societal impact of the internet and web, or of e-commerce. This is far too big a subject for one chapter. The kind of electronic publication considered here, therefore, is that which is at least partially analogous to what we might consider a publication in more conventional form, such as a book, a dictionary, a bibliography or a newspaper, as opposed to one which might be compared to a bank, a café or a shop in the non-virtual world.

Electronic publishing – predictions

When electronic publications first began to be widely available in the late 1980s and early 1990s, some sweeping predictions were made about the impact that this would have. It was thought that our lives, the publishing industry and publication media would be changed forever. Collections of academic articles appeared in which the death of the book was discussed, and journalists predicted that in a very short time paper would be forgotten as a publication medium for their newspapers (Tuman, 1992; Nunberg, 1996; Finneran, 1996). Even relatively recent articles have predicted that libraries will become presentational warehouses for rare and antiquated books, while all new stock will be in electronic form (Friend, 2000). Meanwhile commercial interests have generated large amounts of promotional copy extolling the virtue of e-books, whether delivered via specialist readers, downloaded onto a PC desktop or a Palmtop, or even sent to a mobile phone. Such texts continue to be actively promoted by booksellers such as Barnes and Noble's online bookshop (www.barnesandnoble.com).

However, most of the predictions made about the obsolescence of the book have floundered because the needs of users have been ignored, and as Norman (1999) observes, such disregard for the users of technology can quickly endanger the success of even the best products. Commentators who predicted the imminent dominance of the electronic text ignored the considerable obstacle to the use of electronic publications, which is the move from the familiar, convenient delivery mechanism of print to the far less convenient computer screen. The problems presented by reading on a screen should not be underestimated, but remain unsolved. It is still not comfortable to read large amounts of text on screen (Benson, 2001). Even laptop computers are, in truth, not very portable, because of their size and weight and because the screen size and quality makes it hard to read much text at a time. Flat reading devices for e-books, such as the Gemstar Rocket e-bookman (www.ebook-gemstar.com) have also been developed. Xerox is even trying to develop electronic paper, which can be used in a kind of quasi-book fashion (Cleyle, 2001). However, none of these is as light, portable and comfortable on the eye as a book. Users have as yet not flocked to use such devices in significant numbers, for what may seem obvious reasons to all but the e-book industry.

Electronic books

Firms such as Adobe, Microsoft and Xerox remain committed to developing further e-book hardware and software. However, even if a lightweight reading device is developed it is not guaranteed to replace the printed book or newspaper. As Bolter (1991) observes, 'no one technology of writing has ever proven adequate for all needs'. Even if a technology ceases to be dominant it may survive because it fills a need. For certain types of text, print may always be the best method of delivery. This does not mean that it cannot coexist with the electronic text. The pencil still works perfectly well, despite the invention of the word-processor, because in certain conditions it is more suitable for the task in hand (Dauguid, 1996). When taking notes to write this chapter, for example, it was more convenient to use printed material and write notes on paper with a biro. Users stubbornly insist on choosing to read fiction in printed, paperback form and there is evidence that even experienced computer and internet users have not been inspired by the promise of online, electronic fiction (Rennie, 2001).

Electronic reference tools

Despite the ability to integrate annotation functions and text searching into e-books, most of them are just that, a book in electronic form. Some publishers realized relatively early on in the existence of electronic publications that this may not be the best way to capitalize on the advantages of electronic delivery (Landow, 1996a, 1996b). It was, they realized, preferable to offer users the ability to search the equivalent of thousands of books in seconds. Electronic production of information does, then, endanger the existence of the printed book as a reference source. Bibliographies and other reference works are much easier to consult online than in book form. Databases may also aggregate full-text content as well as reference listings. It is not surprising that such products as MEDLINE, Lexis Nexis and OCLC's citations indexes have been successful. It is simply much easier for users to search for information in an electronic database or collection than to flick through perhaps multiple volumes of a reference work. There is however an important difference between these products and e-books, and it lies in the method of their use. Information is retrieved from a reference source, which is not designed to be read. An e-book is usually the result of digitizing a source that was designed for reading, and print is still better suited to this complex activity.

Catullus marvels at how much information can be packed into three sheets, but he makes it clear that he admires the writer as a poet rather than merely an information provider. It may seem banal to say that when we read we are looking for more than information, but this is a fact that electronic delivery makes us reconsider. A scholarly monograph is judged on its argument not just the number of facts in it, a literary novel is judged by the artistry of the writer.

Electronic media can deliver far more information than a human mind can recall, and can search it far faster then our brains. This ability must have an impact on the work pattern of those who use electronic publications. Organizational roles where data are simply collected, organized or presented must be affected by this. However, human agency is still key to this process of using such electronic sources. As Jonscher (1999) observes, databases are an ideal ways of organizing informational content. However, the significance of such content must be processed by the human brain, and it is this step which is almost impossible to automate. A database like Lexis Nexis can be searched for records in a matter of seconds, but it will still need a lawyer's accumulated experience and powers of reasoning to decide how such information might be used to win a case. Both Jonscher (1999) and Stoll (2000) are concerned that the dominance of computers and electronic resources in schools is, ironically, in danger of producing a population which is ill equipped to use such resources in their working lives. If time in the curriculum is made available for teaching ICT, then other subjects must suffer. It is history, literature and other humanities subjects, they argue, that teach students to reason, analyse and evaluate large amounts of complex information. It is these skills that will be even more crucial when electronic delivery allows access to ever growing amounts of information. Yet there is a risk that students are being trained to use a computer to retrieve data, but not to perform the kind of analysis of it that can only be done by the human brain.

It appears that it is important not to be too radical in the use of electronic publications, and to remember that the same traditional skills and practices are vital in the use of electronic materials as they were in printed text. This kind of conservatism of practice may help to explain why one particular type of electronic publication is arguably the most successful type of all. That is the electronic journal.

Electronic journals

E-journals and their methods of usage are perhaps midway between the e-book and the full-text or reference collection. Users still read journal articles, but traditionally it was relatively rare for a user to read the whole of a given journal issue. Users also need to search for articles on a certain topic across a range of journals or from a back run of issues. Electronic delivery of journals allows this kind of searching to be performed much more easily than when dealing with multiple title pages of a print journal. Access to articles is also facilitated when users can access an article online, as opposed to having to deal with large bound volumes of several issues at a time. Libraries also favour electronic delivery, since it saves shelf space and the cost of binding volumes. However, the actual usage of the material remains very similar to that of printed articles (Tomney and Burton, 1998). In essence users tend to read the contents having first printed them out.

Although some journals are electronic only, the most prestigious in any given field are usually those that appear in print as well. Even those journals that appear only in electronic form tend still to adhere to conventions such as having release dates for discrete, numbered issues. There is no reason why an electronic-only journal should do this, except that users are accustomed to such practices, and alerting them to the production of a new issue is a way of informing them about new material being produced (Wilson, 1999). Some electronic-only journals have also tried the use of innovative practices such as adding discussion forums or staging online seminars. But these have not proven to be a success. Hopkins (2000) speculates that, at least in the case of humanities users, this is because users feel uncomfortable about opening up their ideas to public discussion in an unfinished form. They prefer to wait until they are sure of what they want to say, then publish it in a conventional article. Once again it seems that the impact electronic publications have is driven not so much by the technology and its potential, but by the users and the culture and expectations they bring to the use of such publications.

It is also theoretically possible for articles produced in electronic form to depart from traditional models as seen in printed journals. However, despite some early experiments in online journals such as *JIME* (www-jime.open.ac.uk/), this is rarely the case. Ayers (2002) feels that the form of online scholarly journal articles has quickly settled for the most conservative option, despite the possibilities offered by the electronic medium. He has therefore set out to prove that historical research done as part of his Valley of the Shadow project (www.iath.virginia.edu/vshadow2/) can indeed be presented in an article which makes radical departures from the traditional linear argument. Accordingly he and Mark Thomas have produced an article (2002) which is structured as a hypertext, and can be entered at several different points. It allows them to link together key findings, and also to include complex coloured maps and tables which would be unlikely to be included in a print publication. The response of the historical community is not yet known, but the article is now under review, and it will be fascinating to see whether this changes the way that scholarly articles are written, or remains an interesting but isolated experiment.

Multimedia

The Ayers and Thomas article makes use of the potential of electronic media to easily integrate other media. There is, however, a danger of multimedia being integrated just because it is possible to do so, and with no clear idea why it adds to the experience of reading a text. It is, for example, possible to appreciate the Yeats poem 'Lapis Lazuli' without seeing a photograph of a sculpture in the stone or hearing a reading of the poem, as is possible in the edition by O'Donnell and Thrush (1996). Indeed this may be the point of reading a poem, that it makes users exercise their visual imagination as a result of the words they have read. It is important to consider whether an electronic edition of a literary text, including every single image of the original manuscript, or pictures of the author and where they lived, is so much better than a traditional printed book, or whether it is any more useful to most users (Flanders, 1997; Robinson, 1997). This becomes especially important when the cost of the electronic products to an individual, library or institution is much higher than the same items in print.

Some early critics saw the possibility of the integrated multimedia text as disturbing. Bolter (1996) feels that the image is in danger of taking over electronic text and rendering us illiterate. He argues that as a result of the importance of the web and the number of images it uses, the image may become more important than the word. Bolter complains that 'nobody' now creates web pages that contain text alone, and seems to take this as a symbol of the death knell of text in electronic form. As with many predictions about electronic publishing, this has so far failed to happen, perhaps ironically, because of the technological limitation of the internet as a delivery mechanism. Web designers are now well aware of the problems caused by large image files which make the page slow to load and thus deter users (Gillespie, 2002).

Bolter and critics like him who become fixated on the technology often seem to forget that whether they are delivered on the internet or on paper, not all publications are alike, simply because there are words in them, and nor is the way that they are used. It would seem ridiculous to assert that a newspaper, a novel and an academic monograph are seen merely as publications, and that they are used in the same way, by the same type of person. If a magazine uses a large number of photos, this is not taken as proof of the death of printed crime fiction. Once more, it appears that the effects of electronic publication technology are less radical than some commentators thought they might be.

The integration of multimedia into publications is also not something that we should be surprised about. As print technology progressed, authors took the opportunity to integrate what we might now call multimedia into their text. By the 17th century the ability to make prints of images led to the popularity of emblem books, which integrated poetry with pictures, neither or which could be fully interpreted without the other. It is not surprising that there are already electronic versions of emblem books, such as those produced by Adams and Graham (2000), and Barker, Feltham and Guthrie (2001). In the 19th and 20th centuries the cases of the *Illustrated London News* or *Life* magazine or *Picture Post* show how popular journalism integrated the image into news gathering a long time before the BBC website was produced.

Commercial e-publications

Electronic delivery has the potential to change the way that academic publications are produced. This was initially a market in which commercial publishers were very interested. Some of the earliest forays into commercial electronic publication were made by Chadwyck-Healey. Rather like Cornelius who is celebrated for producing the whole history of the world in one publication, they grasped the potential of the CD-ROM to make available large amount of textual data. Early publications were not simply reference listings or numerical data but comprised the whole of English poetry from 900 AD to 1900, or the entire works of Goethe. Thus allowing readers not simply to access literature in books, but to search it.

The *Canterbury tales* was an early venture into this kind of publishing, a collaboration between an academic research team and a commercial publisher, Cambridge University Press (Robinson et al., 1996; Solopova, 2000). It is planned to produce all of the *Canterbury tales* on CD-ROM and that each tale will include all possible manuscript sources. This was originally greeted with much excitement by libraries, publishers and some academics. However the planned series is taking a considerable time to produce, given the small editorial team. CUP also seems to have lost faith in such products, and while later titles in the series may appear in due course, it has failed to increase its list of similar humanities titles. This may be due to doubt that there is enough demand for such products for them to make a profit. This seems to be because while a small number of medieval literature scholars were delighted by the Chaucer CD-ROM, it failed to attract the vast majority of academics, teachers or students in the wider field. Most students and teachers did not change the culture of reading Chaucer in book form, and did not perceive a necessity to use the text in electronic form, thus demand remained small. This must have been disappointing for the publishers when Chaucer is an author who is central to the curriculum at both school and university level. And it must have served as a deterrent to the development of further electronic publications of a more specialist nature. CUP therefore appear to be moving towards the journal market, where users have been easily convinced of the merits, and crucially the necessity, of electronic products as a way of improving their working lives.

Other projects, both commercial and those based in university research teams, used the medium to present different variations of one text. Editors of printed texts have to choose which one of the texts they feel is the 'best', print that, and present variants from it in note form. It is usually impossible for the reader to make comparison with the actual sources. An electronic edition allows all the manuscripts, or variants, to be displayed and linked together. This allows the reader to construct their own hybrid edition, which they might change every time they use it (Bolter, 1992).

Hypertext

In the early to mid-1990s there was great excitement about the possibility of hypertext editions of literary work, or of fiction. Users could make the most of the possibilities of hypertext linking to wander from one lexia to the next, ignoring the constraints placed on them by the traditional narrative which is so much more suited to the printed book (Doss, 1996). However, this ability to make associative links was not really as new as it appeared. As Nelson (1992) has pointed out, when not reading fiction we read few books in a straightforwardly linear fashion. We are likely to move around from one part to another, ignore some chapters, read some parts in more depth than others, move associatively from a footnote to another text entirely, and above all use navigational devices like indices and contents pages to help us make choices about what to read. When we read a book we are also making associations, whether conscious or unconscious, to our own private hypertext of knowledge, which comes from other texts. Catullus deliberately places his poem within the poetic tradition of his time, which valued the presentation of a large amount of information, with the utmost elegance, within a small space. When classicists read his poem they recognize this because they have read other texts, whether by other classical poets, or by scholars who comment upon them. A hypertext edition of Catullus, as for example can be found at the Perseus project (medusa.perseus.tufts.edu/), will make links to such information, but in doing so, is in a sense stressing the connection to the printed past just as much as it is pointing towards an electronic future (Landow, 1992).

Nevertheless, it seems difficult for many users to transfer skills from the print to the electronic medium (Warwick, 1999). Perhaps as a result of this, such facilities in a novel or edition have not proved very popular. The experience of 'reading' a hypertext can leave users disorientated (Nielson, 1998), and it seems that when reading we rather like the beginning, middle and end that printed texts can offer us, or to be guided through a myriad of possibilities by the unseen hand of the expert editor.

Although specialized scholarly products, such as the *Canterbury tales*, are not finding a mass market, electronic research resources are being produced by specialist academic research teams situated in universities, and funded by research grants, which means that they do not have to make a projected profit to exist. However, as argued elsewhere (Warwick, 2002), while the project teams are doing fascinating work, in the humanities there is very little evidence that research culture has changed to accommodate the use of these publications. Some electronic products such as Bell and Howell's Literature Online site (http://lion.chadwyck.co.uk) are used at university level to support teaching and learning, at least where there is money to pay the large cost of resources. However, electronic resources for teaching and learning do not yet appear to be perceived as a necessity, nor to have enjoyed the success of the electronic journal. This seems to be because, far from replacing books in education, electronic resources have not became part of the mainstream culture since users have yet to be convinced of their overwhelming importance. There seems to be no 'killer app' that distracts them from the book as the essential tool for learning.

Technological watershed

In the Catullus poem, we saw that he expresses a concern about how the text he has produced may be received. As suggested at the beginning of this chapter, this is in part a testimony to being at a technological watershed. When poetic culture was largely oral, and philosophical debate was held 'live' rather than on the pages of journals and monographs, this is an understandable anxiety, but it is one with which we had come to terms in the age of print. The author of a printed book is largely resigned to the idea that they have no contact with the reader. However, the electronic text delivered on the web makes a return to the connectedness of author and reader more likely. The common practice of adding e-mail addresses or discussion forums to the site of an electronic publication means that the editors, publishers and authors all invite the readers to communicate with them, and indeed with each other. Thus the editor may not be sure of a 'suitable' reader, but they are able to find out about the response to their publication in a more immediate way than by doing an anxious search for citations in future learned journals. It has also become obvious that just by putting up a website anyone can become a publisher, or an author, and communicate with millions of others, and indeed this has been held responsible for the low quality of much on the web, and of people's perception of it as an unreliable and low-status medium.

Once again, however, the connectedness of writers, publishers and their audience, as well as the low status of publication, are hardly new. In the early days of the book, in the 16th and 17th centuries, the activity of publication in print was thought to be a very low-status activity, and certainly not something that a serious writer ought to be proud of. As a result, authors would circulate material to their friends, in what became known as coterie publishing. Perhaps the most famous example of this is Shakespeare's sonnets (Marotti, 1986). This allowed close contact between the author and his readers, and enabled those involved to comment on ideas quickly and share knowledge within a small community. All of these ideas predate the pre-print archive, such as the Los Alamos archive for particle physics, by about 300 years. In time, of course, the status of print publication rose, as it became a more common activity. It is possible that the status of web publication will also change as the medium matures and changes, in response not only to technical, but societal changes.

Access to information

It is possible to see that electronic publishing has indeed affected the way users gain access to information. Electronic delivery has revolutionized access to data and information that may be stored and searched in a database. Reference information has become far more accessible, more quickly, to a wider range of people. Electronic journals have been a success, since they provide for the needs of a particular community, and make it easier to search for and access articles. Yet ultimately the way that information is used has not changed. Whether a doctor accesses information from a medical textbook or MEDLINE, it is still up to them to make the diagnosis. Whether a particle physicist reads an article in the printed or electronic version of *Nature* its relevance to their particular research will be a matter for their own judgement.

Both the doctor and the physicist need to relax, and they may do this by reading novels on a beach which they found in a holiday guide. They may have booked the holiday online, but it is most likely that the book will be a paperback, and so will the guidebook. Though these two people are perfectly capable of using computers and electronic publication technology, they will probably choose to access many if not most of the publications that they need in traditional format, because they find printed books cheaper, easier and more convenient to use than the electronic alternatives, should they even exist. Other people on the beach may hardly use electronic publications at all. This does not make them Luddites, it may simply be that they do not read academic journals, work in education or need to consult databases of reference or business information. Despite what technology enthusiasts might think, this category is still a large one.

Conclusion

Electronic publication is still a relatively new technology. The effect of the internet as such has obviously been enormous, but that of electronic publishing is still somewhat limited. As has been shown, in certain areas it has made a significant impact, but these are still relatively small. Books and other printed publications are still very much with us. Far from having superseded print, electronic delivery still remains a relatively minor part of the entire book market. This does not make e-books, for example, a complete failure, but they are not the runaway success that had been predicted. None of this should, however, surprise us. It has been stressed throughout this chapter that it is important to consider the needs of users and the culture in which they work, and also to remember that there is far more continuity with the methods and practices of the past in electronic publication than many had at first thought. As Catullus found, it is hard to look to the future and predict whether your work will be a success, but at least he was thinking about who his readers might be. The effects of reading and literacy changed society, but did so slowly. We should not, therefore, be surprised that it is taking time for the effects of electronic publishing to be felt. Change will happen, but it may be more gradual than had been thought, because although computer processing power may double every 18 months, it takes much longer for humans to upgrade themselves, even if they want to.

Acknowledgement

The work for this chapter was completed while I was lecturing at the University of Sheffield Department of Information Studies. I would like to thank my students and colleagues for discussing with me some of the ideas that I have used here.

References

Adams, A. and Graham, D. (2000) *The Glasgow University Emblem Website*, available at www.emblems.arts.gla.ac.uk/.

Ayers, E. L. (2002) Professor of American History, University of Virginia, USA. Interview conducted 14/01/02.

Ayers, E. L. and Thomas, W. G. (2002) *Two American communities on the eve of the Civil War: an experiment on form and analysis*, available at lincoln.vcdh. virginia.edu/article_front.html.

Barker, W., Feltham, M. and Guthrie, J. (2001) *Alciato's book of emblems*, available at www.mun.ca/alciato/index.html.

Benson, P. J. (2001) The more things change. paper is still with us, *The Journal of Electronic Publishing*, **7** (2), available at www.press.umich.edu/jep/07-02/ benson0702.html

Bolter, S. J. (1991) *Writing space: the computer, hypertext and the history of writing*, New Jersey, Laurence Erlbaum.

Bolter, S. J. (1992) Literature in the electronic writing space. In Tuman, M. (ed.), *Literacy online: the promise (and peril) of reading and writing with computers*, Pittsburg and London: University of Pittsburg Press, 19–42.

Bolter, S. J. (1996) Ekphrasis, virtual reality and the future of writing. In Nunberg, G. (ed.), *The future of the book*, Berkeley, University of California Press, 253–72.

Catullus, G. (1893) Poem 1. In Merill, E. (ed.), *Poems*, London/Boston, Ginn (translation by Claire Warwick).

Cleyle, S. (2001) E-ink boost for mobile electronic reading, *Biblio Tech Review*, available at www.biblio-tech.com/BTR901/January_2001/e-ink_for_e-books__.html.

Dauguid, P. (1996) Material matters: the past and futurology of the book. In Nunberg, G. (ed.) *The future of the book*, Berkeley, University of California Press, 63–102.

Doss, P. E. (1996) Traditional theory and innovative practice: the electronic editor as poststructuralist reader. In Nunberg, G. (ed.) *The future of the book*, Berkeley, University of California Press, 213–24.

Finneran, R. J. (1996) *The literary text in the digital age*, Ann Arbor: University of Michigan Press.

Flanders, J. (1997) The body encoded: questions of gender and the electronic text. In Sutherland, K. (ed.) *Electronic text: investigations in method and theory*, Oxford, Clarendon Press, 127–44.

Friend, F. J. (2000) Keeping your head in a revolution, *The Journal of Electronic Publishing*, **5** (3), available at www.press.umich.edu/jep/05-03/friend.html.

Gillespie, J. (2002) Graphics and palettes, *The Web Page for Designers*, available at www.wpdfd.com/wpdgraph.htm.

Hopkins, L. (2000) Early modern literary studies: future developments. Paper presented at the Digital Resources for the Humanities conference, 10–13 September 2000, University of Sheffield, UK.

Jonscher, C. (1999) *The evolution of wired life: from the alphabet to the soul-catcher chip – how information technologies change our world*, New York, Wiley.

Landow, G. P. (1992) Hypertext, metatext and the electronic canon. In Tuman, M. C. (ed.), *Literacy online: the promise (and peril) of reading and writing with computers*, Pittsburg and London, University of Pittsburg Press, 67–94.

Landow, G. P. (1996a) Twenty minutes into the future, or how we are moving beyond the book. In Nunberg, G. (ed.), *The future of the book*, Berkeley, University of California Press, 209–38.

Landow, G. P. (1996b) We are already beyond the book. In Chernaik, W., Deegan, M, and Gibson, A. (eds) *Beyond the book: theory, culture and the politics of cyberspace*, London, Office for Humanities Communication, 23–32.

Lee, S. D. (2001) *Digital imaging: a practical handbook*, London, Library Association Publishing.

Marotti, A. F. (1986) *John Donne, coterie poet*, Madison, University of Wisconsin Press.

Nelson, T. E. (1992) Opening hypertext: a memoir. In Tuman, M. C. (ed.), *Literacy online: the promise (and peril) of reading and writing with computers*, Pittsburg and London, University of Pittsburg Press, 43–58.

Nielson, J. (1998) Using link titles to help users predict where they are going, *The Alertbox: Current Issues in Web Usability*, available at www.useit.com/alertbox/980111.html

Norman, D. A.(1999) *The invisible computer: why good products can fail, the personal computer is so complex, and information appliances are the solution*, Boston, MA, MIT Press.

Nunberg, G. (ed.) (1996) *The future of the book*, Berkeley, University of California Press.

O'Donnell, W. and Thrush, E. A. (1996) Designing a hypertext edition of a modern poem. In Finneran, R. J. (ed.) *The literary text in the digital age*, Ann Arbor, University of Michigan Press, 193–212.

Rennie, I. (2001) *Bad books: an investigation into the unpopularity of online fiction and the future of the e-book*, unpublished MA dissertation, Sheffield University.

Robinson, P. M. W. (1997) New directions in critical editing. In Sutherland, K. (ed.) *Electronic text: investigations in method and theory*, Oxford, Clarendon Press, 145–72.

Robinson, P. M. W, et al. (eds) (1996) *Chaucer: The wife of Bath's prologue on CD-ROM*, Cambridge, Cambridge University Press.

Solopova, E. (ed.) (2000) *Chaucer: the general prologue on CD-ROM*, Cambridge, Cambridge University Press.

Stoll, C. (2000) *High tech heretic: reflections of a computer contrarian*, New York, Random House.

Tomney, H. and Burton, P. F. (1998) Electronic journals: a study of usage and attitudes among academics, *Journal of Information Science*, **24** (6), 419–29.

Tuman, M. C. (ed.) (1992) *Literacy online: the promise (and peril) of reading and writing with computers*, Pittsburg and London, University of Pittsburg Press.

Warwick, C. (1999) The lowest canonical denominator: electronic literary texts, and their publication, collection and preservation. In Klasson, M., Loughridge, B. and Loof, S. (eds) *New fields for research in the 21st century, proceedings of the anglo nordic conference 1999*, Swedish School of Library and Information Studies, Boras, Sweden, 133–41.

Warwick, C. (2002) English literature, electronic text and computer analysis: an unlikely combination, forthcoming in *Computers and the Humanities*.

Wilson, T. D. (1999) Information research: a case study in the free electronic publication of research, *Vine*, **111**, 10–16.

12

The role of the professional in the information society

Peter Brophy

Overview

This chapter considers the ways in which the responsibilities of 'professionals' are changing in the information society. It explores what is meant by a 'profession' and the application of this concept to library and information science. The impact of information and communications technologies has been profound, raising new challenges and new dilemmas for professionals. The tension between 'professional' and 'managerial' perspectives needs to be considered carefully and it is suggested that much work is needed to redefine professionalism in the information society.

Introduction

There is something a little presumptuous in a 'professional' writing about his own profession, for the range of concerns and the plethora of viewpoints render any individual account partial and incomplete. Francis Bacon (1613), in *The elements of the common lawes of England*, commented 'I hold every man a debtor to his profession' but each of our debts is different. Our profession – be it that of doctor, lawyer, accountant, architect, engineer, surveyor or even librarian or information scientist – has helped make each of us what we are. Commentary from the inside looking in is a perilous process!

George Bernard Shaw had much to say about professions and professional accreditation – well, he had much to say about everything! The former he castigated in his famous phrase 'All professions are conspiracies against the laity' (Shaw, 1913) but the latter, professional accreditation, he seemed to favour if only to protect the customers. He chose one of the most common occupations of all and remarked, 'Parentage is a very important profession; but no test of fitness for it is ever imposed in the interests of children' (Shaw, 1944).

But what is a 'profession'? The dictionary tells us that it is a 'paid occupation, especially one involving training and a formal qualification' (Pearsall, 2001). Dale (2001) suggests two other definitions:

- a calling requiring specialized knowledge and often long and intensive academic preparation
- an occupation, such as law, medicine, or engineering, that requires considerable training and specialized study.

A point which does not emerge from these quotations, but is surely of the utmost importance, is that professions are validated by the societies that support them. We speak of the profession of medicine and value doctors highly, yet it has not always been so. We respect architects, even if we do not always admire what they produce. For a profession to be accorded societal recognition, it would seem that a number of criteria have to be met:

- There must be an identifiable subject with reasonably clear boundaries which is not immediately accessible to the uninitiated lay person.
- There must be a long apprenticeship involving the learning of both theory and practice (though the balance may vary hugely) and the application of the latter.
- The application of the subject matter of this apprenticeship must be useful to society.
- The profession must promulgate standards for the products or services that are produced and delivered by its members.
- Members of the profession are individually responsible for the standards of their work and for their professional conduct but are overseen by a professional body which has powers to ensure compliance.

The information professions: subject focus

The application of these criteria to the 'information profession' – the quotation marks will be omitted in the rest of this chapter – has always been problematic. If we take librarianship as one of the more clearly definable of the information professions (the plural itself, of course, introducing yet another note of uncertainty or ambiguity) then we can find ways to define its subject matter which would meet the first of the above criteria. Thus Harrison (2000, 48) lists the professional 'practices' of librarianship as including:

- abstracting and indexing
- acquisition of stock and materials selection
- bibliography work
- cataloguing and classification
- enquiry desk work
- information services
- library organization
- local library co-operation
- promotion of the services
- professional awareness of new services
- reference work.

It is immediately apparent that, while the uninitiated lay person would probably accept his or her inability to perform brain surgery and thus the inaccessibility of at least parts of medicine to those who have not served the required apprenticeship, the same is probably not true of the subject matter that Harrison lists. Faced with the challenge, many non-librarians would have a go at organizing a library – and at least in corporate environments many do. As Dale (2001, 440) remarks, 'Untrained staff seem to do the job to a standard that satisfies their employers. I would maintain (and can usually demonstrate) that information professionals can add huge value, but it is an uphill struggle.'

The Association of Research Libraries (ARL) in the USA recently undertook a study on the changing roles of library professionals (Simmons-Welburn, 2000). The methodology involved sending questionnaires to 122 member libraries, with 55 (45%) being returned. The study team examined job descriptions which had been 'posted' by the member libraries over the previous three years. They concluded:

The new skills requested in position descriptions revolve around technology and include knowledge of educational and instructional technologies (or teaching technologies), especially for public institutions. It is common to find postings for reference positions seeking individuals with knowledge of electronic resources and products . . . Other new positions reported include information technology specialist and digital projects librarian.

A significant number of the descriptions collected indicate that the positions have been redefined to fit within new or reengineered organizational configurations. . . . Many positions ask for the possession of team skills – the ability to work in 'team-based' or 'team-oriented', 'client-centered' environments.

An earlier ARL report by Wilder (2000) is quoted. The changes represent:

a movement away from traditional library skills and library education generally. One is left with the overpowering sense that while the individuals who are about to leave this population may be replaced, their skills and professional training may not.

The boundaries of the subject area are thus changing rapidly. Information technology now dominates the information production/organization/access/ use arena to an extent that is not true of other professions. Riggs (2000, 1), in a review of library and information work, speaks for most information professionals in observing, 'Never before in the history of librarianship and information work have there been the high rapidity of change and the growing magnitude of ambiguity as we are experiencing today. We can no longer rely on what worked in libraries in the past to be the best approach in the future.'

Yet this is not the only change. The distinction between professional and 'other' (the terminology is always problematic: 'non-professional' is clearly unsatisfactory if not downright insulting; 'paraprofessional' is meaningful only to aficionados of the debate) library staff has always been difficult to draw. Now the onset of information and communications technology (ICT) based services is making the distinction even more difficult to define since the skills a team requires are partly 'professional', and they come from a variety of different disciplinary bases. There is a lack of confidence among information professionals which denies them the ability to operate alongside those with different knowledge bases. The nervousness that this has engendered among library professionals, at least in the public library sector, was summed up in Jones et al. (1999, 22–3):

> Many librarians were unsure of their role and were less enthusiastic than library assistants about changes in their jobs. They felt that the introduction of technologies to service provision might devalue the skills they already have, and they will be marginalised.

The same report suggested that information professionals will need to adopt (and adapt to) five new roles of:

- *intermediaries*: helping customers to find their way through the 'information maze'
- *information experts*: interpreting information requests, finding information sources; repackaging information, and so on
- *advisers*: providing help, for example assistance in using computers
- *learner support*: acting as coaches, trainers and mentors
- *management and support*.

A somewhat earlier study of the academic sector (Oldroyd, 1996, 138) examined staff development and training needs, and suggested that the focus would need to be on:

- the development of interpersonal skills
- the ability to exploit information technology
- team working
- understanding of learning theory, course design and delivery methods
- management skills
- changing roles in relation to the convergence of libraries and computing services
- working within work-based learning contexts.

Both of these accounts stress the team and managerial roles that characterize so much information work. Yet this is as much part of the problem as of its solution. Most information professionals work in significantly sized organizations, where their role is concerned with management as well as with the application of their professional skills. As many writers have pointed out, the skills of a good professional are not necessarily those of a good manager – Peter Drucker goes so far as to suggest that a good professional rarely makes a good manager (Drucker, 1955, 335). Since the management of information is so much a part of the information professional's job, it is not perhaps all that surprising that difficulties are encountered – a good, yet 'unqualified', manager may have enough skills to be, or to appear to be, a good information professional. What is more there could be real conflict between professional behaviour and the organization's legitimate expectations of those who have been charged with managing its affairs – an issue considered in more detail below.

The information professions: apprenticeship

The former Library Association in the UK – the picture is much the same elsewhere – has in fact been quite successful in securing recognition for its accreditation of courses, and for its own processes but within a fairly tightly defined sub-field. The merger with the Institute of Information Scientists, in April 2002, to create the Chartered Institute of Library and Information Professionals (CILIP) has in some ways reinforced this element of professionalism. It explicitly uses the term 'Chartered' which in the UK implies national recognition of professional status. It has also emphasized its continued commitment to what had been increasingly joint activity between the two organizations in course accreditation as well as in testing and recognizing individual professional achievement. The standard of an undergraduate degree in the field, or a postgraduate qualification built upon a degree in another subject, both followed by a period of professional practice, reflection and reporting – or a longer period where candidates do not have a formal qualification in the field – is now well established. Despite a decline in the popularity of undergraduate degrees in librarianship (a trend not shared by other information-related subjects) this pattern seems likely to continue.

However, the breaking down of the recognizable boundaries of the information profession – if they ever existed – has made any claim to exclusive territory very difficult to sustain. Clearly, in an 'information society', where information is created, organized, delivered and used by many players, and where highly complex information and telecommunications technologies are employed, there will be many active 'professions' represented. For example, since the world wide web became the medium of choice for delivering online information, new 'professions' (the quotation marks have been reintroduced here to emphasize that the term may be questionable in this context) have emerged – web designers being just one example. It is unlikely that many of these people would yet see their natural home as within an organization like CILIP, though that of course is one of the challenges for the new body. Many of these new professionals will look elsewhere for their professional accreditation. They may look to a sister (or competing?) professional body, like the British Computer Society (BCS) or they may rely on commercial accreditation, as for example by gaining Microsoft or Lotus Certification.

It follows that, while patterns of professional apprenticeship are established in traditional areas and new patterns are starting to appear in emerging fields, the situation is fluid and must be expected to remain so. The challenge for any professional body in this field will be to remain influential across a broad sweep of activity while filling at least one niche which represents a skill which is key and which is recognized as such by society, including employers. Further, that niche must be one which is not immediately accessible to the uninitiated lay person.

The information professions: usefulness to society

Perhaps this issue can be dealt with swiftly. While some professions may be of doubtful usefulness (one has to be careful with examples, but perhaps phrenology might be an uncontroversial candidate these days!) it is hard to believe that many would question that the organization of information has a key role in current societies. Of course, what may be questioned is the need for professionals to handle this role – but that is a separate issue. Using this criterion the information professions would seem to occupy one of the strongest places in modern society. However, on its own this is not enough.

The information professions: professional standards

A feature of most professional bodies is that they set standards for the work that their members carry out. We are not talking here of the ethical standards of members (which are dealt with in the next section) but rather of the standard that a customer should be able to expect of a service or product.

Accountants, for example, have detailed standards on accounting practice and the presentation of accounts; engineers have a wide variety of technical standards they must follow, and so on.

Information professionals have been quite well served in this area. Professional associations have been active, for example in the development of cataloguing rules and classification schemes. The Library Association stated that 'the constant maintenance and improvement of standards of service are central to The Library Association's mission' (Library Association, 2002). [Following the formation of CILIP, from April 2002 the LA website remains frozen; see the CILIP website (www.cilip.org.uk) for developments.] Both CILIP in the UK and The American Library Association in the USA publish many standards and guidelines, most of which are freely available from their websites. In the academic sector there are the then Library Association's *Library and learning resources provision for franchized and other collaborative courses* (Library Association, 1999a) and the Association of College and Research Libraries (part of the ALA) offers *Objectives for information literacy instruction: a model statement for academic librarians* (Association of College and Research Libraries, 2001) – to give just two, randomly selected, examples from many.

Linked to the setting of standards is the engagement of most professional associations in lobbying and advocacy. Standards need to be accepted not just by members, but by society at large and the broader interests of the profession need to be promulgated. The American Library Association, for example, has defined five Key Action Areas (American Library Association, 2001):

Diversity

Diversity is a fundamental value of the Association and its members, and is reflected in its commitment to recruiting people of color and people with disabilities to the profession and to the promotion and development of library collections and services for all people.

Education and Continuous Learning

The Association provides opportunities for the professional development and education of librarians, library staff, and trustees; it promotes continuous, lifelong learning for all people through library and information services of all types.

Equity of Access

The Association advocates funding and policies that support libraries as a great democratic institution, serving people of all ages, income level, location, or ethnicity, and providing the full range of information resources needed to live, learn, govern, and work.

Intellectual Freedom

Intellectual freedom is a basic right in a democratic society and a core value of the library profession. The American Library Association actively defends the right of library users to read, seek information, and speak freely as guaranteed by the First Amendment.

21st Century Literacy

The American Library Association assists and promotes libraries in helping children and adults develop the skills they need – whether the ability to read or use computers – understanding that the ability to seek and effectively utilize information resources (information literacy) is essential in a global information society.

Looking to the future, this role of the professional associations seems secure provided that they can maintain public credibility. The values illustrated in the above quotation are closely aligned with the late 20th century liberal consensus. Whether they will remain aligned with public opinion remains to be seen.

The information professions: personal responsibility and ethical standards

One of the hallmarks of professionals is the way in which they take personal responsibility for their work. Professional bodies provide advice and guidance to enable their members to act in this way. They also 'police' their members' activities. The then Library Association's Code of Professional Conduct (Library Association, 2001; see CILIP website, www.cilip.org.uk, for developments) sets out the issue in the negative, defining professional conduct in terms – very imprecise terms – of what a member should not do:

> Members of the Association must conduct themselves in such a way that their conduct would not be reasonably regarded by their professional colleagues within

> the field of librarianship . . . as serious professional misconduct or as professional misconduct. It is by this overall test that the conduct will be judged.

However, the surrounding text is perhaps more helpful in helping to define the scope of 'professionalism'. So:

> The professional librarian's prime duty is to facilitate access to materials and information in order to meet the requirement of the client, irrespective of the librarian's personal interests and views on the content of the materials and the client's requirement.

A particularly important clause in the Code of Professional Conduct relates to the locus of professional responsibility.

> In all professional considerations the interests of the clients within their prescribed or legitimate requirements take precedence over all other interests. . . . Circumstances may arise when the public interest or the reputation of the profession itself may be at variance with the narrower interests of an employer. If it is found impossible to rectify such differences then the public interest and the maintenance of professional standards must be the primary considerations.

The attempt is made here to answer one of the questions raised earlier, namely how the relationship between the information professional *qua* professional and the information professional *qua* employee should be reconciled. The professional body takes a clear stance: the professional duty comes first.

However, practice does not always follow the rhetoric in the information professions. As was noted earlier, many information professionals perform a dual role, also acting as managers within their organizations. The idealistic stance of the professional body sometimes conflicts with organizational values and demands. If we take one of the clearer examples of the impacts of ICTs on the profession, that of internet filtering, the tensions become apparent. The Library Association's Code of Professional Conduct states:

> In places to which the public has right of access, save where the flow of information must be restricted by reason of confidentiality, members have an obligation to

facilitate the flow of information and ideas and to protect and promote the rights of every individual to have free and equal access to sources of information without discrimination and within the limits of the law.

The Association's Policy Statement in this area is quite explicit (Library Association, 1999b):

> The Library Association does not endorse the use of filtering software in libraries. The use of such software is inconsistent with the commitment or duty of a library or information service to provide all publicly available information in which its users claim legitimate interest. Access to information should not be restricted except as required by law.

Notes of guidance on the use of internet filtering, issued by the Library Association (Library Association, 2000), make the following statement:

> Whilst not endorsing the use of filtering technologies, The Library Association recognises that ultimately decisions on their use frequently rests [sic] with the governing body or local authority respectively.

However, this is not a get-out clause. This last statement refers only to *children's* use of the internet, and relates to situations (such as in schools) where librarians may be acting in loco parentis or may have an explicit duty of care. In the UK, unlike the situation in the USA, there has been no outcry among public librarians over the installation of internet filters on PCs that are publicly available to adults. It seems that they go along with the view that filtering is acceptable. For example, a message from one local authority librarian to the People's Network e-mail list in August 2001 simply reports that 'Use is filtered for staff as well as public, as a matter of corporate policy, so trying to access worst sites gets an "Access Denied" message' (Drewitt, 2001). In this case the librarians seem to accept that even their own access to the internet should be filtered!

It would be easy to castigate librarians who find themselves in these situations for failing to follow their professional duties as laid out by their professional body's advice and standards. Yet maybe all is not as it seems. One part of the reason for the different approach is undoubtedly the clash between professional and managerial responsibilities. Perhaps, however, the key reasons go deeper.

The example of internet filtering is no more than one instance of the more general question of the information professional's ethical responsibilities. Traditionally, the key ethical principle of the information professional has been one of 'value neutrality' – what Foskett referred to in the title of his 1962 book as *The creed of a librarian: no politics, no religion, no morals* (Foskett, 1962). According to this theory it is the customer's values that must be allowed to prevail; the librarian is there to facilitate, not take sides. This idea was illustrated most graphically in Hauptman's study of 'reference ethics' (Hauptman, 1976). He visited 13 academic and public libraries and asked for help in locating information on how to make a bomb. Only one librarian refused to help – and that was on the basis that he wasn't a registered student there! However, as Alfino and Pierce (1997) point out in their excellent monograph, *Information ethics for librarians*, this is not 'value-neutral' conduct at all. The idea that librarians can somehow step aside from society is misguided. By acceding to the request, librarians contribute to the state of society. They may pretend to be unbiased automata, yet their decisions and actions will profoundly affect other people's lives – and thus they cannot avoid the ethical dilemma simply by providing anything for which they are asked. Furthermore by refusing to engage with the requestor, perhaps by offering alternatives and adjunct works, such as – in this case – a volume on peaceful protest or even a first aid manual, they make a value judgement. The very notion that 'everyone has a right to know how to build a bomb' is itself value laden. 'The problem is not just that it is hard to be neutral, but rather that it is an impossible, fundamentally self-deceptive goal' (Alfino and Pierce, 1997, 10).

Wengert (2001, 500) points out that professional associations habitually give precedence to rules when they address ethics:

> Rules provide the demanding call of obligation, they identify something that *must* be done. In addition rules tend to be short enough that one can understand them well enough to know when they have been followed and when not. In this way they provide relatively clear norms to follow and something short and specific to which one can appeal when criticized.

The alternative formulation of an ethical stance, which is by the *results* of an action, is far more difficult to define and far more ambiguous in guiding actions that should or should not be taken. Yet, Wengert continues,

> thinking that the rules that get followed exhaust the ethical content of the situation is an ugly trait that occurs in some of the worst forms of bureaucracy. When rules get disconnected from the consequences that result from following those rules, people can be very badly treated. Insisting that one's obligation is merely to follow the rules leads one to see one's ethical life as a life of avoiding the blame . . . Our sole goal ought not to be morally blameless; we would also like to contribute to making better the lives of those around us and who share our communities.

The information professions need to engage in a much higher level of debate about these issues than has been apparent to date. The librarian who introduces or allows internet filtering may be acting in a 'more ethical' manner than a professional association which tries to pretend that its members can stand aside from engagement with real ethical dilemmas and merely apply some simple rules. He or she, provided the decision to filter has been carefully argued, is accepting the inevitability of engaging with society as it exists, and is taking moral responsibility as a member of that society for the well-being of its members.

The picture is, of course, complicated by the legislative frameworks within which an information professional operates. In the USA, freedom of information legislation and the First Amendment to the Constitution, which guarantees freedom of expression, provide a more certain backdrop to professional ethics than is available in the UK. In the UK the recent and much-criticized Freedom of Information Act and the incorporation of the *European convention on the protection of human rights* into UK law are as yet untested in this area, and our reliance on case law for guidance makes the position uncertain. This should not, however, prevent information professionals from engaging in debate about the issue.

The dilemma over value neutrality and societal engagement can only become more marked as our society becomes more dominated by ICTs. The very design of information systems – and especially those which are central rather than peripheral to the ways in which people choose to live their lives

– is value laden. The idea of 'quality assured' information, now frequently cited as the reason behind the continuing need for librarians and other information professionals, is self-evidently itself a value judgement, for it assumes that a central role will be to select some, and reject other, information objects. Even the seemingly 'neutral' search engines are laden with implied values – the basis of the design of Google, perhaps the highest-regarded of the search engines and one that minimizes the display of advertising – is that resources which attract the most external links are the most valuable. Should we accept such judgements at face value?

Conclusion

There can be little doubt that the information society requires professional approaches. On the one hand its technological structures require people who can act as information engineers and information architects with all the skills and standards that such terms imply, while on the other the complexity of information organization and use necessitates expert information advisers and teachers. Yet professionalism in these areas is ill defined. Engagement with the issues outlined in this chapter, and with others, will provide a rich and engaging agenda as the 21st century progresses.

References

Alfino, M. and Pierce, L. (1997) *Information ethics for librarians*, Jefferson, NC, McFarland & Co.

American Library Association (2001) *ALA interests and activities*, available at www.ala.org/work/.

Association of College and Research Libraries (2001) *Objectives for information literacy instruction: a model statement for academic librarians*, available at www.ala.org/acrl/guides/objinfolit.html.

Bacon, F. (1613) *The elements of the common lawes of England*, London, Assignes of I. More, Esq.

Dale, A. (2001) Dispatches: Letters from the Corporanian war zone: Letter 7 – meeting the demands of Chartered status, *Journal of Information Science*, **27** (6), 439–41.

Drewitt, D. (2001) Displaying acceptable use policies. Message to the

PEOPLESNETWORK@JISCMAIL.AC.UK list, 20.8.2001.

Drucker, P. (1955) *The practice of management*, London, Heinemann.

Foskett, D. J. (1962) *The creed of a librarian: no politics, no religion, no morals*, London, Library Association.

Harrison, C. T. (2000) Writing a professional development report. In Wood, K. (comp.), *A chartership reader*, London, Career Development Group (of the Library Association).

Hauptman, R. (1976) Professionalism or culpability? An experiment in ethics, *Wilson Library Bulletin*, **50**, 626–7.

Jones, B. et al. (1999) *Staff in the new library: skill needs and learning choices: findings from Training the Future, a public library research project*, British Library Research and Innovation Report 152, London, British Library Research and Innovation Centre.

Library Association (1999a) *Library & learning resources provision for franchised and other collaborative courses*, available at www.la-hq.org.uk/directory/prof_issues/franchise.html.

Library Association (1999b) *The use of filtering software in libraries: policy statement*, available at www.la-hq.org.uk/directory/prof_issues/filter2.html.

Library Association (2000) *The use of filtering software in libraries: guidance notes*, available at www.la-hq.org.uk/directory/prof_issues/filter.html .

Library Association (2001) Code of professional conduct. In *The Library Association yearbook 2001–2002*, London, Library Association Publishing, 216–18.

Library Association (2002) *About the Library Association: who we are*, available at www.la-hq.org.uk/directory/about.html.

Oldroyd, M. (ed.) (1996) *Staff development in academic libraries: present practice and future challenges*, London, Library Association Publishing.

Pearsall, J. (ed.) (2001) *The concise Oxford dictionary*, 10th edn rev, Oxford, Oxford University Press.

Riggs, D. E. (2000) Library and information work in context. In Line, M. (ed.), *Librarianship and information work worldwide 2000*, London, Bowker Saur, 1–17.

Shaw, G. B. (1913) *The doctor's dilemma: a tragedy*, London, Constable.

Shaw, G. B. (1944) *Miscellaneous works: everybody's political what's what?*, London, Constable.

Simmons-Welburn, J. (comp.). (2000) *Changing roles of library professionals: a SPEC kit*, Washington, DC, Association of Research Libraries.

Wengert, R. G. (2001) Some ethical aspects of being an information professional, *Library Trends*, **49** (3), 486–509.

Wilder, S. (2000) The changing profile of research library professional staff, *ARL: a Bimonthly Report on Research Library Issues and Actions from ARL, CNI, and SPARC*, (208/209) (February/April). Cited in Simmons-Welburn (2000).

Index